T0330021

Liberalism in Crisis?

ISPI

ISTITUTO PER GLI STUDI DI POLITICA INTERNAZIONALE

Founded in 1934 upon the initiative of a group of companies and scholars from the Universities of Milan and Pavia, ISPI is one of the oldest and most prestigious research Institutes in Italy.

The vocation of the Institute is to promote the study of international affairs and strategic problems, train young men and women intending to work in international surroundings, as well as supply a forum for discussion and debate at a high level.

In particular ISPI's Research Area carries out studies in the fields of international politics and economics, strategic studies and history of international relations, whose aim is to further awareness and broaden understanding of international relations and foreign policy. Specific attention is devoted to the European Union and to its current challenges in the economic and political fields.

This volume – supported by the Compagnia di San Paolo – is realised in the framework of the European Economic Governance Monitor (EEGM) which is a network of leading European think-tanks. The EEGM partner Institutes contributing to this volume are: European Policy Centre (EPC, Brussels); Istitut Français des Relations Internationales (IFRI, Paris); Stiftung und Wissenschaft Politik (SWP, Berlin); Istituto per gli Studi di Politica Internazionale (ISPI, Milan).

Liberalism in Crisis?

European Economic Governance in the
Age of Turbulence

Edited by

Carlo Secchi
*Vice President, ISPI and Professor of European Economic
Policy, Bocconi University, Milan, Italy*

Antonio Villafranca
Senior Research Fellow, ISPI, Milan, Italy

In Association with

Edward Elgar
Cheltenham, UK • Northampton, MA, USA

ISPI
ISTITUTO PER GLI STUDI DI POLITICA INTERNAZIONALE

Published by
Edward Elgar Publishing Limited
The Lypiatts
15 Lansdown Road
Cheltenham
Glos GL50 2JA
UK

Edward Elgar Publishing, Inc.
William Pratt House
9 Dewey Court
Northampton
Massachusetts 01060
USA

A catalogue record for this book
is available from the British Library

Library of Congress Control Number: 2009930856

ISBN 978 1 84844 530 7

Printed and bound by MPG Books Group, UK

Contents

Figures

Tables

Abbreviations

AAU	Assigned Amount Unit
ABI	Bankers Association of Italy
ABS	Asset-Backet Securities
AIG	American International Group
ASEAN	Association of South-East Asian Nations
BEPG	Broad Economic Policy Guidelines
BINGO	Business and Industry Non-Governmental Organizations
BIS	Bank for International Settlements
BSC	Banking Supervision Committee
CDM	Clean Development Mechanism
CEBS	Committee of European Banking Supervisors
CEEC	Central and Eastern European Countries
CEIF	Clean Energy Investment Framework
CEIOPS	Committee of European Insurance and Occupational pensions Supervisors
CEPS	Centre for European Policy Studies
CESR	Committee of European Securities Regulators
COP	Conference of the Parties
COREP	Common Reporting Framework
CRD	Capital Requirements Directive
ECB	European Central Bank
ECOFIN	Economic and Financial Affairs Council
ECT	European Communities Treaty
EDP	Excessive Deficit Procedure
EEA	European Economic Area
EFC	Economic Financial Committee
EIB	European Investment Bank
EMS	European Monetary System
EMU	Economic and Monetary Union
ENGO	Environmental Non-Governmental Organizations
EOFS	European Organization for Financial Supervision
ERU	Emission Reduction Unit
ESCB	European System of Central Banks
ESFS	European System of Financial Supervisors

ETS	Emission Trading Scheme
EU	European Union
EUA	European Union Allowance
EWG	Eurogroup Working Group
FAO	Food and Agriculture Organization
FED	Federal Reserve
FSA	Financial Services Association
FSAP	Financial Sector Assessments Programme
FSF	Financial Stability Forum
GAO	General Accountability Office
GDP	Gross Domestic Product
GEF	Global Environment Facility
GO	Guarantees of Origin
IAEA	International Atomic Energy Agency
IASB	International Accounting Standards Board
IFAD	International Fund for Agricultural Development
IFRI	Institut Français des Relations Internationales
IFRS	International Financial Regulatory Standards
IMF	International Monetary Fund
IPCC	Intergovernmental Panel on Climate Change
IPO	Indigenous People's Organizations
JI	Joint Implementation
LGMA	Local Government and Municipal Authorities
LGTT	Loan Guarantee of the Trans-European Transport
LoLR	Lending of Last Resort
LULUCF	Land Use, Land-Use Change and Forestry
MBS	Mortgage-Backed Securities
MEA	Multilateral Environmental Agreement
MERCOSUR	Mercado Común del Cono Sur
NAFTA	North American Free Trade Agreement
NGO	Non-Governmental Organization
NIC	National Intelligence Council
NYSE	New York Stock Exchange
OCA	Optimum Currency Area
OECD	Organisation for Economic Co-operation and Development
PCA	Prompt Corrective Action
RGGI	Regional Greenhouse Gas Initiative
RINGO	Research and Independent Non-governmental Organization
RU	Removal Unit
SEC	Security and Exchange Commission
SGP	Stability and Growth Pact
SIV	Special Investments Vehicles
TCC	Total Compliance Cost

TEC	Treaty establishing the European Community
TEU	Treaty on European Union
UN	United Nations
UNCED	United Nations Conference on Environment and Development
UNCTAD	United Nations Conference on Trade and Development
UNDP	United Nations Development Programme
UNEP	United Nations Environment Programme
UNESCO	United Nations Educational Scientific and Cultural Organization
UNFCCC	United Nations Framework Convention on Climate Change
UNICEF	United Nations Children's Fund
UNIDO	United Nations Industrial Development Organization
US	United States
USA	Unites States of America
WB	World Bank
WCI	Western Climate Initiative
WMO	World Meteorological Organization
WMO	World Meteorological Organization
WTO	World Trade Organization

Contributors

Carlo Altomonte is Assistant Professor of Economics of European Integration (Jean Monnet Chair) at Bocconi University, Milan and Associate Senior Research Fellow at ISPI. He has held visiting posts in programmes on Economics of European Integration, among others, at NYU and Keio University (Tokyo). He has published extensively in top journals in the field of international and industrial economics.

Franco Bruni is Professor of Economics at Bocconi University and Vice President of Milan's Istituto per gli Studi di Politica Internazionale (ISPI). He is past-President and member of the Council of Management of the Société Universitaire Européenne de Recherches Financières (SUERF) and member of the European Shadow Financial Regulatory Committee. He is author of many publications on monetary economics and financial regulation

Karel Lannoo is Chief Executive of the Centre for European Policy Studies (CEPS) and Independent Director of BME (Bolsas y Mercados Espanoles), the company which runs the Madrid stock exchange. He has published some books and numerous articles in specialised magazines and journals on EU, financial regulation and corporate governance matters. He has spoken at several European Parliament, Commission and related institutions hearings and participated in studies for national and international bodies (EU institutions, OECD, ADB, World Bank). He is a regular speaker at international conferences and in executive training programmes.

Hans Martens is the Chief Executive of the European Policy Centre, responsible for the overall management of the EPC and its human and financial resources, liaison with members and representing the EPC at events and meetings across Europe. He also contributes research and analysis in the economic and social area. His career includes experience in leading an economic, research and training consultancy business and working in banking as a Chief Economist and Head of international private banking.

Jacques Mistral is a Professor of Economics, Head of Economic Research at the Institut Français des Relations Internationales (IFRI); he served as Financial Counselor to the Embassy of France in the United States of America from 2001 to 2006. He recently published two books on the American economy, a report on reforming financial accounting and numerous articles on recent global and financial issues.

Francesco Passarelli is Associate Professor of Economics at the University of Teramo and at Bocconi University, Milan. Recently, he has published several studies on voting, collective choice and political economics, with special reference to the EU.

Daniela Schwarzer is Head of the EU integration division of the German Institute for International and Security Affairs (SWP). She is co-founder and co-editor of the *European Political Economy Review* and of www.eurozonewatch.eu. Previously, she worked for the *Financial Times Deutschland*.

Carlo Secchi is Professor of European Economic Policy at Bocconi University in Milan, where he is Director of ISLA (Institute for Latin American Studies and Transition Economies). He is chairman of the Italian Group of the Trilateral Commission and Vice President of ISPI. He has been a consultant of the Italian Government, the European Union and various research institutions worldwide. He has extensively published articles and books on international trade, economic integration and European economic policy.

Antonio Villafranca is Senior Research Fellow and Head of the European Programme at ISPI. He is lecturer of International Relations at the Bocconi University in Milan. He has published several articles and edited volumes on European governance and EU policies.

Fabian Zuleeg is Senior Policy Analyst at the European Policy Centre (EPC). He is an economist by training and at the EPC he is responsible for the political economy programme, which covers topics such as future European competitiveness, social Europe, climate change and better policy making and economic governance.

Foreword

The general issue of economic governance in a multi-level system such as the European Union is, nowadays, crucial. This book is a very timely one, because it discusses the current economic crisis and the best ways of addressing it, showing that there is no single solution to it. Instead, it highlights the need for policy measures that will have to be taken and coordinated at supranational, national and local levels, in line with subsidiarity, one of the key principles underpinning the process of European integration. Indeed, optimum management of the crisis constitutes a vital 'stress test' for the Union, since failing to strike the right balance between European and national policies would ultimately serve to call into question the very viability of the European economic system built up over the last 50 years. This volume, apart from discussing the best ways to manage these processes, also offers important insights into the lessons that we can learn from these testing times to help us define a better system of economic governance for future generations.

The book is the result of joint efforts by some of the most prestigious national think tanks in Europe, such as CEPS, EPC, IFRI, ISPI and SWP. They have been working for more than a year on these issues of governance, each one contributing on the basis of its own national and international experience, in order to define a common, truly European approach to the problem. I had the pleasure of attending the first workshop held in connection with this project, on 28 May 2008, and found much to learn from it. The book constitutes a natural further step in this extremely fruitful direction.

In congratulating the authors and the editors Carlo Secchi and Antonio Villafranca on their excellent work, my hope is that the book will stimulate further debates and research programmes on these issues which will prove useful in helping us to develop our common European home. I also hope that other European think tanks will seize on this form of cooperation, of which this book is such a brilliant example, when addressing issues of equal importance. Free exchanges of ideas and sensibilities of this kind are fundamental to building a closer and stronger European Union.

Hans-Gert Pöttering,
President of the European Parliament

Introduction

Carlo Secchi and Antonio Villafranca

The beginning of the new millennium appeared to pave the way to the success of the liberal model on a global scale. The striking growth of the emerging economies, together with positive growth rates in developed countries, was expected to give rise to a win-win situation which could make significant pay-offs available to everybody.

The current severe economic crisis may represent a rude awakening from this 'liberal dream'. A crisis that originally seemed to be rooted in American problems and miscalculations, has shown its seriousness by affecting the entire world and changing its nature from a strictly financial to an economic crisis. The race towards continuous growth has come to a halt and a period of systemic crisis has started.

In other words, the most striking features of the current crisis are not only its systemic dimension but also the clear-cut demonstration of impressive and strict linkages between the international financial system and the real economy. An analysis exploring these linkages and the effectiveness/sustainability of the measures undertaken by states (particularly the European ones) to face the crisis is therefore required.

The initial bankruptcy of Lehman Brothers and the ensuing negative spiral in the banking system may represent a good starting point for such an analysis. These events have led to sweeping changes and unexpected state interventionism in the economy in just a few weeks.

In an increasingly uncertain context verging on real panic, some people have raised doubts about the liberal system itself and its own future sustainability. As a consequence, the crisis has engulfed not only the international markets but also the liberal approach itself, which showed unexpected drawbacks in what is a truly global economy (not to mention the problem of its sustainability in environmental terms).

But this view seems too extreme. Rather, the crisis is bringing back to the surface recurring, if not old, questions on the liberal economic system:

the presence of the state in the economy; market failures; proactive use of fiscal policies; participation in international economic governance; the environmental sustainability of capitalism etc.

These questions are not particularly original as they have characterized the capitalist system since its origins, but the depth and size of the current crisis are placing new emphasis on their importance.

This is particularly true if one considers that national responses to the current crisis run the risk of using traditional 'recipes' instead of searching for wide-ranging and original solutions (requiring strong political commitment). Indeed, state debts have been dramatically increased since the crisis exploded in October 2008. The message sent by national authorities is crystal clear: extraordinary times require extraordinary interventions. But growing national debts raise many problems in terms of national income redistribution in the short/medium run and sustainability in the long run. In addition, the perceived need to stimulate the economy by raising new national debt may give rise to harmful competition among states (which would be obviously more disappointing in the European Union). The situation may be aggravated by the return of a recurrent 'spectre' in times of crisis: economic nationalism and protectionism.

In contrast to these approaches, the need for coordinated measures to exit the crisis still exists, not only for fiscal policies but also for regulation. Financial markets are regulated mostly at the national level but they operate on a global scale. They require more coordinated, if not centralized, institutions and regulation.

In order to outline these new coordinated measures, it is not necessary to criticize the entire model of economic development that we have been experiencing so far. However, a demand for an urgent rethinking of global economic governance is emerging. Therefore the approach to economic governance is not strictly economic but also political. A growing widespread consensus is surfacing as a consequence of the surge of new economic powers (China, India and Brazil). This process should lead to a new Bretton Woods redefining the rules in a truly globalized world.

The fact that the crisis broke out in the United States, which has been unable to tackle it effectively and prevent it from acquiring a systemic nature, may be interpreted as the diminishing power of the US. Today, at least in the economic field, this power needs to be shared not only with the United States' traditional and trusted European allies but also with the big emerging powers. In a nutshell, the outburst of the crisis has made the search for a new world economic governance more urgent.

This volume attaches great importance to the role the European Union can play in this search. The unpreparedness to face such a severe crisis was clear not only in the United States but also in Europe, where a lack of real federal bodies and competencies has made the political leaders' task even more difficult, though not necessarily less effective.

The rationale for such a European difficulty lies primarily in the EU's continuous search for a balance between the potentially federal competencies given to European institutions and the preservation of national sovereignty that is not merely formal.

Several decades ago, some of the European Union's historical goals in the economic field were simply considered impossible (that is the Single Market and above all the Economic and Monetary Union) but they are now a reality.

Even at the political level, some important steps have been taken (such as the 'co-decision' procedure which puts the European Parliament and the European Council on an equal footing). But it has not been possible to repeat the pace and importance of economic cooperation in the political realm.

The European Union is an unfinished puzzle to which new pieces are constantly added. This feeling of continuous 'work in progress' is more evident when the EU is confronted with serious international problems, such as the current economic crisis. In such cases, the European Union shows the inconsistencies of an incomplete job: a common currency which has not yet created an optimal currency area; a monetary policy given to a 'federal body' (the European Central Bank) but with few tools at its disposal for effective bank supervision (still in the hands of the national central banks); fiscal policies undertaken at the national level (despite the efforts made by the Stability and Growth Pact).

These institutional problems have made the identification of a common policy very difficult in the wake of the crisis, thus leaving room for the member states' initiative (under the active leadership of Mr Sarkozy, President of the EU in the second half of 2008).

Indeed, the interventions decided in the European financial system in October/November and the subsequent recovery plans may be regarded as a simple sum of national interventions, or in the best case an attempt to coordinate them.

In addition to these institutional constraints, member states' 'atomistic' answers have also originated from the effects of the crisis not being spread evenly across the European countries. The risk of the above-mentioned harmful competition raising new debt to finance national packages has made things even worse.

Bearing all this in mind, many questions arise concerning completion of the European puzzle, including during the crisis: the institutional development of the European Union; its role in the new world order; the coherence of its common monetary policy with national fiscal policies; the regulation of the financial system; the future sustainability of the measures adopted to support national economies; the coherence of the current measures with ambitious future targets (such as those addressing climate change).

This volume intends to tackle all these issues by relating them to the main features of the current crisis: its systemic dimension and the strict financial markets/real economy linkage.

Chapter 1 by Jacques Mistral starts this analysis by providing an interpretation of the challenges facing the world economy today. The author maintains that we are not facing a cyclical adjustment after which we should go back to 'business as usual' but rather a severe crisis jeopardizing the entire globalization process. An open world economy now calls for better international governance. The author devotes the second part of his chapter to the search for this would-be governance of the world economy. In this regard, the G20 initiative should not go through a series of successive rounds of negotiation, as it should be placed in the context of a 'global grand bargain'. Evidently, this approach would imply a bold strategy bringing many issues into the hands of political leaders but at the same time leaving room for possible trade-offs. Mistral concludes his chapter by proposing the creation of a new 'United Nations Economic Security Council' and by analysing a viable role for the European Union in this new context.

These proposals provide a general framework but they need to be further developed to include specific sectors. As far as the financial system is concerned, the current crisis, and above all the options for a viable solution to it, are still a conundrum for many financial authorities and operators, politicians and academic economists. They are still striving to understand the core of the problem. Franco Bruni attempts to contribute to this understanding by stressing 'forbidden' questions instead of elaborating complete answers, in Chapter 2. According to Bruni, it is extremely important to raise these questions as at least for the time being it does not seem possible to answer them in a clear-cut way. In addition, this allows us to emphasize 'left-aside' issues and show the drawbacks and weaknesses of economic and financial theory. Firstly, Bruni lists the arguments in favour of and against an explanation of the crisis centred on an alleged 'excessive liberalization'. He stresses that many express the desire to increase the regulation and supervision of financial markets or expand the role of governments in placing constraints to 'wild free markets', whereas requests for considering improvements in monetary strategies are less noticeable. In this case, the 'forbidden' question is the role of monetary policy in crisis prevention, even in the normal long run. Secondly, Bruni wonders whether we are experiencing a lack of qualitatively adequate regulation, or also quantitatively scarce regulation. Indeed, regulation cannot be simply considered a limitation of market mechanisms as it often allows for their reinforcement. Simply put, the cure does not necessarily consist of adding and reinforcing regulations, as it may also imply changed, reformed and streamlined rules. Thirdly, attention is placed on today's widespread criticism of new financial instruments. Bruni does not deny the excessive reliance on opaque over-the-counter transactions, but at the same time he states that innovative instruments are extremely important for the economy since they contribute to risk management and allocation and to the efficiency of forward-looking, expectation-driven financial markets. Moreover, Bruni tackles the issue of adequate level of supervision. The absence of strict supervision has been a fact, but it is not the same thing as the lack of regulatory powers. Building on these and other 'forbidden' questions, the author concludes his chapter by highlighting some implications and suggestions for European monetary and financial governance.

Chapter 3 by Karel Lannoo is closely linked to Bruni's chapter, but more particularly presents policy recommendations aimed at identifying steps to be made towards a more integrated financial oversight. In the first two sections, Lannoo provides an overview of the impact of the crisis on the entire European financial system. He stresses the effects on the European banking system by presenting estimates of the total losses related to the subprime crisis and recent trends in profitability and capital/liquidity ratios. In addition, he makes a comparison between the EU and the US banking systems, particularly in terms of recent leverage levels. The analysis also encompasses the impact of the crisis on the European insurance sector, which is quite a small actor in the financial system as compared to banks (its total assets being about one-fifth of the banking sector). In this regard, Lannoo points out that the insurance sector has been less affected by the crisis due to limited transparency of the published accounts. Besides, the author provides an analysis of the most severe effects of the crisis on the activity of the financial markets, and international and European policy responses to the full-blown systemic crisis. Following this detailed description, Lannoo discusses models of European regulatory and supervisory reform. He aims at highlighting the shortcomings and inconsistencies of proposals which have been debated for some time: upgrading the Level 3 Committees, strengthening the role of the supervisory colleges, expanding European supervisory cooperation through memoranda of understanding, and a clearer role of the European Central Bank (ECB). Lannoo proposes to overcome these limits by establishing a new and effective supervisory system to deal with today's and tomorrow's European challenges. But EU policy-makers will be required to take a quantum step in terms of institutional changes, to take full account of these limits. Following the example of the creation of the European System of Central Banks in 1998, Lannoo suggests preparing a roadmap leading to a European System of Financial Supervisors (ESFS). This roadmap would require the European Council to mandate the High Level Expert Group on EU financial supervision to make concrete proposals for the creation of the ESFS, the groundwork of which should be laid by a European Financial Institute. Finally, a European Resolution Trust would be a necessary corollary to an ESFS and would represent a safety net for the short-term financial problems of EU-based financial institutions.

The analysis of the financial and monetary aspects of the current crisis is completed in Chapter 4. Daniela Schwarzer focuses on the evolution of the Economic and Monetary Union (EMU) in the first euro decade, and further changes EMU governance may go through as a result of the crisis. The first part of the chapter is devoted to the internal governance dimensions of the EMU. The author presents the EMU's economic record in terms of growth, inflation and employment from 1999 to 2008. She underlines that the ECB has delivered solid monetary policy results in the first decade of the EMU but also stresses that divergence in Europe has increased, and that the 'one-size-fits-all' monetary policy has consequently intensified cyclical developments in some regions and member states. In 2005, the European Stability and Growth Pact (SGP) – which lays down rules for fiscal policy coordination – was reformed in order to enable more political discretion in its application. In other words, governments were allowed to take cyclical conditions into account, as the stabilizing role of fiscal policy had become a concern. Schwarzer also considers the institutional innovations of the EMU and attaches great importance to the creation and evolution of the Eurogroup (which the Lisbon Treaty will give a legal basis in an EU treaty for the first time). After her analysis of this first decade, the author stresses the impact of the crisis on the EMU in the second half of 2008, by analysing the first Eurozone summit and the role played by the ECB and member states in stabilizing European financial markets. In the second section, Schwarzer analyses the external dimension of the euro, underlining its international success in terms of its attraction for the opt-out countries, safe haven for Central and Eastern Europe, external value etc. The author concludes that a different view has been taken on the role of discretionary fiscal policy in the EMU in the last years, especially as it turned out that the EMU is not evolving towards an optimum currency area as quickly as was expected when the Maastricht Treaty was drafted. These problems may be aggravated by future challenges for the Eurozone (the up-coming Eastern enlargements, the impact of the Lisbon Treaty etc.). Particularly within the context of the current crisis, it is striking that risk and benefit evaluation still runs along national lines rather than in view of EMU aggregates. The world's second largest economy cannot count on instruments which are habitually available for truly integrated economies.

Chapter 5 by Altomonte, Passarelli and Secchi, and Chapter 6 by Zuleeg and Martens, move the analysis to another relevant aspect of the current crisis: fiscal policy and the spreading of the crisis beyond the borders of financial markets. These two chapters can be considered complementary. Indeed, Chapter 5 provides a detailed examination of the impact of the crisis on EU fiscal policy and the compatibility of the fiscal stimulus with the Lisbon agenda, whilst Chapter 6 examines the long-term implications of the crisis on European fiscal policy, by stressing the need for more prudent public finance once the current crisis has passed. In particular, Altomonte, Passarelli and Secchi place emphasis on the conventional wisdom behind the EMU: discretionary fiscal policy should not be used as a tool to stabilize output over the cycle (the stabilization role being normally left to monetary policy in the entire euro area, with the condition that price stability is not endangered). Only automatic stabilizers will work in the case of asymmetric shocks among member states. As a consequence, the euro 200 billion set of common discretionary fiscal policy actions (Recovery Plan) suggested by the European Commission to limit the effects of the crisis on the real economy can be considered a veritable 'revolution' in the traditional economic set-up of the EMU. Therefore, the authors assess the 'extraordinary' nature of these measures, if not for their size at least for the nature of the policy under consideration. The reasons behind the Recovery Plan can be found in the peculiar aspects of the current crisis; a liquidity crisis transformed into a solvency crisis with ensuing consequences in terms of the drying up of credit for new investments, and hence low growth rates in the medium run. These reasons make monetary policy virtually useless in stimulating the economy. But the authors are well aware of the problems discretionary fiscal policies can create and they provide a detailed analysis of the significant lags traditionally shown: information, decision and implementation lags. These lags are obviously considered within the context of the current crisis, whilst the Recovery Plan is also assessed in terms of its coherence with the aims of the Lisbon Agenda. Finally, the authors stress the fact that the structure of national incentives for national governments (to minimize debt and maximize employment) is not in line with EU-wide needs, the ideal solution being a federal set-up for fiscal policy and deficits in the Union's budget. But this is clearly not possible, hence the authors suggest multi-level coordination of economic policy actions: a strengthened role for the Eurogroup (also used more frequently at the head of state and government levels); a clear link between fiscal policy actions and the Commission's annual monitoring of the Lisbon Agenda; some explicit form of centralization of fiscal policy at the EU level, namely the possibility to raise EU-level debt managed by the EU institutions.

This analysis is completed in Chapter 6, where Zuleeg and Martens highlight the political economy of discretionary fiscal policy, examining its interaction with fiscal consolidation and the long-term sustainability of public finances. The authors do not argue against the Recovery Plan and a proactive use of fiscal policy, as the current crisis is not a 'normal' cyclical downturn and government responses need to be adapted accordingly. But they do warn against the longer-term effects, and suggest a careful assessment of the principles that should underpin long-term fiscal policy in the EU. In particular, in order to examine the EU's current and future position on fiscal policy, the authors contrast the EU position with that of the US (from bad to slightly better and from bad to worse, respectively). Building on the insights provided by this comparison, Zuleeg and Martens suggest some policy recommendations for the EU: the SGP should focus on longer term sustainability, and national fiscal sustainability programmes should be drawn up in order to assess whether any level of deficit or surplus in a member state is in line with the long-term trends and the current state of the economic cycle (with economic prospects preferably assessed by an independent expert body); fiscal policies should be considered one of the key components of structural reform; a European Futures Fund should be established to start accumulating assets in order to deal with future challenges (ageing population, pollution etc.).

The final chapter of the volume, written by Antonio Villafranca, deals with climate change and more particularly with the search for a revised multilevel governance in fighting climate change. This issue is particularly significant in the context of the current crisis for at least two reasons. On the one hand, the enormous problems created by the crisis must not hide the urgent need to fight global warming, partly as there are some important deadlines just round the corner (identification of the post-Kyoto targets, hopefully at the United Nations Framework Convention on Climate Change (UNFCCC) Copenhagen Conference in December 2009). With the aim of playing a leading role in fighting climate change and developing new 'green technologies', the European Union is the first region to have already identified binding targets for its members in the post-Kyoto period. Its aims and mechanisms (including the European Trading Scheme) can be an example for other areas around the world.

On the other hand, the search for a new global economic order urged by the crisis may be considered an unprecedented occasion to include the issue of a better-shared governance of climate change (involving the US and large emerging countries). This is perfectly in line with Jacques Mistral's 'global grand bargain'. In particular, this chapter places emphasis on the current 'spontaneous' governance by analysing all levels of intervention (global, regional, state and sub-state) with the aim of highlighting inconsistencies at any level. The author suggests 'non-revolutionary' changes which can potentially make fighting climate change more effective. The UN system should be reformed and developed countries should provide emerging countries with 'all-inclusive packages' (including financial aid, new trade agreements and qualified participation in international institutions). Regional actors (that is the EU) can be regarded as 'transmission belts' to help make global targets coherent with national constraints and have their members respect a solidarity principle, if requested. State and sub-state levels should strengthen their cooperation (possibly through an 'internal pact') to increase the magnitude of their intervention and its coherence with regional and international targets.

The following conclusion can be drawn from the seven chapters: we are still deep in the 'age of turbulence' and it is hard, if not impossible, to predict when this will be completely over. Therefore, this volume does not attempt to identify a possible deadline for the crisis, but it does shed light on its nature and on viable options for facing it. The reader is thus given a number of insights and policy recommendations which could improve European governance, not only in the context of the current economic crisis but also in view of the future recovery.

This volume has been realized within the framework of the EEGM (European Economic Governance Monitor), a network of leading European think-tanks: Istituto per gli Studi di Politica Internazionale (ISPI) in Milan, European Policy Centre (EPC) in Brussels, Istitut Français des Relations Internationales (IFRI) in Paris, Stiftung und Wissenschaft Politik (SWP) in Berlin, and Chatham House in London. Chapter 3 has been provided by the Centre for European Policy Studies (CEPS) in Brussels.

The editors wish to wholeheartedly thank Compagnia di San Paolo for its support for this volume and other EEGM initiatives, through which it demonstrates its constant, special attention to the European Union and its integration process.

Special thanks are also extended to Mr Pöttering for his Foreword and to all the authors for their chapters. Their suggestions, constant help and enthusiasm have ultimately made this volume a reality.

1. Shaping a New World Economic Governance: a Challenge for America and Europe

Jacques Mistral

Globalization has been the driving force of the world economy for two decades. Economic growth, expansion of trade and capital flows, a broad diffusion of wealth, tens of millions of people lifted out of poverty – these are testimonies of its impressive success. The fall of the Berlin Wall marked the dawn of a new era based on an unprecedented combination of free market and political democracy. For a decade – to risk oversimplification – we relied on the visions of Francis Fukuyama (1992) and Thomas Friedman (2005). The political economy of globalization looked as simple as that:

Democracy + Market = Peace + Prosperity

The results in 2009 are not exactly those which were expected. The world economy has certainly grown much richer, but it is not as homogeneous as it was once expected to become. The success of emerging powers means that we are entering an era of competition among different forms of capitalism. A backlash against globalization is simmering in many quarters. The financial crisis highlights a dramatic shift in the contours and the promises of the global economy.

What a difference a year makes! When G8 leaders met in June 2007 in Heiligendamm, they had no clue about the impending financial crisis, skyrocketing oil prices, global food shortage or mass lay-offs. One year later, facing a much more difficult economic environment, the question of how much power the G8 wielded was explicitly raised after its meeting in Hokkaido: How could they discuss, in 2008, food without India or Brazil, oil without Saudi Arabia, aid policies without Africa, exchange rates or climate without China?

Now, leaders of the G20 countries (whose share in world output has been stable for decades at about 90 per cent) gathered for the first time in Washington on 15 November 2008 to address the consequences of the financial crisis. Is this the beginning of a new steering committee? Is this the proper way to address the many challenges facing the world? How will Europe respond to these new challenges?

Europe is seen by many as a protection against the winds of global change. And the need for security will only increase should economic difficulties continue. Europe is consequently much weaker on the world scene that what one would expect from the 'soft power' deriving from its size, weight and influence. Europe too frequently remains an 'accidental player' (Pisani-Ferry 2005) in a fast-changing world. In the best interest of Europeans, the Union should be actively contributing to shaping its environment. A severe economic crisis in that sense is both the highest challenge and an opportunity to design a strategic vision and a more effective presence in world affairs. Facing the initial shock of the financial crisis in the autumn of 2008, the action of European leaders under the French Presidency proved appropriate and inspiring and should be followed by other steps; will Europe be up to the task in the context created by the deepening of the crisis and by the inauguration of a new administration in the US?

In what follows, I shall give a broad interpretation of the challenges facing the world economy today; the conclusion is that we are not facing a cyclical adjustment after which we should come back to 'business as usual', we face a severe crisis and globalization as we knew it is under threat, an open world economy now calls for a better international governance. The second part is devoted to some aspects of this would-be governance of the world economy; the G20 initiative is placed in the context of a 'global grand bargain' with special focus on the European contribution.

1. CYCLICAL ADJUSTMENT OR SEVERE CRISIS?

As evidenced by Martin Wolf, 'globalization worked'. It fueled an unprecedented period of rapid growth; simultaneously, a greater flexibility of labor markets in industrialized countries and the lowering impact of Chinese costs on manufactured goods prices delivered a long period of low inflation. This conjunction opened new options in the design of monetary policy which the FED (Federal Reserve) under Alan Greenspan was quick to seize. Yet these were, and could only be, extraordinary conditions. And the follow-up proved to be an extraordinary crisis. This is the background of so many recent discussions about a 'Bretton Woods II'. The answers are naturally extremely different depending on the views one adopts about the crisis: is this a cyclical adjustment similar to (even if more violent than) the many previous ones? Is this a more significant turning point which calls for structural transformations? The chapter adopts the latter view for two reasons: one, the deep roots and severe consequences of the financial crisis; second, the connection of different high profile challenges (even without entering the climate change issue which is the matter of Chapter 7). An aggressive use of monetary and tax policies is certainly more than needed to avoid the risk of the recession turning to depression; but short-term measures are not sufficient to restart a vibrant international economy. The present crisis should rather be seen as an opportunity to reassess global economic arrangements and prevalent economic doctrines.

1.1 Liquidity, Innovation, Imbalances

The easy and cheap financing of the US deficit is the most prominent demonstration of excess liquidity in the first decade of the twenty-first century. The persistence of the so-called 'global imbalances' has been one of the decade's major conundrums. Pessimists have prophesied a 'hard landing', only to be regularly proved incorrect. As a consequence, the opposite argument, based on a savings glut, demography and the diversification of global portfolios, has gained more credibility over time – perhaps too much. On the one hand, investors were in effect accumulating treasury paper to finance the deficit. On the other hand, liquidity was pushing demand to extraordinary levels, not only in the US ('the consumer of last resort') but in emerging economies, which were catching up at an unprecedented rate. Accelerated growth in emerging economies, above all in China and India, necessarily drew massively on world resources and a bottleneck slowly built up.

In short, asset markets as well as commodity markets have sent clear warnings. These warnings have been expressed on many occasions by central bankers (in particular the ECB (European Central Bank) and the BIS (Bank for International Settlements) focusing on asset prices), finance ministers (in particular the German and French ones, emphasizing the inadequate pricing of risk at regular G7 meetings) or experts (both in Washington and Europe emphasizing the unsustainability of continuously increasing deficits). These warnings have been systematically put aside.

The whole story of economic growth in the last decade thus starts with excessive liquidity, which is at the root of both financial excesses in the US and soaring commodity prices. Faced with these unexpected developments in 2008, many experts drew – during the first semester – a parallel with the 1970s and raised the specter of 'stagflation'. Subsequently, as of September 2008, commodity markets having started to fall and the threat of recession growing more serious, parallels are more frequently drawn with the depression of the 1930s. Anyway, macroeconomic disorder is the major aspect of the global outlook today; restoring an appropriate framework for future global growth is the first item on the international economic agenda which means and cooperatively fighting recession, reducing global imbalances, controlling global liquidity.

The recent financial turmoil has also brought into sharp relief the need to rethink many aspects of financial regulation and supervision. The broad concept of financial innovation should certainly not be imperiled. Innovation as always improves, in principle, the efficacy of financial intermediation. But nice principles have proved far from reality as the former chairman Greenspan candidly recognized in his testimony before Congress. The range of failures retrospectively appears wide-ranging: imprudent behaviors when dealing with exotic products, perverse incentives, inappropriate regulations and negligent supervision allowing, in the most extreme cases, pure outright fraud. Recent events in the US prove that confidence in self-regulation and lax public oversight in a context of abundant liquidity has gone too far and allowed excessive risk-taking. The key challenge for financial regulation now is to strike a good balance between allowing innovation while keeping systemic risks under control. It is certainly well intentioned to warn against the potential dangers of a return to too rigid regulations. But following the financial disaster, about which the complete credit freeze speaks volumes, confidence will not be durably restored without caution being more systematically embedded by regulation and supervision into financial flows and transactions (more on that in Chapter 2).

An excessive faith in the virtues of self-regulating markets, the whole concept of self-regulation to which US authorities have been so strongly committed for years, is severely damaged. The question of rules and enforcement has to be newly answered. In this process, governments are back; their support, in particular, is massively needed to rescue the financial industry. State intervention is welcome as far as it is the answer to the risk of a systemic crisis, but with the size and range of this intervention come extensive power of governments who are increasingly interfering with the economy which in turn increases the danger of 'patriotic' or nationalist postures: all this could easily turn into a threat to open markets.

1.2 Emerging Economies Don't 'Decouple'

An interesting development of the globalization story has been the creed that emerging economies were not only a success story of the past but could become, as of 2007–2008, the very engine of future world growth. During two quarters, emerging countries (and even Europe) in effect continued to grow despite the weakening of the US economy. In early 2008, the buzz-word among economists was *decoupling*. As we presently know, this was short-sighted. Given that the US is the largest economy, with close to 30 per cent of global GDP (Gross Domestic Product), it remains, for good or ill, the core of the world economy: the idea that the rest of the world could be immune from American turbulences, specifically in the framework of a systemic financial crisis, should always have looked hardly credible. Now, the economic crisis in the industrialized countries is clearly creating new challenges for emerging countries.

Following the reduction of world demand the output gap increases everywhere; political decisions will be much more difficult under strong fiscal and social pressures. Credit conditions are deteriorating with much higher spreads than one year ago. Capital flows are retracting at a dramatic pace as the Institute for International Finance recently warned: private capital flows to emerging economies could retract as much as from more than \$900bn in 2007 to less than \$200bn in 2009: such figures illustrate the extent to which the banking crisis and risk-aversion among international investors are shaking fragile countries, (the Ue should devote specific attention to Central European States). For commodity dependent countries, the downturn of prices in the second half of 2008 reduces the room for maneuver. On top of that, because emerging countries as well as industrialized countries face the risk of recession, they do not enjoy the flexibility to design countercyclical policies as is the case in OECD (Organisation for Economic Co-operation and Development) countries. The result could be a major setback for development goals, in particular poverty reduction. Confidence in the free market economy could also be imperiled: in his history of globalization, Jeff Frieden recalls that Latin American countries, which had benefited immensely from external trade since 1914, turned to their 'import-substitution' strategy for a quarter of a century after the collapse of world trade in the 1930s. Avoiding major setbacks in the integration of emerging countries in the world economy, stabilizing their outlook in the midst of a deep international crisis and reducing poverty should consequently be important and specific items on the G20 agenda.

1.3 No Time for Malthusian Fears

In the second half of the twentieth century, the challenge of a rapidly growing population was met by boosting agricultural productivity through the so-called 'green revolution'. The results were impressive, providing nearly 40 years of abundant food supply. It is interesting to observe that the last time the G7 leaders discussed the issue was in Ottawa in 1981. The communiqué from this meeting emphasized 'the importance of accelerated food production in the developing world and of greater world food security' (G7 communiqué, 1981, art. 19). The terms *production* and *security* are still relevant today. Food made a spectacular comeback on the world scene in 2008. Prices for basic products have been on the rise for two years. At first, they mainly gave rise to humanitarian concerns, but then became a far-reaching socio-economic problem. In 2008, increased prices have drawn millions of poor people into deeper poverty and sparked riots and unrest in many countries. The most ancient specter in economic life – food shortages – is back. Due to deteriorating financial conditions in the second half of 2008, governments are reported to be securing food supplies through secretive barter deals (some of them amounting to as high as $500mn), a revival of forgotten trade practices which suggest that the food crisis, even if it is no longer in the headlines, is deepening rather than having been solved as the UN Food and Agricultural Organization recently warned. This has deep political consequences for governments who simply cannot accept transferring for their responsibility in this particular issue to world markets without preserving some safeguard clauses.

Food in effect is such a sensitive political issue that protectionist measures quickly arise as an urgent reaction. Yet that is fundamentally wrongheaded. Malthus has been proven wrong repeatedly over the past two centuries; and there is little reason to think that his fears could be more pertinent now. Emphasis on free trade is an important part of the solution, not of the problem. On the other hand, political realities need to be recognized and it would be pure ideology to argue that world markets are always and everywhere the only way to feed people. Industrialized countries have proven to always rely on much less simplistic views regarding their own agricultural products and farmers. Agriculture has always been a major dividing line in the globalization process – and it recently explained a significant part of the failure of the Doha Round. A more sophisticated approach to the agricultural division of labor is needed: 'free trade' cannot be the only policy prescription given to governments exposed to pressing domestic needs.

The food issue has recently been made more divisive due to different views regarding the recent trend to develop biofuels. International institutions, the IMF (International Monetary Fund), the World Bank as well as the OECD, agreed that most of the growth in global corn production in recent years stemmed from price increases due to American ethanol production. Longstanding farm subsidies in wealthy countries have also contributed to the crisis, ruining small farmers and decreasing agricultural investment.

The good news, however, is that higher prices provide an opportunity to put an end to decades of neglect of agricultural policies in the developing world. A major contribution will come from the roughly 500 million smallholdings, which have a significant potential to increase productivity and supply while improving social stability; policies should create the favorable environment needed to stimulate investment, be it by securing property rights or bolstering infrastructure. W. Arthur Lewis (1978) had already emphasized that 'if we can make this domestic change (in the agriculture) we shall automatically have a new international economic order'. This avenue is certainly much more promising than any reference to a new Malthusianism that would entail the notion of absolute limits to economic growth. The same holds for commodities, particularly energy.

1.4 Commodities and the Success of Globalization

High commodity prices pose a serious challenge to stable growth worldwide and increase inflationary pressures. Market pressures are timely warnings of the importance of long-term challenges. Even if the 2009 slowdown naturally eases the pressure on world resources, the first semester of 2008 has been a clear demonstration that a successful globalization puts strong pressure on resources: western countries suddenly felt the effect of forces and policies from elsewhere. While the G8 generates approximately half the global GDP, emerging economies now account for three-quarters of the world's economic growth which clearly calls for better strategies to ensure viable growth in the long run.

The fact is that in recent years political and security problems have discouraged investment in many resource-rich countries, such as Iran, Iraq, Nigeria, Venezuela, and Russia. The downturn in that sense is bad news as regards adaptation of capacity to a growing world economy. New energy sources are naturally considered to be essential, and the 44th President of the United States, for one, strongly supports them, but significant differences remain over what these new sources might be. Many countries consider a fresh start to the nuclear industry to be an important part of the solution – though Germany does not share that view. Many also remain suspicious about the development of biofuels, which have been accused, as we previously mentioned, of contributing to increased food prices.

The solution to market tensions entails a curb on energy demand, in particular in the industrialized world, and especially in the US where energy efficiency is much lower than in the EU and Japan. But countries that subsidize fuel consumption will also have to cut that support; China, for one, raised its prices in the spring. Nevertheless, such policies are difficult to implement because consumers consider energy consumption to be a kind of constitutional right and governments are reluctant to imperil what they consider a key element of political stability.

In short, 2008 has not only been a year of despair in the financial sphere, it has been an acid test of the consequences of a successful globalization on world resources. When the economy hopefully rises out of the present recession, there is no doubt that a resurrecting demand will quickly hit capacity limits. Even if the economic outlook in the winter of 2009 remains deeply uncertain, it is not too early to prepare, qualitatively but also quantitatively, the resources we will need in the future.

1.5 Trade and Jobs, Patriotism and Protectionism

Trade and capital flows will decrease in 2009; these were the natural engines of globalization and their downturn could pose a major threat to open world markets. Countries that have relied on export-driven growth, from China to Germany, already are and will be severely hurt. Capital-importing countries will face major difficulties in financing current account deficits; the IMF has already started its traditional business *vis-à-vis* some of these countries and this trend can only go further in 2009. Governments are under increasing pressure to prop up domestic demand and jobs. With the global economy facing its worst recession in decades, protectionism is now a growing risk and it is no surprise that it became a major theme of the 2009 Davos World Forum. To understand the deep reasons for these dangers, one has to understand how the world economy has worked over the last decade.

Increasing trade and capital flows, as we have already noticed, have gone hand in hand with ballooning 'global imbalances'. These are the result of a polarized world divided between countries with huge savings surpluses and other ones, mostly the US, with deficits. There is a fascinating link between the technicalities of international finance and the protests against outsourcing. On the one hand, we have leverage finance, capital flows, a "new class of investors" as Alan Greenspan said. On the other hand, we have workers struck by the consequences of the new division of labor: 'outsourcing is a 'new industrial revolution' threatening not less than 40 million jobs in the US, according to Alan Blinder (2006), the Princeton Professor and former governor of the FED. The backlash against globalization is becoming more pronounced every day in many countries, in particular in the US. We see it in rising nationalism and protectionist temptations. It has been simmering in the 2006 and 2008 elections; it has been manifest in the eruptions in Congress against a Chinese company buying American oil assets or in the virulent response to an attempt by an Arabic group to invest in US harburs.

The same is true when it comes to the suspicions raised in Europe *vis-à-vis* sovereign wealth funds or anger in business and political circles when the euro reached an all-time high of 1.6$ in July 2008. Economic openness – which served the free world so well for decades – is today too frequently perceived as a threat to national security. These are not the reactions one would expect from the world's dominant economic powers, the ones that bear a special responsibility for promoting the agenda of globalization. Americans or Europeans have proved not to be protectionist by nature. What they probably want looks like a level playing field; otherwise, we are faced with the danger of mercantilist policies, not only tariffs but more surreptitious channels, like introducing social or environmental clauses in trade agreements, or the more aggressive form of competitive devaluations.

*

Finally, this survey of difficult challenges currently facing the world economy should have nothing to surprise anyone familiar with economic history. Even without referring to the first half of the twentieth century, the last 40 years look like a golden age only if one forgets the breakdown of the gold-exchange standard, the oil crises, stagflation in the industrialized world, and financial crises everywhere in emerging countries. From a long-term perspective, however, what is fascinating about these episodes is the flexibility with which adaptations have occurred, offering solutions to seemingly intractable problems. This is where we are again, with higher stakes than anytime since World War II. But the economy will not recover today following the previous lines of easy credit and cheap commodities, and continuously increasing outsourcing and global imbalances. Globalization as we knew it has lost momentum; the financial crisis, commodity prices and protectionist reactions reveal the collision course between mutual dependence, with its costs and benefits, and the return of nationalism, with its prejudices and fears. We are definitely entering a new phase of globalization. We need better governance of globalization, and we need it urgently.

2. 'GOVERNING' THE GLOBAL ECONOMY

Globalization is frequently presented as a product of market forces and technological innovation. True enough. But this should never erase the other side of the picture: globalization is also the result of a political process. A huge amount of political capital has been spent year after year to sell to public opinions the merits of openness, industrial restructurings and competitive wages. It became common wisdom that, as painful as it can be, labor flexibility is necessary for better and higher value added jobs to replace low-skilled and low-paid ones. The financial (and then economic) crisis, as well as previous ongoing trends towards rising inequalities, have sown doubts about whether globalization could live up to those promises particularly in industrialized countries. There are widespread doubts, too, about the international community's ability to find the right path to rescue the world economy and restore a virtuous circle of development, trade and increasing living standards. Facing this globalization fatigue, choices made today will shape our future.

2.1 Between Global Order and International Instability

The divide facing us in 2009 can simply be summarized as a choice between the build-up of a new global order and the propagation of international tensions. Despite the deepening of the financial crisis, the autumn of 2008 and winter of 2009 brought some reassuring good news. Taken together, they create the conditions for an unprecedented exercise in international political economy. First, leaders everywhere perceive a common vital interest in averting the worst case scenario and in placing the world economy on a stronger footing for a more inclusive and sustainable globalization. Second, the election of Barack Obama places America on a completely new footing in world affairs – America is back and will be strongly involved. Third, the French Presidency of the European Union has exemplified what Europe could bring to the world: initiatives, flexibility, working institutions (in particular regarding the role of the ECB) and above all a visible political existence. Fourth, the G20 meeting in Washington in November 2008, short-circuiting esoteric debates about refreshing of the G7, proved timely and effective.

Speaking of 'an effective G20' could sound a little strange and deserves some comments. Following an initiative by Nicholas Sarkozy, this meeting was initially received with skepticism. Papers volubly described the unlikely meeting of a US 'lame-duck' President days after the election of his successor with European leaders bickering as usual about arcane matters and emerging countries, leaders watching from the side without any willingness to take bigger responsibility for fixing problems not of their making. At best a distraction, at worst a costly failure. Well, it did not turn out that way. The communiqué is surprisingly substantial (even perhaps excessively technical for leaders) if compared with so many previous exercises. Most importantly, it summarizes a vision backed by commitments… and summons the next meeting five months later. These are only a meeting and a communiqué and it is easy to mock language and photos, but it is a step in the right direction and one has to remember that the Bretton Woods agreements have been in the making for years. Where are we going from there?

The first difficulty is that we are at a turning point not only economically but also ideologically: we have nothing to fear except to be prisoners of old thoughts and prejudices. The fundamental political economy choice we face today is not, as conservatives have said for a quarter century, between market economy and 'socialism', it is between dysfunctional policies and enabling governments. 1989 is an historical year because it marked a decisive victory of the free world and the supremacy of a pure-market form of capitalism; 2008 could force everyone to recognize the limits of this extreme form of unbridled capitalism. Now, the question is not so much with the diagnosis than with prescriptions. We can solve the problems facing us only by collective action and by restoring a multilateral system in which all are bound by the same rules. Unfortunately, multilateralism has been discredited and rejected by the US administration for too long, we have fewer materials on the shelves than we would wish and governments are ill-equipped to discuss these issues and design the solutions. What can Europe, the heartland of law-based international governance, bring to the table? In short, a lot of good will and experience but also the weaknesses due to its divisions.

2.2 Coordinating Stimulus

We are in the grip of the most severe crisis for eight decades. Reinhart and Rogoff (2008) summarized how the 'average crisis' unfolds. Asset markets collapse (equity prices retreat by half), house prices fall (by one third), output falls (by 10 per cent), unemployment rises (by 7 per cent). How far will we follow this path? The answer will result from our ability to provide both short-term stabilization and structural reforms. The buzz in this context is to 'avoid the mistakes of the 30s' which, more or less, correctly inspire the initial reactions of the governments. In so doing, central banks and treasuries are not expected to invent new strategies, they have to use all their policy tools and most importantly they have to do so in unison: what we need now is a coordinated monetary expansion and a coordinated fiscal expansion across the globe. Everyone familiar with the books of Charles Kindleberger knows that the main danger of a severe crisis is that it is protracted, that difficulties are accumulating, that the number of options progressively diminishes, that the temptation of 'beggar-my-neighbor' policies inevitably increases.

We know that. What makes the rescue so difficult is the magnitude of the action. German initial unwillingness to go that far in the autumn of 2008 has, for example, been criticized as well as Barack Obama's huge stimulus for being not big enough. Following a quick U-turn of the economic profession, huge deficits are now considered wise policies. The G20 was right in November to confirm that there are times for virtue and times for boldness. Looking forward, the following question is: how long will markets finance public debts if they run out of control? 2009 will see tax revenues starting to collapse; a bad news which is not priced since markets until now have been fully supportive of aggressive policy actions to restart the economy. But it can be extremely costly as it is shown by countries like Greece or Spain whose credit spreads have quickly and widely increased (if compared with what the German treasury pays) in early 2009. Those countries have quickly been qualified as 'fragile', which is true. But it would be foolish to think that the 'flight for safety' is a definitive protection for bigger countries, either other European ones or even the US. This recalls another aspect of the 1930s: the absolute chaos in the management of state expenditures and revenues, every government trying to design its optimal mix so as to preserve a better credit than others (see Kindleberger 1973; Kindleberger and Aliber 1978, among others). The lack of successful coordination at the time certainly ranks among the causes of the disaster. No one certainly wants to repeat the errors of the 1930s. But it is not sufficient to call, as most economists do today, for ever higher deficits: a smooth financing of deficits will continuously require a concerted monitoring of tax policies facing unexpected developments of credit conditions.

Contrary to many negative critics, the reaction of tax policies in autumn 2008 in the EU have been reasonably rapid, appropriate and coordinated, especially if one has in mind that such a quick and massive answer was a sort of a revolution as compared with the traditional set-up of the EMU (Economic and Monetary Union). Now, this was only the first step, the future of public debts for every country in the world will be under market scrutiny. American and European governments are the bigger debtors to come; both sides should agree that huge deficits are extraordinary measures, not the engine of future growth, and assess the long-term sustainability of their fiscal deficits. Proposals by Fabian Zuleeg and Hans Martens (Chapter 6) are not only the backbone of wise European policies but, were we be able to improve our own policy framework, offer the basis for a much needed coordination with the US administration.

2.3 The Future of Financial Regulation

The initial reactions and measures taken to contain the financial crisis everywhere include massive injections of government money; they have had at best mixed results. Following the failure of Lehman, those measures avoided a complete collapse of the financial sector in the autumn of 2008. The danger is that with the government being given this sudden and huge influence in the economy, this new power could quickly be misused. All these interventions are undoubtedly justifiable but where is the intellectual construction we need to design them properly? Populist or nationalist comments – which are inevitably rising with the injection of tax-payers', money into a failed financial system – are alarming. The need of a more adequate regulation, not necessarily a more intrusive one, and of its forceful enforcement, rather than a negligent one, is no more debated. This is precisely what European Ministers (more precisely those from continental Europe) regularly suggested to their colleagues at G7 Finance Ministers meetings; at the end of the day, they were not proven wrong!

The solution to the financial crisis will not lie in the accumulation of emergency measures but rather in structural reforms embedding the banking industry and financial markets into a binding international framework. When it becomes flagrant that 'government is not part of the problem', we suddenly discover that we do not have the tools to make the government an efficient part of the solution. This is the task facing us now, and it is urgent. The key challenge for designing these regulations will be to exercise prudence and discipline without discouraging innovation and repudiating its benefits. The best inspiration to achieve this sensitive balance is to be found in an open-minded and result-oriented transatlantic financial dialog. It had a good start years ago because the success of a global economy is linked to a greater harmonization of capitalist infrastructures: accounting standards, market supervision, ratings methodology... But the prevailing, sometimes ideological, vision in the US of self-regulating markets limited the fruits of this dialog. With a new US administration, this time is over. Prior bias can now be overcome and the two continents usefully bring to the table different perceptions and experiences. Washington is ready to move, but make no mistake – Washington is certainly ready to exercise leadership. We have had a first sense of this new dynamics with the publication of the 'Volcker Report' on January 15, 2009. The report is the most extensive and detailed available proposal: it redesigns the boundaries of financial supervision, the tasks facing the regulators and supervisors, the governance and reform of infrastructures and strongly emphasizes the need for greater international cooperation. Paul Volcker now being the closest advisor to President Obama as regards financial reform, it will not take long for the administration to transform the report into materials for G20 meetings.

Despite frequent skepticism, there are consequently good reasons to think that an improved global coordination of financial regulation is feasible. The 'unipolar approach of the Bush Administration' (remember the Sarbanes–Oxley law and its extra-territorial measures) being over, there is no more excuse for European unpreparedness to productively enter this dialog. But American authorities need empowered counterparts; there is no dialog if one part of the table is divided into 27 conflicting views! This is a second aspect where the negative consequences of a still fragmented Europe are all too visible. Discussion in Chapters 2 by Franco Bruni and 3 by Karel Lannoo exemplify different pieces which would build a more integrated framework of regulation and supervision (see also regular publications by Nicolas Véron from Bruegel). The silence of the Commission in this regard since the beginning of the banking and financial crisis speaks volumes; the European Central Bank by contrast demonstrated its effectiveness. It is time to send a wake-up call to Brussels ('but whom should I call there?') and quickly entrust Frankfurt with bigger responsibilities, it would be good for Europe and reinforce European positions in coming international debates.

2.4 Trade and Exchange Rates

The rise of protectionism is not the most likely development of the crisis in 2009 but it possibly stands as the greatest threat to the future of the world economy. Lessons from the great depression are clear: the economic isolationism of the 1930s dramatically reinforced the depression (the spiral of contracting world trade from 1929 to 1933 as drawn by Kindleberger is probably one of the most illustrious graphs related to this period). For sure, there is nothing similar to the detestable Smoot–Hawley tariff in sight. But the modern economy is much more complex and trade flows could be severely damaged by more discrete measures. Following a long period of tariff disarmament, many countries for example have lower tariffs than the 'ceilings' rates agreed under WTO (World Trade Organization) rules. This leaves ample room to maneuver to raise levies while respecting the rules. Calls to help troubled industries will introduce discriminatory subsidies as we have already seen for the car manufacturing industry. The proposals to use 'social' or 'environmental' clauses to stop 'unfair' trade practices could have more appeal to politicians than crude tariffs barriers but they could also prove damaging to world trade and investment decisions. In a social and ideological context where support to free trade could be more fragile than before, the G20 commitment in November 2008 to avoid any new trade barrier was more than welcome. Commitments are what they are and disappointedly, Russia or India took restrictive measures a few days after the G20. But the most significant gesture is the move by the US Congress to include in January 2009 in its stimulus package fragments of a 'buy American act'; even if modest in scope, this is more than a negative signal; Chancelor Merkel and others were well inspired to strongly disapprove. A revival of the Doha negotiations would bring a renewed momentum and push back these temptations for a beggar-my-neighbor policy but seems for now to be off the table. A less ambitious but more easily reachable goal for the leaders would be to reinforce the role of the WTO in order to 'name and shame' any cut to the commitments of free trade and to possibly reinforce the role of the organization to repress the more serious ones. This is what the European Union could endorse and propose in order to maintain trade policies on the right tracks. A more serious threat could come from the 'manipulation' of exchange rates which recalls the 'competitive devaluations' of the 1930s.

The theory of international trade explains the benefits of free trade under the condition that trade flows are balanced; in that case, outsourcing can require structural adjustments, which are costly for those involved, but import flows are counterbalanced by increased export opportunities so that the policy problem is to find a balance between winners and losers of free trade. This condition is not fulfilled by countries continuously accumulating huge surpluses. Increasing imbalances between China and the US have fueled many proposals to call the IMF to duty in restoring more discipline in the management of balance of payments and exchange rates, without success. The reason is that the effectiveness of the Fund is asymmetric. Its power is linked to its ability to finance deficit countries when external funding dries; being the creditor of last resort, its credit is conditional to the adoption of new economic policies. There is nothing similar when dealing with surplus countries or with a deficit country enjoying, like the US, the privilege of a reserve currency. The prerequisite to face this problem is to recognize that trade and exchange rates have to be seized together, so that the solution relies on the IMF and the WTO working together to exercise judgement, propose solutions and be able to enforce appropriate measures. Could such a scheme work? Technical solutions certainly exist; an exchange of views between Pascal Lamy and Dominique Strauss-Kahn would certainly prove productive and deliver practical proposals for diagnosing countries with excessive structural surpluses, as well as for recording excessive fluctuations of exchange rates which distort trade flows. The IMF would as of today propose policy recommendations; implementation could be more forceful than now by using the WTO's toolbox and its lot of pressures and sanctions. Such a process is fully in line with the philosophy of free trade embedded in the Bretton Woods institutions and trade agreements; it would offer a legal and rational framework for dealing with issues which, uncontrolled, could dangerously threaten the future of liberal trade.

2.5 Capitalism, Capitalisms

However, the future of globalization will not be dictated by economic considerations alone. Two events which occurred in the summer of 2008, the Olympic Games in Beijing and the Russian invasion of Georgia, exemplify if needed the weight of geo-politics in our world, a trend that has been emphasized by Thierry de Montbrial for years. The issue has been raised in economic terms, before the financial crisis, at a conference devoted to the 'war of capitalisms' which had been organized by Le Cercle des économistes in Aix en Provence in July 2007 and more recently, in political terms, at the World Policy Conference organized by IFRI (Institut Français des Relations Internationales) in Evian in September 2008. These conferences have argued that the primacy of the American form of capitalism has been incorrectly interpreted as having become the only possible form through some sort of socio-economic Darwinian evolution. In principle, it is true that superior efficiency could have forced companies, cultures, and policies onto the same track, summed up in the phrase 'shareholder value'. Yet the world economy did not develop that way. Other forms of capitalist development have proven more resilient than initially thought. Critics of the American way had been for example quite frequent among German officials for years (remember the qualification of Wall Street bankers as 'locusts' by a German Economic Minister) and Chancellor Merkel for one recently celebrated the permanent value of Sozial-*Markt Wirtschaft* in reconciling economic efficiency and social fairness. More recent forms of capitalisms even became more dynamic in the context of globalization. Family capitalism regained strength; private equity capitalism has not been (until now?) undermined by the financial crisis. State capitalisms, especially due to their geopolitical leverage, have become prominent actors on the world stage.

Many believe that this latest trend is reinforced by the economic crisis which could speed up the decline of western dominance of the world. The *Financial Times*, for example, (January 29, 2009) heralded that 'Wen and Putin lectured western leaders at Davos'. The two leaders in effect used the world economic forum in January 2009 to criticize what they see as an 'unsustainable model of development', to attack greedy financial institutions and to denounce macroeconomic policies which led to the financial crisis. The implications of such a state of world affairs have yet to be fully grasped. But whatever they are, and however they are to be understood, the effects of the present crisis will clearly extend much farther than pure economic considerations. It casts a shadow over the US, and more generally western, dominance. As numerous publications now recognize (one particularly noticeable originating from the US National Intelligence Council) (NIC 2008), America's absolute power remains huge but its relative power will crumble: the world that Barack Obama will face is completely different from the one Bill Clinton inherited from President Bush senior.

It is now recognized, even among top US analysts, that we are entering a 'multipolar world'. The international system as we knew it following the fall of the Berlin Wall will be almost unrecognizable following the rise of emerging powers and the growing influence of non-state actors (see Slaughter 2004). The NIC report adopts the view that relative wealth and economic power will move from west to east. In many aspects, this has recently become common wisdom. We should nevertheless think twice before adopting this view without reservation: the 'multipolar world' is not still a given for two reasons. First, extrapolating recent trends of economic growth could prove a poor predictor of the future performance of these countries; we have already commented what happened in 2008 to the too optimistic theory of 'decoupling' (as the worsening financial and socio-economic situation in Russia and China demonstrates). Second, it remains unclear what we mean when speaking of other 'poles' than the US. The BRICs (Brazil, Russia, India and China) are from now on important players at the top table; without them, older industrial nations will have difficulties in handling the global crisis, but they have still to confirm that they are willing to continue to be part of the game, respecting existing rules and contributing to the design of new rules. In fact, what we know most clearly about a 'multipolar world' is that it is not intrinsically stable. Think of the US Congress moves to forbid Chinese or Arabic investments in US so-called strategic assets or to the Russians using gas as a bargaining tool *vis-à-vis* Ukraine and the west and you easily see how the strategic behaviors of big players could have a disruptive effect on market forces. This is also a world where the dispersion of power means in practice that more actors have the effective capacity to block collective action. The collapse of the Doha Round, the first not to come to a conclusion since World War II, speaks volumes about the new challenges facing a de-centered world where a few well-placed particular interests can derail a vast global process.

2.6 The Political Economy of Global Governance

Globalization has been interpreted until now as a product of market forces. International institutions, especially under the Bush Administration, have come to be considered less and less relevant. While critics were right that international organizations should be more focused, they were wrong in concluding that they could simply be bypassed. It was simply premature to declare the death of 'embedded capitalism' which was such an essential part of the second half of the twentieth century. But it is hardly surprising that, following this war of attrition, there are few supranational bodies able to enforce reciprocity today. It is certainly noteworthy that the cooperation among central banks after August 2007 proved an important asset for rescuing the world's financial sphere. But what about other institutions? The IMF has been a bystander of sorts, powerless in the face of increasing global imbalances and the recent financial crisis. The WTO's latest Doha Round was derailed. And the G8 became impotent, sort of an anachronism.

Global problems require global solutions. But what do we really know about institutions delivering 'global solutions'? The predominant answer a few years ago relied on self-regulated markets; is it sufficient that this reference be now discredited to jump to the opposite argument and call for a world government? This solution has surprisingly been (nominally) endorsed as a desirable move by Gideon Rachman, a prominent commentator of the *Financial Times*. Unfortunately, as Rachman (2008)emphasizes, it is not sufficient that the most pressing political problems, like the financial crisis or climate change, are unequivocally requiring global solutions to see national governments surrender sovereignty. Everywhere, the average citizen's political identity remains (at best) national, an American proverb captures it eloquently: 'all politics is local'. We should consequently not expect the world running to adopt a global government. But Rachman is wrong when suggesting that international governance necessarily means international government.

Turning to history, we see two other solutions bringing peace and prosperity to the world, hegemony and balance of power. Contemporary history shows economic leadership under the two successive forms of the Pax Britannica and the Pax Americana, both of them combining, according to the classic analysis of Robert Keohane (1984), hegemony and cooperation. As for the balance of power, the most interesting example remains Europe following the Congress of Vienna which organized one of the longer periods of peace in European history. Unfortunately, none of these references seems to apply today. Contrary to so many received opinions, the United States today has not an 'excessive' power; the risk is rather that the country becomes too narrowly concentrated on its own difficulties. But its relative power remains so high that it makes the idea of a balance of power with other 'poles' in the world a sort of fantasy. The world we are entering into is neither the 'unipolar' one, which will remain in history as the brief moment of a neo-conservative dream, nor the 'multipolar' one, which the French diplomacy has sometimes imprudently and prematurely trumpeted. This invites an alarming comparison with the great depression whose amplitude has been correctly attributed to the lack of appropriate international cooperation, 'the UK being unable and the US unwilling' to organize it. Should we today be afraid that the US is unable to do the job alone and that no other country is ready to contribute? Globalization today needs leadership and international cooperation.

2.7 The G20 and the Coming Grand Bargain

Global governance is a question of political economy which raises three questions: are existing institutions the ones we need? To what extent will participants be willing to uphold multilateral commitments? How will collective decisions be implemented? The short answer reads as follows. No one can reasonably expect international institutions suddenly to solve intractable problems; there is no 'magic bullet'. On the other hand, international institutions, rules, and networks are so important to the proper functioning of globalization that there is no alternative to them. The notion of building 'better' international arrangements from scratch is pure fantasy. The real point is political: international institutions should reflect the world economy in its present form, in full cognizance of the ways in which it has changed.

In this context, the G20 summit really is a breakthrough for three reasons. First, it has finally enlarged to major emerging countries the obsolete G7 which was trying to square the circle with infamous G8+5 formulas. Second, it convened the leaders, even to tackle the issue of their finance ministers' responsibility; this is good news because building new international arrangements is a question of political will and power-sharing, which only leaders can deal with. Third, it decided to meet again in April in London, which means that it is the beginning of a process from which results are expected. Where are we going from there? The April meeting will be focused – according to the host, Prime Minister Gordon Brown – on three issues: stabilizing the banking system, agreeing on a worldwide stimulus and reigniting credit to business and households; that is great, but not enough. Substantially, this is the job of finance ministers. For leaders, it might seem logical to attack the formidable international agenda by going through a series of successive issues: finance, climate, energy, trade, exchange rates, food, development… But trying to close each of the issues one after the other could prove the wrong method. This piecemeal approach, tackling problems in isolation from the others, will soon lead to the same difficulties we have been experiencing for years.

This is why the G20 must adopt more ambitious goals. It should focus on the true job of leaders: act on impulse, compromise and enforce. As compared with ministers, they are solely able to make compromises regarding power-sharing (for example the question of seats in the governing bodies of international organizations, the UN security council or the Board of the Bretton-Woods institutions); they are also sole able to accept trade-offs between different sectors, agreeing to concede one thing in a trade negotiation against another involving climate. Leaders now have to embrace the design of a more integrated architecture of international organizations. Former President Eisenhower once advised: 'if a problem cannot be solved, enlarge it': this is a bold strategy but it can work because it brings more political stuff into the hands of the leaders and consequently opens more room for possible trade-offs. And, in effect, many of the challenges facing the world economy today are interconnected as we amply demonstrated earlier.

A radical step to transform 'governance' into a reality would be the creation of a new United Nations Economic Security Council which (probably) originated in the 1995 Report of the Commission on Global Governance (under the name of a 'Global Council'); in 2002 Jacques Chirac introduced the expression 'Economic and Social Security Council' which was subsequently adopted by Kemal Dervis in 2005 and finally endorsed by Chancellor Angela Merkel in January 2009 in Paris and then in Davos. Is this reference to the UN to be taken seriously? Well, President Bush and the neo-conservatives, for sure, are not the only ones to deplore the too frequent ineffectiveness of the institution. But it is time now to bring to the end with eight years of contempt; the world is better with the United Nations than without. Listening, for example, to Jean-Marie Guéhenno (Under-Secretary of the UN for peacekeeping operations) at a Weatherhead Conference in Talloires in June 2008 makes crystal clear that the dangers posed by destabilized states makes peacekeeping a strategic necessity in the present era and that the United Nations is the only organization to have the legitimacy and track record to maintain civil order amidst political and social crises. Chancellor Merkel's proposal has to be taken seriously and offers a clear basis for a strong European proposal.

The hope raised by Barack Obama being elected is that the arrogant and brutal stance of the Bush presidency will give way to the moral leadership of an open and progressive society. In his book, *The Audacity of Hope*, he argued that 'when the world sole superpower willingly restraints its power and abides by internationally agreed-upon standards of conduct, it send a message that these are rules worth following'. The importance that President Obama attaches to the UN system is shown by the fact that he appointed Susan Rice, one of his closest aides, as America's ambassador to the UN. There is a clear recognition in Washington today that the major factors affecting America's security and well-being in the long run are: reforming the global financial system, enhancing energy security, addressing climate change, managing the anti-globalization backlash and finally restoring the role of international institutions. This is an Acheson moment: Dean Acheson, Secretary of State of President Truman, summarized his role in shaping the post-World War II world as being 'present at the creation of the world', a new world following the ruins of the depression and the war. Today, again, is a time requiring bold responses to the world disorder.

3. CONCLUSIONS

Hopes that we could come back to the previous trends of globalization are wrong. The present crisis is not a cyclical one; it will extend much beyond economic considerations. The world has a choice: either to defend short-term interests and stick to past solutions, or to recognize new realities, share power, design common goals, and accept symmetrical responsi-bilities and constraints. The choices we will make will shape the world for decades. Entangled in the financial crisis, we face the unpleasant truth that we were not able to avoid sort of a repetition of 1929. The following question is: will we be able to jump from 1929 to 1945? 2009 may well go down in history as a pivotal era, like 1989 (the fall of the Berlin wall), 1944 (Bretton Woods), 1919 (the Treaty of Versailles) or 1815 (the Congress of Vienna). Those momentous events marked the end of an era and opened a new epoch in the history of the world. A new America is ready to do its part of the job and to exercise leadership, it cannot do the job alone. America re-engage the world, America needs partners, this is a challenging demand vis à vis Europe! Europe is naturally a prominent player in international economics, trade, finance, aid, agriculture, climate and so forth. But Europe is too frequently ineffective due to its weak internal governance, its lack of strategic perspective and the contradictions of its external representation(s). Its role now is not to offer a moral grand-mastership; there is no more excuse for standing at ease on the side of world affairs. The European Union is a 'work in progress'; it is frequently said that it never progress quicker than when facing challenges, the highest the challenges, the quicker the progresses! Nobody in the 80s believed that the single currency could be a reality in a generation; the fall of the Berlin wall did it in a decade. Europe, not France, Germany or Italy, is called to duty, it's called now. This should be used as a huge opportunity to complete the 'European puzzle'.

BIBLIOGRAPHY

Aglietta, Michel (2008), *Macroéconomie financière*, La Découverte.

Altman, Roger (2009), 'The Great Crash, 2008, a geo-political setback for the West', *Foreign Affairs*, **88** (1), January–February.

Artus, Patrick (2007), *Les incendiaires: Les banques centrales dépassées par la globalisation*, Paris: Librairie Académique Perrin.

Bank for International Settlements (BIS) (2008), *78th Annual Report, 1 April 2007– 31 March 2008*.

Baumol, William J., Robert E. Littan and Carl J. Schramm (2007), *Good Capitalism, Bad Capitalisms*, London: Yale University Press.

Blinder, Alan (2006), 'Offshoring, the next industrial revolution', *Foreign Affairs*, **85** (2), March–April.

Bradford Colin I. and Johannes F. Linn (2007), *Global Governance Reform, Breaking the Stalemate*, The Brookings Institution Press.

Bradford, Colin I., Johannes F. Linn and Paul Martin (2008), *Global Governance Breakthrough: the G20 Summit and the Future Agenda*, Brookings Policy Brief no. 168, Brookings Institution Press, December.

Brender, Anton and Florence Pisani (2007), *Les déséquilibres financiers internationaux*, La Découverte.

Brookings Global Economy and Development (2008), *The G-20 Financial Summit: Seven Issues at Stake*.

Cooper, Richard (2008), 'Global imbalances, globalization, demography and sustainability', *Journal of Economic Perspectives*, **22** (3), Summer.

Dervis, Kemal and Ceren Ozer (2005), *A Better Globalization: Legitimacy, Governance, and Reform*, Center for Global Development, April.

European Commission (2006), *Global Europe, Competing in the World, a Contribution to the Growth and Sobs Strategy*, December.

Food and Agricultural Organization (FAO) (2008), *The State of Food and Agriculture Report – Biofuels: Prospects, Risks and Opportunities*.

Frieden Jeff (2006), *Global Capitalism*, New York: Norton.

Friedman, Thomas L. (2005), *The World Is Flat: a Brief History of the Twenty-first Century*, Farrar, New York: Straus & Giroux.

Fukuyama, Francis (1992), *The End of History and the Last Man*, New York: Free Press.

FTChinese.com (2009), *Wen and Putin Lecture Western Leaders at Davos*.

Greenspan, Alan (2008), *Testimony before the Committee of Government Oversight and Reform*, US Congress, 23 October.

Grieco, Joseph M. and G. John Ikenberry (2003), *State Power and World Markets*, New York: Norton.

Group of Thirty (2009), *Financial Reform, a Framework for Financial Stability*, 15 January.

International Monetary Fund (IMF) (2008), *World Economic Outlook: Housing and the Business Cycle*, www.imf.org, 26 August.

Institute of International Finance (2009), *Capital Flows to Emerging Markets Economies*, 27 January.

James, Harold (2001), *The End of Globalization*, Cambridge, MA: Harvard University Press.

Kahler, Miles and David A. Lake (eds) (2003), *Governance in a Global Economy*, Princeton, NJ: Princeton University Press.

Keohane, Robert (1984), *After Hegemony, Cooperation and Discord in the World Political Economy*, Princeton, NJ: Princeton University Press.

Kindleberger, Charles (1973), *The World in Depression*, Berkeley, CA: University of California Press.

Kindleberger, Charles and Robert Aliber (1978), *Manias, Panics and Crashes, a History of Financial Crises*, Wiley Investment Classics.

Le Cercle des Économistes (2008a), *Un Monde de Ressources Rares*, Paris: Librairie Académique Perrin.

Le Cercle des Économistes (2008b), *La Crise Financière: Causes, Effets et Réformes Nécessaires*, Presses Universitaires de France (PUF).

Le Cercle des Économistes (2008c), *La Guerre des Capitalismes Aura Lieu*, Paris: Librairie Académique Perrin.

Lewis, W. Arthur (1978), *The Evolution of the International Economic Order*, Princeton, NJ: Princeton University Press.

Mistral, Jacques (2006a), 'Growing inequality is turning America inward', *Financial Times*, 16 July.

Mistral, Jacques (2006b), *Market Forces and Fair Institutions, The Political Economy of Europe and the US Revisited*, CES Working Paper no. 138, Center for European Studies, Harvard University.

Mistral, Jacques (2007), *Comment Réformer la Gouvernance Mondiale,* in Le Cercle des Économistes, *Un Monde de Ressources Rares*, Paris: Librairie Académique Perrin.

Mistral, Jacques (2008–2009), *La Troisième Révolution Américaine*, Paris: Librairie Académique Perrin, 2ᵉ édition enrichie.

Montbrial, Thierry de (2008a), *L'action et le Système du Monde*, Presses Universitaires de France (PUF).

Montbrial, Thierry de (ed.) (2008b), *RAMSES 2009, Introduction*, Paris: Dunod.

Montbrial, Thierry de (ed.) (2008c), 'World policy conference', *Politique étrangère*, numéro special Evian.

National Intelligence Council (NIC) (2008), *Global Trends 2025, a Transformed World*, US Government Printing Office.

Obama, Barack (2006), *The Audacity of Hope: Thoughts on Reclaiming the American Dream*, New York: Crown Publisher.

Organisation for Economic Co-operation and Development (OECD) (2008a), *Economic Assessment of Biofuel Support Policies*, OECD Working Papers, 26 August.

Organisation for Economic Co-operation and Development (2008b), *Rising Food Prices: Causes and Consequences*, OECD Working Papers, 26 August.

Pisani-Ferry, Jean (2005), *The Accidental Player, the EU and the Global Economy*, www.Bruegel.org.

Sapir, André (ed.) (2007), *Fragmented Power, Europe and the Global Economy*, Bruxelles: Bruegel.

Rachman, Gideon (2008) 'And now for a world government', *Financial Times*, 8 December.

Reinhart, Carmen and Kenneth Rogoff (2008), *The Aftermath of Financial Crises*, www.economics.harvard.edu./rogoff

Ruggie, John (1983), *International Regimes, Transactions, and Change: Embedded Liberalism in the Postwar Economic Order*, in St. Krasner (ed.), *International Regimes*, Ithaca, NY: Cornell University Press.

Slaughter, Anne-Marie (2004), *A New World Order*, Princeton, NJ: Princeton University Press.

Truman, Edwin (ed.) (2006), *Reforming the IMF in the 21st Century*, Washington, D.C.: Peterson Institute for International Affairs.

Véron, Nicolas (2008), *Europe's Banking Challenge: Reregulation without Refragmentation*, CESifo Forum, 4.

Wilkinson, Rorden (2006), *The WTO: Crisis and the Governance of Global Trade*, New York: Routledge.

Wolf, Martin (2004), *Why Globalization Works?*, London: Yale University Press.

Wolf, Martin (2008), 'Why agreeing a new Bretton Woods is vital and so hard', *Financial Times*, 5 November.

2. Do We Understand It? Forbidden Questions on the Financial Crisis

Franco Bruni*

1. INTRODUCTION

The international economic crisis started during the summer of 2007 (Gorton 2008) in a specific section of the US financial markets and then spread rapidly everywhere in the financial world and in the global real economy.[1] The desire to understand with precision its causes and consequences is still premature. Reflections, plans and deliberations have started, in an effort to render the world economy more resilient and to prevent new crises, by correcting the rules, the institutions and the behaviours that contributed to the present one. The priority, though, is the immediate cure of the current turmoil. Financial authorities and operators, politicians and academic economists are still trying to better understand what is happening and where the heart of the problem is.

To contribute a stimulus to this understanding, this chapter briefly discusses some specific issues. The idea is more to stress questions than to elaborate the answers. In fact, questions are posed that can be called 'forbidden'. They are forbidden for at least three reasons: because it still looks impossible to answer them in a clear-cut way, while they tend to inspire half-baked non-orthodox answers; because they deal with issues and aspects of the crisis that are often 'left aside' by the typical discussions on the crisis; and because they reveal weaknesses and uncertainties of some relevant parts of economic and financial theory.

* The author is grateful to Charles Goodhart and to the other participants in a workshop of the LSE Financial Regulatory Group for a useful discussion of a previous draft of the chapter. He also thanks Niccolò Biancheri, George Kopits, David Llewellyn, Giovanna Nicodano, and other friends and colleagues that have read the draft and contributed criticism and suggestions.

The following three sections concentrate, respectively, on monetary policy, financial regulation and crisis management. Section 2 asks the question of how much monetary policy is responsible for the crisis. It discusses the relationship between the risk-free interest rates manoeuvred by central banks and the size and sensitivity of the risk premia that are included in spread-augmented market interest rates. Certain weaknesses of the received monetary orthodoxy are then listed, in an effort to understand to what extent they have contributed to the mistakes that triggered the crisis. The last forbidden questions of section 2 are about the potential role that reforms of monetary policymaking might have in curing the crisis and avoiding new ones.

Section 3 is a discussion of a widely held opinion: that the responsibility for the crisis has been an insufficient amount of financial regulation[2] and that financial markets can be more stable only if they are subjected to stricter regulations. According to this idea, the crisis proves the weaknesses of the market mechanism and the dangers of liberalization. The discussion in the section is organized by listing the arguments that can be made in favour of and against an explanation of the crisis centred on an alleged 'excessive liberalization'. As the questions posed are of the 'forbidden' type, no clear-cut answer is offered, while the importance of quantitatively insufficient regulation is contrasted with that of qualitatively inadequate rules.

Section 4 looks at how crisis management has been conducted worldwide, especially in the US and in the EU, during the first 5–6 quarters of the crisis. Authorities have taken decisions that have certainly contributed to limit some of the worst possible consequences of the financial mess. But their decisions have also proceeded in a controversial and disorderly fashion, showing the limits of the crisis management tools that have been used and disorienting many analysts and market participants. The forbidden question is then: can we state that, in spite of some reassuring results obtained by the interventions of central banks, prudential authorities and governments, the overall observation of crisis management has been a depressing experience? Three specific crisis management tools are considered in the section: lending of last resort, bailouts and deposit insurance.

The considerations springing from the forbidden questions of this chapter are certainly relevant to discuss the European monetary and financial governance in the scenery of the crisis. The institutional and operational evolution of monetary policy in the euro-area and of European financial regulation, supervision and crisis management, depends on how some of the questions are answered and on how Europe is able to share with the global financial system the best part of its answers. With this in mind, section 5 concludes the chapter.

2. IS MONETARY POLICY AT THE ROOT OF THE CRISIS, AND OF THE CURE?

Excessively low interest rates, for too much time, are often cited among the causes of the crisis. There is a significant degree of consensus, in particular, on the fact that US monetary policy, from 2002 to 2005, has been nourishing the bubble in housing and other asset prices, which started to precipitate as soon as the Fed started to target a higher cost of liquidity. Many commentators also agree on the idea that the pegging of the renmimbi has been at the roots of the transmission of excess liquidity to China and the Far East, contributing to the inflated global growth that eventually resulted in the financial crisis. The opinion on European monetary policy is usually one of a more cautious behaviour, keeping interest rates less low for less time. But also ECB (European Central Bank) moves have been influenced by the expansionary stance initiated in Washington, perhaps via some very implicit targeting of the dollar price of the euro, that European lobbies wanted to prevent from increasing too much.

The connection between excessive monetary laxity and financial instability is often presented as obvious and self-evident. On one side excess liquidity pushes up asset prices, directly initiating the bubbles. On the other side, too low short-term central-bank-controlled risk-free interest rates are an incentive to run higher risks in search of decent expected returns. Portfolios will therefore be pushed towards riskier structures and 'the price of risk' will decrease leading to an imprudent allocation of resources.

While the responsibility of monetary policy for the crisis is widely accepted and understood, there is an insufficient elaboration of the idea and of its consequences for future policy making. One should try to reach a more precise and explicit understanding of the various channels through which the allocation of resources becomes riskier when liquidity is overabundant. One should also link the analysis of this issue to an effort in explaining why monetary policies erred in the direction of excessive laxity, to the point of causing the crisis. Conclusions should then be drawn on what to do to avoid analogous mistakes in the future: what kind of monetary policy strategies can help to avoid bubbles and financial crises?

The only relevant literature is the one that deals with the role of asset prices in monetary strategies. Arguments in favour of 'leaning against the wind' are contrasted with reasons suggesting that monetary policy should not impede the development of bubbles.[3] But no strong conclusion is reached. Some related work, mainly developed at the Bank for International Settlements, tries to link optimal monetary policy with prudential policies, advocating a countercyclical framework for monetary and financial stability.

The rest of this section offers three kind of considerations that might be helpful for thinking about these issues. First, a very simple analytical reasoning is used to show how the combination of opaque intermediation with low risk-free rates results in a flattening of risk premia and in a weakening of their relation to the increase of underlying risks. Second, those weak points of today's monetary orthodoxy are pointed out that may have contributed to the strategies that triggered the crisis. Third, some comments are made on how monetary policy could enter the set of 'global reforms' that will try to increase the stability and the efficiency of the future international monetary and financial system. European monetary governance can obviously influence this reform process but the latter can in turn impact on the evolution of the former.

2.1 Risk-Free Rates and Spreads

In a beautiful short paper Raghuram Rajan (2006) explained how the excess liquidity that resulted from global disequilibria (including the US balance of payments) acted as an incentive for asset managers to compete in promising α-type returns (that is, excess returns for given levels of risk) by 'buying illiquidity'. He observed that their competition came to the point of pretending that β-type returns (that is, higher returns compensated by higher risks) were α-type. In particular, they tended to hide (sometimes even to themselves) that the probability distributions of their investment strategies had fat tails (that is, relevant probabilities of resulting in high losses).

The information asymmetries in asset management and the opaqueness of financial intermediation can in fact explain a perverse link between the level of risk free rates and the behaviour of risk premia. Let us look at this link with the simplest possible analytical apparatus.[4] Let i be the policy-determined risk-free rate and r the equilibrium rate on a set of risky investments that have probability of default p and loss-given-default $L\%$. Suppose pure competition (zero expected profit) between risk-neutral, opaque intermediaries, able to borrow at rates driven much more by the risk-free rate than by the risks implicit in their investments. For simplicity, consider the extreme case where i is their borrowing cost. The following relationship will result:

$$(1+i) = (1-p)(1+r) + p(1-L)(1+r), \text{ or}$$
$$r - i = (1+i)pL/(1-pL).$$

The spread between r and i ('risk premium') is positively related to the level of the risk-free rate: a low interest rate policy favours the flattening of the spreads. Note that this happens with risk-neutral intermediaries: with $L > 0$ a decrease in i, if matched by an equal decrease in r, allows an expected profit to be competed away leading to a larger decrease in r and a smaller spread.

The derivative of the spread with respect to pL is $(1+i)/(1 - pL)^2$, also increasing with i: low risk-free rates, besides flattening the spreads, favour a decrease of the sensitivity of spreads to credit risk.

The first two graphs in Figure 2.1 show how the period of low US risk-free rates (2002–2005) is reflected with a short lag in an impressive lowering of risk premia on both investment grade and speculative grade corporate bonds. Obviously, when the decrease in risk-free rates is a reaction to a crisis that follows a bubble, the lag becomes much longer, as pL increases in the expression above: this is the reason why in late 2008 very low US rates go together with very high risk premia. The third graph in Figure 2.1 shows how the distribution of spreads became concentrated and 'without tails' (compared to the average 1997–2006) in early 2005, just after the maximum monetary expansion; in May of the following year the higher interest rates had already widened a bit the range of the bond spreads.

The reasoning can be extended to the case where the funding of the 'intermediary' comes also from its own capital, in a proportion $k < 1$. Competition pushes r towards a level allowing a minimum required yield y on capital:

$$k(1+y)=(1 - p)(1+r)+p(1\text{-}L)(1+r)\text{-}(1 - k)(1+i), \text{ or:}$$
$$r - i = [i(pL - k) + ky + pL]/(1 - pL).$$

The positive relation between the risk-free rate and the spread still holds when the capital ratio is smaller than the expected loss (or when, for a given capital, the opaque gamble looks riskier). Note that a lower i also allows a higher y for any given spread: easy money has in fact favoured an (unsustainable) increase of the profitability of opaque intermediation. On the contrary, if we interpret a decrease in y as an increase in the degree of competition within the industry of opaque intermediation, the expression is in accord with the intuition that higher competition reduces risk premia. Competition is also the reason why, for $k > pL$, the relationship between i and the spread becomes negative.

When the intermediaries' capital is considered, the derivative of the spread with respect to pL is

$$[i(1 - k)+(1+ky)]/(1 - pL)^2,$$

always increasing with the risk-free rate: a lowering of the latter decreases the sensitivity of the spread to credit risks even with high capital ratios ($k > pL$).

Option-adjusted spreads over government bond yields, in basis points

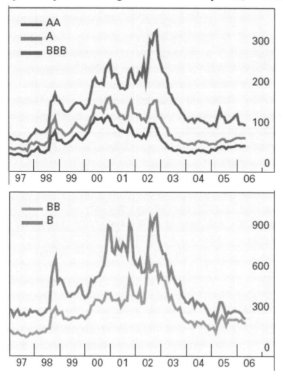

Distribution of bond spreads at various dates; the average refers to the
period January 1997–May 2006

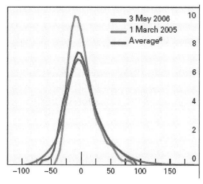

Source: Bank for International Settlements.

Figure 2.1 Corporate Bond Spreads

2.2 The Weaknesses of Received Monetary Orthodoxy

As a reaction to the 'great inflation' of the 1970s, both academics and policymakers gradually developed a worldwide monetary orthodoxy that backed the successful worldwide effort to restore price stability. The subprime crisis exploded, in the summer of 2007, when the convergence towards a common view of the optimal monetary policy strategy appeared high and growing. After one year and a half of FED (Federal Reserve) presidency, professor Ben Bernanke was even expected to start making some concrete steps towards a more formal adoption of his beloved 'inflation targeting' by the United States. 'How the world achieved consensus on monetary policy'[5] might still be considered a story difficult to spell out convincingly but, for instance, that consensus contrasted strikingly with the weak and controversial state of the economics and politics of financial regulation. This is perhaps among the reasons why, after admitting the responsibilities of monetary policy in causing the bubble and the crisis, there is a general tendency to avoid a follow-up in this field and concentrate analyses and plans on the regulatory and supervisory front.

Some doubts, to be sure, have been raised about the merits of global monetary management in obtaining low rates of inflation. The effects of globalization and higher productivity have been contrasted with the evidence of an increase of world liquidity that appeared suspect of being out of control. Increases in asset and raw material prices have also been considered as challenges to the textbook models of monetary policy, with some disagreements on how to deal with them. But the overall scenario of pre-crisis monetary policy discussions was much less controversial than 'in the 1970s, [when] conferences provided a forum for heated debates, academics were divided … with many different facets, … central bankers represented institutions with very heterogeneous views, … against … [an] intellectual and institutional background which had all signs of chaos' (Issing 2008).

It is probably fair to say that the strength and coherence of pre-crisis monetary orthodoxy were in fact smaller than it was generally felt. One could also argue that some of the weaknesses of the orthodoxy explain part of the monetary mismanagement that contributed to the crisis. A list of issues on which monetary theory and practices were insufficiently strong and homogeneous or agreed principles lacked enforcement, would be long and varied. It would certainly include, among several other points: the role and the meaning of price stability as the primary objective of monetary strategies; the robustness of a national relationship between money and prices when globalization strengthens the relationship between the world-wide output gap and the individual national inflation rates;[6] the role of asset prices as targets or indicators; the degree of 'de facto' independence and accountability of central banks; the institutional relation of central banks with macro and micro financial stability policies; the sustainability of international macroeconomic dynamics making use of a single dominant national currency; the stability of international financial markets with floating exchange rates and significantly different national monetary policy styles; the optimal relationship between the financial and real development of an economy and the degree of flexibility of its exchange rate.

It is clear how some of the issues in this list have complicated the life of monetary policies in the years before the crisis and caused mistakes in monetary control. The most obvious and widely discussed problem has been the role of asset prices. But it is worthwhile here to add a few comments on a couple of additional items on the list that point at deep controversies but have perhaps received insufficient attention.

The first is the well known problem of the role of monetary and credit aggregates. The orthodox approach has been progressively deemphasizing the usefulness of taking into account statistical measures of the rates of growth of money and credit when deciding changes of the interest rates targeted by central banks. The old 'monetarist' view that the behaviour of the money stock is a crucial variable in deciding monetary policy has been abandoned for several reasons, including the fact that financial innovation has rendered increasingly difficult the same definition of 'money'. The defining characteristic of monetary instruments is their 'liquidity', but innovative financial techniques and changes in the organization of financial markets have increased the potential liquidity of many assets that were traditionally considered illiquid. For some time monetary authorities have tried to pursue this development with continuous changes in the definitions of monetary aggregates (M1, M2, M3 etc.). But their efforts failed to look satisfactory, also as a consequence of the increasing instability of the estimated demand functions of the variously defined aggregates. The result was an orthodoxy, synthesized by Taylor-type rules, prescribing to take decisions on interest rates mainly based on measures of current and expected rates of inflation and real growth.

The European Central Bank has been an exception. In coherence with the inherited German monetary culture and the tradition of the Bundesbank, the ECB has included in its official strategy a special 'pillar', denominated 'monetary analysis', in which the rates of growth of monetary and credit aggregates are given special consideration. A 'critical' value of 4.5 per cent per year for the growth of 'M3' is still officially in force, to indicate the limit beyond which the speed of monetary expansion might be judged excessive, suggesting an increase of targeted interest rates. The use of the monetary pillar has been widely and continuously criticized by ECB-watchers, orthodox macroeconomists, market participants and many central bankers. In 2003 the official strategy downgraded the monetary analysis from the dignity of 'first pillar' to the cross-checking role of a 'second pillar'. In fact the critical value has been systematically exceeded by the rates of growth of M3 and the impact of the 'monetary analysis' on ECB's decisions has been seldom evident, in spite of the insistence with which the Governing Council has always stressed it in explaining the way interest rates were manoeuvred.

The basic empirical support of monetary analysis, the correlation between monetary aggregates and the inflation of consumption prices, has been very weak during the last years. On the contrary, asset prices have clearly signalled the excesses of liquidity creation: a more careful consideration of monetary aggregates and of their credit counterparts would have allowed, particularly in the US, to decide interest rates taking implicitly into account some relevant information contained in asset prices. The information was suggesting the dangers of a post-bubble financial crisis. In fact the crisis is now increasingly understood as a 'credit boom gone wrong' (Eichengreen and Mitchener 2003). The issue of the role of monetary and credit aggregates in monetary policy strategies must therefore 'come back from the wilderness' (Borio and Lowe 2004), while lessons are drawn from the crisis. The reconsideration of this issue should go together with a more parallel, complementary, countercyclical monitoring of price and financial stability, along the lines suggested long ago by the BIS.[7] 'The mutually reinforcing roles of prudential and monetary policy ... could ... allow the authorities to lean jointly against the build-up of imbalances even if near term inflation pressures remain benign' (Borio and Shin 2007, p. 18).

The second issue to be mentioned here, as part of the list of weak points of monetary orthodoxy, is the propensity of monetary management to 'fine-tune' the economy in the short run. The limits and the dangers of fine-tuning can be derived from the theoretical literature as well as from the practice of monetary policymaking. Changes in monetary instruments reach the economy with long and variable lags, so that short-run tuning can destabilize the cycle. Moreover, the evaluation of short-run indicators of the output gap and of inflationary pressures is highly imprecise and can lead to over-reacting, with a natural asymmetric bias towards monetary expansion as the apparent slow-down of aggregate demand commands a stronger political reaction. More generally, it is difficult to conduct monetary policy independently of electoral cycles and other myopic political pressures (see Chapter 5), as well as from the short-run desires of financial intermediaries and asset managers, if the strategy of the central bank shows fine-tuning ambitions and does not oppose a systematic caution in reacting with interest rate changes to any short-term fluctuation of cyclical indicators.

In spite of all these arguments, during the 1980s and 1990s academic and central-bank economists have favoured simplified reaction functions *à la* Taylor, often derived from highly abstract theoretical models, that easily lend themselves to fine-tuning practices. The 'Wicksellian' concept of 'natural rate of interest', or a normal level of interest rates that is coherent with macroeconomic stability, has been somewhat forgotten, while the general attention of the public opinion has been concentrating on interest rate changes. Markets and politicians always expect the right, miraculous 'change' of the key rates without regard for the appropriate level of the real cost of capital. In this atmosphere, monetary policy tends to be nervous and over-reactive creating high waves in the time-path of interest rates. Fine-tuning is the door through which monetary policy can be reached by the destabilizing influence of the short-term desires of politicians and financial market agents. This problem has been particularly strong in US monetary policy and has probably favoured a loss of control of liquidity creation. 'Orthodox' monetary thinking has overlooked the issue of fine-tuning and we lack a robust apparatus of ideas to deal with its temptations.

2.3 Monetary Policy and the Cure

All the comments above seem to speak in favour of giving to monetary policy an important role in the recipe for increasing the stability of the global financial system. Obviously, they are relevant for the long-term worldwide reorganization of money and finance: monetary policy, during the current period of crisis management, is confronted with emergency situations and can hardly be discussed with reference to its optimal long-term strategies to prevent future crises. It might seem paradoxical, for instance, to caution against excessive credit expansion during a crisis troubled by a credit crunch or to discuss fine-tuning when central banks are asking for very strong interventions to limit the immediate damages of a recession.

But, even in the normal long run, the role of monetary policy in crisis prevention remains an issue for a 'forbidden' question. In fact, everybody is expressing the desire to strengthen and improve the regulation and the supervision of financial markets or to expand the role of governments in putting limits to 'wild free markets', while requests for considering an improvement of monetary strategies are much less detectable. On the contrary, exceptional monetary policies are often suggested for the short run, to deal with the crisis, that are in deep contrast with any reasonable long term strategy geared to stability. A typical suggestion of this kind is that, in order to cure deflation, the US 'printing press' should aim at convincing markets that 'inflation is just around the corner' (Boone and Johnson 2008).

As the aim of this chapter is more to point at 'forbidden' questions than to try and answer them, this section will end after two specific additional comments.

First, if a rethinking of monetary policy strategies will take place among academics and policymakers, the most promising starting point is the work done at the BIS during the last ten years. In a number of papers, reports and speeches, easily accessible on the bank's website (some cited above and included in the references below), BIS (Bank for International Settlements) research efforts have tried to design a 'macro-prudential framework for monetary and financial stability', emphasizing the complementary role of monetary and prudential policies in conducting countercyclical pre-emptive actions to moderate the booms in order to avoid the crises that follow the bursting of the bubbles. This work is backed by the study of the past history of financial crises and by a re-reading of the classical theories that, since more than one century ago, have been describing how the behaviour of bank credit can be at the roots of cyclical instability. The message of the BIS has been received with some difficulty by orthodox monetary thinking and little action has followed, in spite of the fact that the bank is an integral part of the heart of the central bankers' community.[8] Paradoxically, the Basel-based institution is often associated, more than with its own policy suggestions, with the Basel II project for banks' capital requirements, even if it only serves as a location for the Secretariat of the Basel Committee on Banking Supervision and in spite of the fact that the BIS countercyclical recipes serve well to highlight some defects of the procyclical, destabilizing formulas of Basel II. It seems desirable that a much wider discussion and research effort develops the basic BIS ideas into a detailed operational version to help frame the monetary strategies of the future.

Second, any reformulation of monetary policy strategy for enhancing financial stability must be global. In today's irreversibly integrated world of money and finance deep differences in national monetary policy styles are unsustainable. National specificities in financial and real markets can justify limited divergences in the reaction functions of monetary authorities. Unprincipled exploitation of apparent national monetary autonomies sooner or later gives rise to disordered dynamics of exchange rates, balances of payments, goods and assets prices, capital flows and adjustments of the global portfolio of financial assets. The disorder is worse if the international monetary system lives in an ambiguous situation where the existence of a *de facto* leading currency and of a dominant country, like the dollar and the US, goes together with a lack of explicit international responsibilities of that country's monetary policy and with the expectation that a progressive shift towards a more symmetric multicurrency world will happen at an unknown speed and in an unknown manner.

It is now common to say that the financial crisis was also the result of an inadequate economic governance of the globalization process. An implication of this idea is that the return to stability requires a higher degree of multilateral cooperation in regulating and monitoring the international economy. The Bretton Woods agreement that opened the post world-war reconstruction period is sometimes cited as an example of the new cooperative setting that is needed: something like a 'Bretton Woods 2'. Monetary and exchange rate policies would be at the heart of such an agreement, together with trade and development policies and, perhaps, international financial regulation. In 1944 Bretton Woods aimed at keeping stable exchange rates with central bank interventions in foreign currency markets. It is difficult to believe that, tomorrow, a new agreement could work in a similar way: the right amount of credible global exchange rate stability could only be obtained indirectly, through the sharing of a global paradigm to harmonize the reaction functions of national and regional monetary authorities.

The 'monetary constitution' of the euro-area is a fundamental input for putting together such a paradigm. Compared to the US, Europe's monetary management has been of help for limiting the instability of the current global turmoil. Monetary policy is one of the fields where the European Union can give a leading contribution to improve the governance of the world's economy.

3. QUALITATIVELY INADEQUATE FINANCIAL REGULATION: ALSO QUANTITATIVELY SCARCE?

To what extent is the financial crisis which started in the summer of 2007 an argument against the reliability of the market mechanism? Information asymmetries and other imperfections are so important in financial markets that many market segments would not even be able to come to existence and survive without some form of regulation. Regulation and supervision are a condition for trust, which is the basis of financial transactions. It is of no use to call markets 'free' only when they are completely unregulated. Regulation can be such as to enhance the effectiveness of the typical functions of a decentralized market system. The easiest example is perhaps the compulsory disclosure of information that would not otherwise be at the disposal of certain market participants: this kind of regulation, obviously, is not aimed at limiting but at reinforcing the market mechanism.

The functioning of a free, decentralized market economy can therefore suffer from insufficient regulation. But market disfunctions can also be caused by excessive regulation or by the presence of bad regulation. Which was the case in the market failures that prompted the crisis? The issue of lack of quantity versus lack of quality of financial regulation seems somewhat relevant and interesting: not so much for its 'ideological' flavour, with anti-market ideas naturally favouring the thesis that regulation was quantitatively scarce, as for the help and the opportunities that the discussion of the problem can offer in singling out the various causes of the crisis and in designing the optimal re-regulation that the experience of the crisis suggests.

The question in the title of this section would not be 'forbidden' if it were possible to answer the quality versus quantity question in an exhaustive way. But there is no clear-cut answer to the question. The best one can do is to list some arguments in favour of the thesis that regulation was quantitatively insufficient ('too free markets, excessive deregulations') and other arguments that, on the contrary, suggest that the crucial problem was one of quality, of bad regulation. In the first case the cure consists in adding and reinforcing regulations, while in the second case the cure must concentrate in changing, reforming and streamlining the rules.

3.1 More Regulation Needed

When the crisis started, international financial authorities were trying to finalise a new, important piece of regulation, the so-called 'Basel II', prescribing more risk-sensitive rules to calculate banks' minimum required capital ratios.[9] The general climate was therefore formally far from one of *de*regulation. Basel II was, in principle, an effort to impose higher capital ratios to riskier banks. But suspicions had been around for some time that within the Basel reform process a permissive tendency was developing, favouring an overall increase of the degree of leverage of the banking system. These suspicions were not completely unwarranted.

In particular, some argued that the new regime of capital ratios was in favour of the largest, internationally active banks. They were the only ones able to set up the complex and expensive modelling system, to calculate and monitor risk, that Basel II required for being allowed to apply the most 'advanced' method to calculate minimum capital ratios. As an incentive to its adoption, the advanced method would have required lower minimum capital ratios. Large internationally active banks would also enjoy the benefits of a number of 'risk mitigating' devices, accounted for by the new proposed rules, including the use of complex derivative products. A far from uniform international application of the regulation was also an opportunity for regulatory arbitrage, much easier to exploit for banks with a wide network of operations. Moreover, the atmosphere of the Basel II reform was one where large banks had an advantage over the authorities in the availability of highly qualified and very well paid human resources, able to manipulate the sophisticated risk management techniques required by the new regulation: the idea of a 'captured' regulation, tailored to the needs and advantages of the regulated, could thus seem plausible also for technical reasons.

In fact, official quantitative simulations of the new method, before its adoption, resulted in significant decreases of minimum capital ratios. While official capital ratios were often kept higher than the minimum prescribed by Basel I, and even if the new capital regulation cannot be responsible of a crisis that exploded before its finalization and adoption, the evidence from the crisis has shown that the years during which the international financial community was concentrating its attention on the complex technical and political process of switching to Basel II were also years of rapid increases of the de facto leverage ratios of many banks, often via off balance-sheet techniques and complex international regulatory arbitrages. Securities were artificially classified in inflated 'trading books', which should have included only assets to be held for short periods before resale, which were favoured by minimum capital requirements rules. Ex post it looks like the system, moving towards the adoption of the complex new Basel system, went through a costly exercise in distraction.

Some groups of academics and independent experts were critical of these developments. For example, the 'shadow financial regulatory committees', both in the US and Europe,[10] have always been active in pointing at the dangers of a captured weakening of the regulation of banks' capital ratios. The members of the shadow committees were far from representing anti-market ideas and from advocating 'more regulation': on the contrary, they were asking for simpler regulations, able to better exploit market discipline and relying less on the discretion of potentially forbearing regulatory authorities. But the spirit of the shadows' statements was one of stopping the trend towards an excessive degree of leverage and adopting 'Prompt Corrective Action' (PCA) procedures, that is, compulsory interventions of the supervisors, triggered by critical levels of the banks' leverage, to impose the recapitalization or the closure of a bank before its capital became negative.

The Basel II reform was also part of a general tendency to increasingly rely on unregulated, privately contracted ratings issued by agencies having an obvious conflict of interest in releasing their risk assessments. Inadequate ratings are misleading for the buyers of securities. Their damage is magnified and can cause systemic instability when they become, as in Basel II, an input of the risk assessment process that determines the amount of banks' regulatory capital. Ratings contributed to wrongly assess the risks inherent in structured products and seriously underestimated the correlation of defaults. Triple As were granted much too generously, also to help in complying with the restrictions on institutional investors' eligible investments. The lack of a regulation of rating agencies is often considered a crucial cause of the crisis. Even those who do not share this opinion, or are sceptical about the feasibility of an effective regulation of rating agencies, agree, after the crisis, that risk regulations should not be based on non regulated ratings.

The crisis exploded in a globally over-levered financial system. The degree of leverage was in fact under-regulated. Banks' minimum required capital ratios are in proportion to their risk-weighted assets. These ratios create an incentive to acquire assets that absorb less capital as they are considered less risky. Capital ratios, though, do not induce banks to refrain from expanding the total size of their balance sheet: for a given amount of capital, banks can fund low-risk assets by increasing leverage. A high leverage worsens the consequences of any underestimation of the assets' risk: with a leverage (ratio of total assets to the bank's capital) of 20, an unexpected loss of 1 per cent of the assets is a loss of 20 per cent of the capital. With a leverage of 40, as was the case in some European banks and US investment banks, losing 2 per cent of the assets means wiping away more than five years of very high profits. Moreover, a high leverage increases the exposure of banks, for any degree of maturity mismatching of their assets and liabilities, to a refunding risk that is not taken into account by the regulation of minimum capital ratios.

The absence of a regulation prescribing a maximum leverage has led European banks to build up increasingly large and leveraged balance sheets, even if with assets of relatively good quality to limit the value of risk-weighted assets used to calculate the Basel ratios. Under the stress of the crisis, the liquidity of their leveraged assets suddenly precipitated, revealing an unexpectedly large funding problem and paralysing the functioning of the inter-bank market. In the US, on the contrary, minimum capital ratios are complemented by a maximum leverage rule for commercial banks. The problem was that the US rule allowed and stimulated the accumulation of risky assets in off-balance sheet Special Investment Vehicles (SIV). The US delayed the adoption of Basel II, which would have prevented SIVs from functioning as a device to reduce capital requirements. As is now well known, the SIV-system absorbed a large portion of the sub-prime securitised mortgage loans, triggering the explosion of the crisis. Moreover, in the US, leverage was not limited for 'investment banks', which caused their unsustainably rapid growth, inflated their profitability during the 'good times' while, as soon as the crisis started, rapidly worsened their solvency and liquidity.

Leverage was also without limits for hedge funds. This was wrongly considered the riskiest aspect of the pre-crisis situation. Ex-post, hedge funds turned out to be more victims of the crisis than responsible for it. The sudden illiquidity of the markets for most securities and financial instruments caused a failure of their portfolio strategies, while preventing their clients from disinvesting. A widely held opinion, to be sure, is that hedge funds, worldwide, should have been left less unregulated, with somewhat stricter requirements to be registered and authorized. Moreover, they should have been better supervized in order, at least, to try and avoid frauds of the Madoff type.

Economic history has often shown the tendency of banks to over-lend during booms, triggering a financial crisis which is then worsened by severe credit rationing. Destabilizing credit cycles can be limited by imposing countercyclical provisioning. Regulations can require banks to increase capital and set aside increasing proportions of liquid reserves when credit expansion is faster. Countercyclical provisioning functions as a disincentive to exaggerate credit booms and secures the funds that allow banks to cope with the descending part of the cycle by compensating the unavoidable losses while avoiding excessive credit rationing. The lack of incentives and rules favouring countercyclical buffers of capital and liquidity[11] is often considered a weak point of the regulatory setting which was in force where the crisis exploded.

Financial innovation has been a protagonist of the crisis and can even be considered its 'ultimate cause' (Llewellyn 2008), as regulation and supervision have been unable to cope in a sufficiently rapid and effective way with the deep changes that took place in financial markets and in the logic of banking and financial intermediation. Innovative and complex financial instruments, such as sophisticated derivatives, credit default swaps and structured bonds, have played an important role in deteriorating the transparency of financial markets, increasing the risks of default and illiquidity and diffusing the financial crisis in the global system. Competent people normally oppose the idea that regulation should have been hostile towards financial innovation and derivative instruments and should now tend to seriously curb their development. In spite of some excesses, innovative instruments are of value for the economy, as they contribute to the management and the allocation of risks and to the efficiency of forward-looking, expectation-driven financial markets. The true problems lie in the way markets for sophisticated instruments are organixed. In particular, an excessive reliance on over-the-counter transactions has caused opaqueness and has dramatically decreased the liquidity of these instruments. Complex instruments were placed and priced in bilateral deals that the crisis turned into illiquid traps. A bank like Lehman was one of the unofficial 'hubs' for the entangled, unsupervised, statistically unsurveyed crossing of a disproportionate number of certain types of these bilateral contracts. When the bank became insolvent, in an enormous part of the market for derivative instruments, trust and liquidity suddenly and completely disappeared and the damage spread like wildfire to large parts of much more standard markets for fixed income securities, commercial paper and inter-bank deposits. Several disastrous aspects of the financial crisis, since the beginning of the US mortgage subprime mess, were triggered by the lack of centrally organized and supervised markets for sophisticated securities. Regulation could have imposed the creation of some of these markets, where transactions and their pricing become more transparent, the execution, clearing and settlement of contracts are better guaranteed and their unwinding becomes easier, thus enhancing the liquidity of the securities and of the various instruments on which they are based.

Note that this aspect of the crisis does not call for less reliance on markets: on the contrary, the problem consisted in the fact that bilateral transactions were *not* constituting a true market mechanism for the pricing, allocation and liquid trading of securities and financial contracts. As elsewhere in the economy, 'markets' hardly exist in nature, as they are highly artificial arrangements requiring conventions, regulations and supervision just to be able to survive. 'More regulation' (and of a better quality) often goes together with a deeper exploitation of the 'free' (where the word does not mean unregulated) market mechanism.

The securitization of bank loans has been a protagonist of the explosion and of the diffusion of the financial crisis, since its very first incidents. The abuse of securitization, leading to a overplay of the 'originate and distribute' scheme, where banks do not hold in their balance sheets the loans they initially extend, was among the most important causes of the breakdown of international banking and of the disappearance of liquidity in securities' markets. From this fact the implication is often derived that securitization operations should have been subject to stricter regulations. In particular it is often said that banks should not be allowed to securitize and sell the 100 per cent of a loan, getting rid of all the incentives to monitor the borrower. European authorities, for instance, have been considering proposals that would constrain banks to hold at least a prescribed percentage of the loans they originate.

Nevertheless, the idea that there has been an excessive freedom to securitize is controversial. The main reason why securitization nourished the crisis is the lack of transparency of the commitments of the originating banks to buy back securitized loans. In principle such commitments can be a sufficient incentive to monitor. The problem was that they were opaque and implicit: the repurchase risk was therefore unaccounted for and invisible for the supervisors, with no impact on the minimum capital and leverage ratios. The banks themselves tended to 'forget' the risk, until they were compelled to step in and refinance the purchasers of securitized loans, with whom they had often deeply connected, as the diffusion of the securities had not gone further than their own Special Investment Vehicles. There is some sense in saying that what failed was the 'originate and *try to* distribute model'. In any case, a lack of regulation of the securitization process was present, as the process could take place intensively without the right amount of transparency, which is a requisite both for market agents and for the authorities to evaluate and monitor securitized lending.

Also the role of ideology deserves some attention in a list of reasons to interpret the crisis as caused by quantitatively insufficient regulation. Political and academic groups, especially in the US, have been arguing with increasing emphasis, during the last decade, that financial market regulation is useless and damaging and that financial operators tend to self-regulate their activities in a socially beneficial way. Their discourse contrasted with a situation where regulation and supervision were present and pervasive, even though in a disorderly and ineffective fashion, with an inefficient and irrational network of dozens of regulatory and supervisory authorities in charge, both at the federal and at the national level. The influence of ideology has been subtle and never resulted in a transparent and official process of 'excessive deregulation'. But ideology has encouraged an attitude which paid insufficient attention to the inefficiency and to the holes of the regulatory and supervisory setting, and tolerated a weak implementation of regulation and a 'captured' negligence of supervision. Ideology was also the basis for supporting the excessive trust in the virtues of 'competition in regulation', the idea that optimal competition can result from competition from different regulatory agencies, which prevented a strong top-down reform of the messy regulatory setting to take place. An analogous idea, even though connected with the political and bureaucratic tendency to keep financial regulation at the national level, prevented the EU from accelerating the building of a supranational strong system of surveillance of the increasingly complicated and internationally integrated financial system.

3.2 Heavier Doses of Regulation is No Remedy

Several considerations, on the contrary, can be used to deemphasize the role of an alleged 'lack of regulation' in explaining the crisis.

First of all, prudential authorities, both in the US and in Europe, have enormous discretionary powers: they can use the framework of regulation to intervene in a deep way and influence the management of financial institutions. The same discretion that has been used to tolerate excessive risk taking could have allowed a much more intrusive attitude on the part of the supervisors.

The absence of adequately strict supervision has been a fact, but it is not the same thing as the lack of regulatory powers. Examples are easy to find:

the FED had the powers to stop the worse practises of sub-prime lending in the US, semi-public Fannie and Freddie could have limited their support of that lending, the European supervisors had the authority to moderate the increase in banks' leverage even in the absence of an officially regulated leverage ratio. Public policies, to be sure, have often stimulated the worse financial behaviours; but the intrusive political pressures that, for instance, have pushed housing finance well beyond prudence, have nothing to do with any looseness in regulating private markets.

Moreover, as already pointed out above, the crisis came in the final phase of a demanding round of worldwide re-regulation of banking: Basel II. The delay of the US in adopting the new rules does not cancel the fact that, if they had been implemented like in the EU, capital requirements would have limited the abuse of the Special Investment Vehicles. As far as Europe is concerned, another example of the fact that the climate where the crisis developed was not one of de-regulation is the enormous effort made, in 2006–2007, by the Committee of European Banking Supervisors,[12] for harmonizing the implementation of Basel II in the different member states, pushing for the more prudent interpretations of the new rules and for a cooperatively transparent sharing of prudential information between national supervisors. The slowness of the process was caused by political and bureaucratic inertia; national authorities were resisting the pressures to release their strong discretionary powers to micromanage banks' risks and were trying to keep acting in a protective way towards the banks based in their jurisdiction; these types of inertia did not favour the building of a more robust European crisis-prevention system, but the show differed a lot from a struggle for more laissez-faire.

The 1999 Gramm–Leach–Biley Act, which repealed the Glass–Steagall regulation that separated commercial from investment banking in the US, is sometimes cited as an example of the de-regulatory trend that eventually brought to the crisis. But the Act cannot, in itself, be interpreted as a move towards a more permissive setting. In fact it has been applied in a permissive way: the FED was kept away from investment banking regulation and supervision and the Security and Exchange Commission (SEC) failed to keep investment banking from developing in an unsustainable, opaque and hazardous way. But the 1999 Act did not deprived the authorities of the powers to exert their surveillance on the stability of commercial and investment banking. This surveillance was crucially important as the possibility of commercial banking groups to include investment banking vehicles extended to the latter the possibility of benefiting from the refinancing facilities provided by the central bank. While some might consider the Act as one of the episodes in a story of gradual deterioration of the de facto *quality* of regulation and supervision, there is no reason to read it as an explicit step towards irresponsible deregulation.

The evolution of accounting rules is another example of a tendency that can hardly be considered permissive. Recent progresses towards marking to market and fair value rules constitute an increasingly stricter discipline for financial and non-financial firms. This fact has been often denied on the basis of two considerations. The first one is that marking to market is procyclical and can inflate profits and net-worth during booms, when it looks permissive. But this is a different issue. The procyclicality of accounting rules made the crisis worse, but enhanced the transparency of its developments. The second consideration is that certain derivative financial instruments are allowed to be 'marked to model', in ways that can often be considered arbitrary. This issue is connected to the lack of a centrally organized counterparty pricing, processing and clearing system for instruments traded 'over the counter': it is the consequence of the lack of a 'true market', more than a weakness of the marking to market discipline. The conceptual and practical difficulties to formulate optimal accounting rules are among the most convincing reasons to think that financial regulation needs more quality improvements than increases in quantity.

The idea that the crisis was caused by quantitatively insufficient regulation often goes together with the opinion that there has been an excessive reliance on the competitive market system. The fact that the crisis was worsened by the lack of 'true markets' for certain financial instruments is an argument against this opinion. The weakness of competitive mechanisms and the want of markets have acted as ingredients of the crisis in several other ways. The correctness of the behaviour of rating agencies would have been enhanced by a higher degree of competition in their industry. It is very difficult to state that a true market existed for rating services, more so when one considers the oligopoly that characterized the investment banking industry demanding the rating services. The quality and soundness of bank management would have benefited from a more vivid, competitive and disciplining market for corporate control in the banking sector.

A very general argument can also be used to deemphasize the idea that more regulation would have resulted in a more stable global financial system. Charles Goodhart (2008b) has labelled this argument the boundary problem. As strict regulation cannot apply to all operations of the whole financial system, a boundary always exists between the activities and sectors that are more regulated and the rest of the financial markets and operations. The greater constraints on the business of the regulated part causes a cycle of flows of operations and funds into the less regulated part of the system during cycle expansions, with sudden and dislocating reversals during crises. Stricter regulation creates disintermediation and regulatory arbitrage in good times and destabilizes the structure of the financial sector as crisis periods push back activities in its more regulated part. This is what happened recently between commercial and investment banking, between banking and non-banking financial markets, between standardized and innovative financial instruments, between underlying and derivative instruments and their markets, between more and less regulated countries etc. The basic message highlighted by the boundary problem is that, for obtaining financial stability, a heavier dose of stricter regulation is a bad substitute for a lighter dose of high quality rules, effectively implemented with careful supervision, sensitive to cyclical conditions in a stabilizing fashion, engineered in such a way as to enhance (as opposed to substitute) the basic mechanisms of free markets by providing the appropriate remedies for their imperfections.

4. CRISIS MANAGEMENT: A DEPRESSING EXPERIENCE?

Governments and central banks have been working hard since the beginning of the crisis to try and cure it (see Chapter 4 for EU governance), managing the various problems caused by the financial turmoil: bank insolvency and illiquidity, credit rationing and the diffusion of the crisis to the real sector, the dilemma of monetary policies in deciding whether to combat deflation or prevent inflation, the dilemma of fiscal policies in stimulating the economies while keeping public debts on sustainable paths.

At the end of 2008 it looks like there is no reason for complacency. The logic and the tools of crisis management were not prepared to cope with such a deep breakdown of financial markets and they have shown their limits. The strategy is opaque and interventions have brought a lot of disorder and uncertainty in the system. On the other hand, some good results have been obtained in limiting the damages. Do these results compensate the shortcomings and the bad side-effects of the reactions that have been decided, or should we be depressed and discouraged by the experience?

This is another 'forbidden question' and cannot receive a clear-cut, concise and exhaustive answer. The best that can be done here is to elaborate a bit around some specific aspects of the experience. With this very limited aim, only three tools of crisis management will be considered here: lending of last resort, bailouts and deposit insurance.

4.1 Lending of Last Resort

As soon as the crisis started, in the summer of 2007, central banks have been quick, generous and innovative in providing liquidity assistance to the banking system. With the exception of the confusing hesitation of the Bank of England in the Northern Rock case, lending of last resort (LoLR) was quickly and efficiently provided, with the hope of preventing illiquidity from becoming insolvency. Interventions were based on the idea that the true problem was confined to the presence of a certain amount of toxic assets – the US sub-prime mortgage loans and their derivatives – in the balance sheet of several banks, worldwide. Neither the amount nor the location of these assets were known with a decent degree of precision, which caused each bank to be doubtful about the soundness of any other bank, thus freezing the inter-bank flow of funds and therefore killing the liquidity of many instruments and markets. Generous LoLR seemed a good solution: it would have allowed buying time for locating the toxic assets, dealing with them and preventing the widespread liquidity problem that the fear of them was causing to develop, with no valid reason, into disastrous insolvencies.

But the logic of central bank lending had many weaknesses. First, information on toxic assets remained largely mysterious and the generosity of LoLR gave no incentive to the system to reveal their amount and location and to become more transparent. Second, the crisis gradually appeared to be much more than a bunch of hidden toxic assets: basically, the entire global financial system was intoxicated by an excess of leverage, overabundant creation of money and credit and underestimation and under-pricing of several types of risk. The inevitable de-leveraging would therefore take much more time and pain than what was deemed necessary to deal with the early culprit, the sub-prime mess. In spite of this changing profile of the crisis, a reconsideration of the strategic role of LoLR was delayed. Third, the quality of the collateral backing central bank financing rapidly deteriorated, causing moral hazard and introducing an anomalous amount of risk in the assets of central banks. Fourth, relatively cheap LoLR, coupled with the possibility – available in the euro-area – of depositing overnight liquidity with the central bank at a non-zero interest rate, acted as a drug for the banks, disintermediating the inter-bank market and discouraging any effort to restart its functioning. Fifth, the progressive use of non-very-short-term LoLR as well as the continuous widening of the set of assets accepted by the central bank as collateral led, especially in the USA, to a degeneration of a highly specific tool of crisis management, and involved the very nature and size of central banks.

While the famous old textbook Bagehot's (1873) golden rules for LoLR were probably too conservative to guide the management of today's big crisis,[13] all rules now seem to have vanished. The use of the instrument is in disarray also for conceptual reasons. 'The crisis has shown that traditional models of banks' liquidity risk and of LoLR require revision. Funding risk now interacts with market liquidity risk, to create difficult challenges for central banks' (Davies 2008). When the worst of the crisis is over, at the latest, deep thoughts will have to be devoted to rebuilding a coherent code of conduct for the LoLR and restoring the credibility of the role of central banks.

With LoLR overflowing its normal banks, the impact of emergency lending on the liquidity of the economy became increasingly indistinguishable from the monetary policy stance. Initially this distinction had been very much stressed, especially by the ECB: abundant, very-short-term facilities to help banks' liquidity problems must not be confused with expansionary monetary policies and are compatible with non-accommodative levels of key interest rates. The intensive use of LoLR weakened the difference and exerted, especially in the US but also in Europe, substantial downward pressure on the manoeuvring of key rates.

4.2 Bailouts

The management of the crisis led in several countries to bailout failing financial institutions, extending well beyond too-big-to-fail deposit-taking commercial banks. The systemic importance of a troubled institution was judged in opaque ways, that cannot be explained on the basis of the received doctrine in money and banking. Paradoxically, one of the most systemic institutions, Lehman Brothers, was denied bailout, causing an enormous shock that started a harder phase of the crisis[14] in mid September 2008.

Bailouts took place in extremely pragmatic ways, very different in the various countries. One cannot detect any procedural coherence in the disparate forms in which taxpayers' money was more or less explicitly committed to prevent bankruptcies of financial operators. The wildest procedures were applied in the US, where also central bank money was created to finance bailouts, with the FED becoming a co-owner of rescued institutions. The opaqueness and improvization of the bailout decision processes also characterize the ex-ante and ex-post evaluation of the social costs of the decisions. Hopefully, governments and parliaments will sooner or later become more sensible to the duty of being accountable for the bailout decisions and will prepare transparent, homogeneous methodologies to assess their costs.

In order to clarify their logic and procedure, bailouts should be examined in the perspective of the concept of 'Prompt Corrective Action'. Some form of PCA is part of any good theory of optimal crisis management and, in certain countries, including the US, it is prescribed by law. PCA requires the authorities to start intervening in increasingly prescriptive forms as soon as a bank begins to show objective symptoms of progressive deterioration of its solvency conditions. The aim of PCA is to correct or stop the operations of the bank before its net-worth becomes negative. PCA should prevent excessive and lengthy forbearance by the authorities, while avoiding bankruptcies as well as bailouts. Bailouts should be the exception: they should be decided, for systemically important institutions, only when the PCA procedure is insufficient or mishandled and fails to deliver its result. They should, in general, be considered an important signal that the action of the supervisor has been inadequate and untimely. Supervisors should be held responsible for having failed to act effectively.

The experience with the current crisis is that the authorities have behaved very differently from how the PCA logic would require. They hesitated a lot before stepping in to constrain the management of troubled institutions, they exercised a great deal of forbearance, they allowed troubled institutions to further spoil their conditions and even to risk danger by 'gambling for resurrection', until they had to choose between allowing bankruptcy and improvising some form of bailout. Their justifications might be: (i) that the crisis developed in a very fast and unpredictable fashion, depending on the moods of the markets: the speed needed to exercise 'early intervention', as required by PCA on several different institutions, contemporaneously, was excessive; (ii) that the difficulties of many individual institutions happened together, being caused more by a macroeconomic crisis than by the typical micro mismanagement that PCA can correct; (iii) that informal, secret PCA was in fact exercised, by pressuring bank managers and offering guidance, help and advice, well before bailouts were decided; the distrustful atmosphere of financial markets was a good reason to adopt secret forms of early intervention, in order to avoid worsening the situation of individual banks by letting the frightened market know that the supervisor was worried about them.

Time will show how farsighted or imprudent have been the bailouts of financial institutions decided by countries during the crisis. In any case, the development of gradually more coherent procedures to decide, execute and evaluate these tools of crisis management seems advisable.

4.3 Deposit Insurance

When the main source of systemic risk in financial markets are the perils of bank runs, caused by the special characteristics of commercial banks, in which information asymmetries go together with high leverage and liabilities that are systematically more liquid than assets, deposit insurance can be thought of as the central tool to enhance financial stability and to manage possible crises.

In spite of the international diffusion of deposit insurance schemes, of a certain amount of experience with their functioning and of a very large literature on the subject, the logic behind the instrument is still somewhat confused and controversial and the way it is organized differs very much in the various countries. Even in the EU's member countries, where deposit insurance has been made compulsory by a Directive, the specific features of the scheme are far from homogeneous. Moreover, the importance of deposit insurance is often in doubt, as the large public is usually unaware of its existence and is never well informed on its features.

During the first part of the current crisis, the most important episode about deposit insurance has been the Northern Rock case,[15] where UK authorities seemed surprised that the existence of the scheme could not stop depositors from running to withdraw their cash from the branches of the bank. In other countries as well, the seriousness of the crisis induced governments to outshine the existing deposit insurance schemes by repeatedly shouting their decision to offer an extraordinary, supplementary and free of charge 100 per cent guarantee for all bank deposits.

These shouts are a reminder that 'explicit' schemes of deposit insurance have always been under suspicion of being superimposed on the 'implicit' insurance that would anyway guarantee bank deposits. One form of implicit insurance is of course the expectation of the bailout of a failing bank. The coexistence of explicit and implicit deposit insurance is among the causes of the fuzziness of the logic of explicit insurance schemes.

One way to see the conceptual problems behind deposit insurance is to observe that it can be aimed at two very different mutually exclusive results.[16] First, it can be thought as a device to protect small deposits of unavoidably uninformed depositors from bank default, thus making bank failures easier to manage and decrease their social cost. Or it can be directed at avoiding bank failures by reassuring the holders of all the deposits. The latter purpose is justified by the special nature of banks that, given the high leverage and the liquidity of their liabilities, can be brought to failure by depositors' runs even if their assets are perfectly sound (Diamond and Dybvig 1983).[26]

The experience of the current crisis suggests that confidence-induced financial melt downs, as well as domino-like contagion effects, are not relevant only for the banking system. They can take place everywhere in the financial markets. The typical bank run, when a more or less justified panic among depositors rapidly exhausts the liquidity of a bank and spreads all over the system, both via the inter-bank market and because other banks' depositors fear that they could suffer the same difficulties as in the first bank, is rather similar to what can happen in the securities market, involving individual investors and brokers, investment banks, mutual, monetary and hedge funds. In fact a panic of this kind has happened, at least in autumn 2008, creating an impressive liquidity crisis in all capital markets worldwide. Securities market 'runs' have proven to be even more probable and dangerous than the classical runs on sight deposits of commercial banks. Correspondingly, the demand for insurance has gone, at least implicitly, much beyond traditionally insured deposits. The supply of insurance has followed, at least implicitly, when authorities started to bail out investment banks and Freddie & Fannie, to pledge public money to increase the capitalization of private banks, to insure bank bonds, to buy toxic securities from various financial intermediaries, to target securities prices and financial markets' stability in deciding how to move central bank interest rates.

Can we conclude that deposit insurance has lost a substantial part of its importance? In particular, can we conclude that the 'first type' of deposit insurance, the one aimed at making bank failures easier and decreasing their social cost, is completely out of fashion? Can we conclude that the problem of deposit insurance can only be considered in connection with a more general issue: which degree and type of financial stability – and how explicitly – are the authorities willing to guarantee to savers, investors and intermediaries? How far are they wanting to risk financial markets inefficiencies and moral hazard in order to prevent or suffocate financial crises?

Are these questions 'forbidden'? Of course. But the problems they contain, in one way or the other, will have to be confronted, also using the experience of the current crisis, in the coming years, by authorities, politicians and by academic research as well, in order to dissipate the depressing sense of confusion caused by the observation of the current status of crisis management practices.

5. CONCLUDING REMARKS: SOME IMPLICATIONS FOR EUROPEAN MONETARY AND FINANCIAL GOVERNANCE

To the extent that monetary policy has been an important cause of the crisis, it can also play a decisive role in curing it and in preventing new ones. There are less reasons to accuse the ECB than the FED of a destabilizing policy behaviour. The European monetary constitution is well equipped, also from a 'cultural' point of view, to be able to deliver monetary and financial stability. But the current crisis, and the experience of the years that immediately preceded it, suggest that European monetary institutions and strategy might benefit from an unprejudiced re-examination. Among the important issues to be discussed there are: the allocative consequences of the impact of monetary policy decisions on the risk-aversion of economic agents and on the level and structure of risk premia in the financial markets; the role of asset prices and of monetary and credit aggregates in the decision process of monetary policy; the complementarity of monetary and financial stability policies in the light of a BIS-type macro-prudential framework; the optimal way of avoiding excessively ambitious 'fine-tuning' of the cycle; the compatibility of floating exchange rates with the increasingly intensive global cooperation and harmonization in monetary policymaking required by financial globalization.

To consider excessive liberalizations and ideological reliance on 'free market' mechanisms as the main causes of the crisis can be a strong and misleading simplification. Markets are never truly 'free' if they do not operate in the framework of a qualitatively adequate regulation. While from certain points of view financial regulation has been quantitatively insufficient, its qualitative inadequateness has been at the heart of the crisis. Moreover, financial regulation was weakly implemented and was assisted by seriously defective supervision. The crisis started in the US but European markets proved to be easily and deeply infected; European banks had increased their leverage even more than American ones; the EU precipitously adopted Basel II, underestimating its limits, using a rather rigid Directive, and paying insufficient attention to the regulation of the leverage ratio that the US had in place; European supervisors were unable to collect and analyse timely information and organize appropriate preventive and early interventions. Europe has no reason for thinking it is simply an innocent victim of a crisis made in the US.

A long list of measures to improve international financial regulation and supervision is now in preparation, under the coordination of the Financial Stability Forum (2008). The Basel Committee is working hard on an 'avalanche of new proposals' (Global Risk Regulator 2008). The European Commission must actively participate in these efforts and EU member countries must adopt and implement European decisions in a rapid, effective and homogeneous way. A high level group of former central bankers and public sector experts has been set up by the Commission with the task of proposing a wide reassessment of Europe's supervisory architecture (ibid.). But the crucial progress that Europe must make, to contribute in a substantial way to the improvement of global financial regulation and supervision, is to accelerate the centralization of the architecture of its regulatory and supervisory powers, that are still detained at the national level. The automatic mutual recognition of national regulations is ineffective and the more-or-less minimum harmonization of nation-based regulations is inconclusive. Moreover European supervisors must realize that limiting their cooperation to a supplementary cross-checking of the surveillance of Europe-wide financial intermediaries and markets is insufficient. The crisis has shown what many people thought was already clear before: that European financial markets need a unified regulation and a centrally supervisory power. Art. 105 of the Maastricht Treaty allows the Council to entrust special coordinating powers to the ECB in the field of financial supervision. The central bank is starting to voice its positive opinion on the idea and its readiness to take these powers.[17] Karel Lannoo in Chapter 3 develops the theme of reforming the supervisory architecture in Europe and explains the work that is currently being done in this direction.

When regulation and supervision fail, crises erupt and crisis management tools have to be used by central banks, financial authorities and governments. Crisis management is now hyperactive everywhere in the world. The experience of observing the way it is operated can sometimes be depressive, as interventions succeed in limiting short-term disasters but lack coherence and seem to move along dangerous directions. Crisis management is another field where European policies must be improved and unified,[18] and then coordinated with the rest of the world. When different and competing national approaches are used to manage the crisis, the single market is usually wounded and the effectiveness of the interventions weakened. When multinational European intermediaries need costly public financial assistance, EU's governments must have the formula for taking rapid decisions and for sharing the burden of the interventions. Bailout policies cannot be simply and hypocritically 'forbidden', as in the EU Treaty. The complete prohibition of bailouts is non-credible. Its violations keep weakening the respect for the basic principles of the Union. In coherence with these principles, a prudent but credible and feasible framework for taking bailout decisions in effective and timely ways must be adopted. The discussion of the preceding section suggests that there are at least two other tools of crisis management that need maintenance, repair and, perhaps, some deep conceptual rethinking, also in the European case: central bank lending of last resort and deposit insurance.

NOTES

1. The stages of the growth and diffusion of the crisis, up until the summer of 2008, are carefully explained in the Annual Report of the Bank for International Settlements (2008), ch. VI.

2. An example is the emphasis by the EU President Sarkozy on the 'US-inspired lack of regulation in the recent years, which was a folly whose price is being paid today', as cited by Cody in the *Washington Post*, 26 September 2008.
3. In favour of activism in confronting asset price evolutions see, for instance, Blanchard (2000), Bordo and Jeanne (2002), Cecchetti, Genberg and Wadhwani (2002); in support of 'benign neglect' see, for instance, Bernanke and Gertler (2001), Mishkin (2008).
4. Developed from Bruni (2007).
5. The title of Goodfriend (2007).
6. See, for instance, Borio and Filardo (2007).
7. See, for instance, Borio and Lowe (2002) and many references in Borio (2006) and Borio and Shim (2007).
8. At the Jackson Hole symposium of October 2008 the chairmen of both the FED and the Financial Stability Forum considered with a lot of caution the idea of macro-prudential policies. 'Should monetary policy itself embody in its objective function the health of the financial system?': Draghi's (2008) answer pointed out several difficulties to do so. As for Bernanke (2008), his definition of a macro-prudential framework disregarded the role of monetary policy. On the contrary, an innovative, stimulating academic presentation was offered by Adrian and Shin (2008).
9. For updated descriptions and documentation on Basel II, see www.bis.org/publ/bcbsca.htm.
10. The statements of the European Shadow Financial Regulatory Committee, starting from no. 1, June 1998, 'Dealing with problem banks in Europe', can be found in a web page hosted by CEPS, www.ceps.eu/Article.php?article_id=266.
11. An exception is Spain, where a regulation of this type exists.
12. www.c-ebs.org.
13. But see, for instance, Vives (2008).
14. See Zingales (2009): 'Lehman's bankruptcy forced the market to reassess risk... [which] is crucial to support market discipline... [but] can degenerate into a panic'.
15. See the introduction and the chapters included in Bruni and Llewellyn (2009).
16. See, for instance, Goodhart (2008a), section B.
17. See, for instance, Atkins, *Financial Times*, 5 January 2009.
18. The reforms of regulation and of crisis management are obviously deeply linked. Alternative regulatory structures may have important implications for resolving failed banking institutions. This fact is emphasized in Eisenbeis and Kaufman (2008), an organic four-step programme for Europe that takes into account the basic views of the Shadow Regulatory Committees.

BIBLIOGRAPHY

Adrian, Tobias and Hyun Song Shin (2008), *Financial Intermediaries, Financial Stability and Monetary Policy*, paper presented at the Federal Reserve Bank of Kansas City Symposium, Jackson Hole, 22 August, www.kc.frb.org/home/subwebnav.cfm?level=3&theID=10697&SubWeb=10660.

Atkins, Ralph (2009), 'Ecb seeks wider policing role', *Financial Times*, 5 January, www.ft.com/cms/s/0/d766f2c0-dac7-11dd-8c28-000077b076 58.html.

Bagehot, Walter (1873), *Lombard Street: a Description of the Money Market*, London: Henry S. King and Co.

Bank for International Settlements (2008), *78th Annual Report*, June.

Bernanke, Ben (2008), *Opening Remarks* at the Federal Reserve Bank of Kansas City Symposium, Jackson Hole, 22 August, www.kc.frb.org/home/subwebnav.cfm?level=3&theID=10697&SubWeb=10660.

Bernanke, Ben and Mark Gertler (2001), 'Should central banks respond to movements in asset prices?' *American Economic Review*, no. 91, 253–257.

Blanchard, Olivier (2000), 'Bubbles, Liquidity Traps, and Monetary Policy', in R. Mikitani and A. Posen (eds), *Japan's Financial Crisis and its Parallels to the US Experience*, Institute for International Economics Special Report no.13.

Boone, Peter and Simon Johnson (2008), 'Inflation should be just around the corner', *Wall Street Journal*, 24 November, www.petersoninstitute.org/publications/opeds/oped.cfm?ResearchID=1062.

Bordo, Michael and Olivier Jeanne (2002), 'Monetary policy and asset prices: does benign neglect make sense?', *International Finance*, **5**, 139–164.

Borio, Claudio E.V. (2006), *Monetary and Prudential Policies at the Crossroads? New Challenges in the New Century*, BIS Working Papers, no. 216, Bank for International Settlements.

Borio, Claudio E.V. and Andrew J. Filardo (2007), *Globalisation and Inflation: New Cross-country Evidence on the Global Determinants of Domestic Inflation*, BIS Working Papers, no. 227, Bank for International Settlements.

Borio, Claudio E.V. and Philip W. Lowe (2002), *Asset Prices, Financial and Monetary Stability: Exploring the Nexus*, BIS Working Papers, no. 114, Bank for International Settlements.

Borio, Claudio E.V. and Philip W. Lowe (2004), *Securing Sustainable Price Stability: Should Credit Come Back from the Wilderness?*, BIS Working Papers, no. 157, Bank for International Settlements.

Borio, Claudio E.V. and Ilhyock Shim (2007), *What Can (Macro-) Prudential Policy do to Support Monetary Policy*, BIS Working Papers, no. 242, Bank for International Settlements.

Bruni, Franco (2007), 'Monetary policy and the allocation of resources: comment on allen', in D.G. Mayes and J. Toporowski (eds), *Open Market Operations and Financial Markets*, London: Routledge.

Bruni, Franco and David T. Llewellyn (eds) (2009), 'The Northern Rock crisis: a multi-dimensional problem', *Suerf Studies*, forthcoming.

Cecchetti, Stephen, Hans Genberg and Sushil Wadhwani (2002), *Asset Prices in a Flexible Inflation Targeting Framework*, in W. Hunter, G. Kaufman and M. Pomerleano (eds), *Asset Price Bubbles*: *the Implications for Monetary, Regulatory and International Policies*, Cambridge, MA: MIT Press.

Cody, Edward (2008), 'Sarkozy advocates systemic change after crisis', *The Washington Post*, 26 September, www.washingtonpost.com/wpdyn/content/article/2008/09/25/AR2008092504285.html.

Davis, E. Philip (2008), *Liquidity, Financial Crises and the Lender of Last Resort: How Much of a Departure Is the Sub-prime Crisis?*, Reserve Bank of Australia Conference on 'Lessons from the financial turmoil of 2007 and 2008', 14–15 July.

Diamond, Douglas W. and Philip H. Dybvig (1983), 'Bank runs, deposit insurance, and liquidity', *Journal of Political Economy*, **91** (3), June, 401–419.

Draghi, Mario (2008), *The Current Crisis and Beyond*, Remarks at the Federal Reserve Bank of Kansas City Symposium, Jackson Hole, 22 August, www.kc.frb.org/home/subwebnav.cfm?level=3&theID=10697&SubWeb=10660.

Eichengreen, Barry and Kris Mitchener (2003), *The Great Depression as a Credit Boom Gone Wrong*, BIS Working Papers, no. 137, Bank for International Settlements.

Eisenbeis Robert A. and George G. Kaufman (2008), 'Cross-border banking and financial stability in the EU', *Journal of Financial Stability*, **4** (3), September, 167–204.

Financial Stability Forum (2008), *Report on Enhancing Market and Institutional Resilience*, April, and Follow up, October, www.fsforum.org.

Global Risk Regulator (2008), **6** (10), November, www.globalriskregulator.com.

Goodfriend, Marvin (2007), *How the World Achieved Consensus on Monetary Policy*, National Bureau of Economic Research, Working Paper no. 13580, November.

Goodhart, Charles A.E. (2008a), *The Regulatory Response to the Financial Crisis*, CESifo Working Paper no. 257, March.

Goodhart, Charles A.E. (2008b), 'The boundary problem in financial regulation', *National Institute Economic Review*, October.

Gorton, Gary B. (2008), *The Panic of 2007*, National Bureau of Economic Research, Working Paper no. 14358, September.

Issing, Otmar (2008), *In Search of Monetary Stability: The Evolution of Monetary Policy*, Seventh BIS Annual Conference, Luzern, 26–27 June.

Llewellyn, David T. (2008), *Financial Innovation and a New Economics of Banking: Lessons from the Financial Crisis*, paper presented at the South African Reserve Bank Conference, November.

Mishkin, Frederic (2008), 'How should we respond to asset price bubbles?', Speech at the Wharton Financial Institutions Center and Oliver Wyman Institute's Annual Financial Risk Roundtable, Philadelphia, 15 May, www.federalreserve.gov/newsevents/speech/mishkin20080515a.htm.

Rajan Raghuram G. (2006), 'Monetary policy and incentives', address at the Bank of Spain Conference on Central Banks in the 21st Century, 8 June, www.imf.org/external/np/speeches/2006/060806.htm.

Vives, Xavier (2008), 'Bagehot, central banking and the financial crisis', *Vox EU*, 31 March, www.voxeu.com/index.php?q=node/1015.

Zingales, Luigi (2009), 'Causes and effects of the Lehman Brothers bankruptcy', oral testimony before the Committee on Oversight and Government Reform, United States House of Representatives, 6 October.

3. Concrete Steps Towards More Integrated Financial Oversight: the EU's Policy Response to the Crisis

Karel Lannoo

1. INTRODUCTION[1]

The financial crisis sounded a rude wake-up call for EU policymakers and confronted them with the limits of the present framework for European financial supervisory cooperation. What had been established and functioned well during good times proved completely inadequate for crisis situations. In the absence of a European safety net or a European crisis coordination mechanism, EU member states fell back on national responses, which now threaten to unravel the single market.

Financial market integration had made powerful strides in the years leading up to the start of the financial crisis. Assets held by the 15 largest EU banks in other EU countries had doubled in the period 1997–2006. Several EU countries had become bridgeheads to a mighty financial services industry, active all across the globe. But financial supervision had not kept pace with these developments. Supervisors are by and large still working within the same structures as before the start of monetary union, with the home country ultimately in charge of the supervisory and lender of last resort functions. In several EU member states, including a country as large as the United Kingdom, the banking sector is five times larger than the GDP (Gross Domestic Product) of the country in question.

The title of this chapter is reminiscent of a CEPS (Centre for European Policy Studies) study published some 18 years ago, entitled *Concrete Steps towards Monetary Union* (Gros and Thygesen 1990). Although we are fully aware of the difference in significance between both plans, now is the time to put in place a realistic roadmap to move to a more integrated structure of financial oversight. The methods and steps that were taken in the run-up to monetary union can serve as a useful model.

This chapter starts with an overview of the 2007–2008 financial crisis from a European perspective. We will thereby often distinguish between two different phases, the period from August 2007 until August 2008, and the period following. In the second section, we analyse the reaction of policymakers to the crisis, focusing initially on the roadmap of the Finance Ministers, and successively on the attempts to unfreeze the interbank market and the large bailout plans of national governments. In the third section, we analyse the proposals for European regulatory and supervisory reform, and put forward a set of concrete proposals.

2. THE 2007–2008 FINANCIAL CRISIS: A EUROPEAN PERSPECTIVE

The impact of the US subprime crisis on the European financial system went far beyond what most had dared to predict. What started as a problem related to one specific asset class in one region, rapidly affected the entire financial system in industrialised countries throughout the world, and the non-financial economy. The market for structured products collapsed, investors withdrew from the asset-backed securities market and the fear that some banks may be in trouble provoked a gridlock in the interbank money market, spreading in a second phase to citizens. The growing mistrust in the financial system led European governments, following the US initiative, to orchestrate a massive bailout of €1,873 billion by mid-October 2008.

The 2007–2008 financial crisis can be subdivided into two phases. During the first, lasting from August 2007 to August 2008, many banks took on ever-increasing amounts of losses related to asset-backed securities. In the second phase, starting in September 2008, with the bailout in the US of Fannie Mae and Freddie Mac, the insurance group AIG (American International Group) and the bankruptcy of Lehman, the crisis became systemic, because of the generalised loss of confidence, leading to the massive bailout plans on both sides of the Atlantic. To date, the costs suffered by the financial system related to the subprime losses and write-downs was estimated to amount to almost $1 trillion, of which over one-quarter was carried by European banks. In the second phase, the issue was no longer the total amount of write-downs, but rather how to keep the system afloat at (almost) any cost.

The financial crisis was not a European crisis, nor was there a European response. Throughout the crisis, the impact on and the response from European countries have been heterogeneous. During the first phase, it was clear that the write-downs and losses concerned some banks more than others: it impacted, in decreasing order of importance, mainly on banks in Switzerland, Germany, the UK and France. Banking sectors were affected in more countries in the second phase, but the response varied, depending upon local circumstances. The UK plan, announced by Gordon Brown on 7 October 2008, was the first large European plan, followed to varying degrees and in different ways by other European states.

Indeed, the financial problems are far from over. The period of de-leveraging and re-capitalisation in the financial sector can be expected to last for a long time. A prominent characteristic of the product to which the financial turmoil is related, real estate, is that prices are sluggish to react to changes in trends and hence cycles tend to be long (Gros 2007).

The question arises what the impact of this crisis will be on financial disintermediation in Europe, which had developed at impressive rates since the start of monetary union. The development of mature capital markets in Europe was one of the hallmarks of the EU's Financial Services Action Plan, but recent developments have put a sharp brake on this process. Recent Commission proposals would reverse the trend, penalise securitisation and strengthen financial intermediation.[2]

2.1 Impact on the European Banking System

The financial sector is going through a lengthy period of de-leveraging, which will take many years to accomplish. As banks need to improve their capital ratios, liquidity premia can be expected to be high for a long period of time. As could be observed in the first year of the crisis, there are several ways in which banks can improve their balance sheets: through rights issues, capital injections by sovereign wealth funds or the state, asset sell-offs and cost-cutting. Banks can be expected to focus more on recurrent forms of income in the retail and corporate lending side of the business. At the same time their profitability will decline considerably from the high levels that were recorded over the last three years.

What is remarkable from a European perspective is not only that the exposure of the European banks to the US subprime market was so pronounced, but also that this vulnerability was not evenly spread across countries. Banks in countries such as Italy and Spain were less affected by the crisis, whereas in others, most notably Switzerland, Germany and the UK, the losses were serious, leading to national debates about bank governance and supervision in the first phase, and large bailouts in the second.

It is difficult to calculate an exact figure for the losses the European banking system incurred in the subprime crisis. The data published to date are mostly based on 2007 annual reports and are thus incomplete, as they do not include the write-downs announced since early 2008. One may have

Liberalism in Crisis?

to wait for the 2008 reporting season to get the full picture. It must be kept in mind that the losses are often write-downs on the value of the asset-backed securities. As long as the banks that purchased them hold on to them, these securities may still be revalued, if the value of the underlying property recovers. In addition, it is difficult to determine what exactly a European bank is. A bank like HSBC, which suffered write-downs of about $33.1 billion, is headquartered in the UK, but has strong south-east Asian roots. IKB, in contrast, which had losses of about $13 billion, is an entirely German bank.

The estimates of the total losses related to the subprime crisis to date amount to $966 billion (Table 3.1), of which more than $272 billion is with banks headquartered in Europe ($206 billion for the EU or 21 per cent).[3] Should this be considered as a huge oversight on behalf of European banks? As the underlying assets are largely based in the US, and mostly in a high-risk segment (subprime), it could be considered as a large exposure of the European banking system to a part of the US market. However, a write-down of $206 (€160) billion on a balance sheet total of €41,072 billion of the EU banking system (2007 data) corresponds to 0.4 per cent, which is not excessive. Moreover, the balance sheet total of the European banking system is four times larger than in the US, which stands at €7,688 billion (2007, only commercial banks). Hence the European exposure to the subprime is, ceteris paribus, limited as compared to that of the US.

Table 3.1 Subprime Losses and Write-downs (up to 17 November 2008)

$ billions	Losses/write-downs	Capital raised
Worldwide	966.1	827.4
Americas	664.4	483
Europe	272.6	303.5
Asia	29.1	40.8
EU27-based banks	206.2	
EU27 % of total	21.3%	

Source: Bloomberg (2008).

A similar situation occurred during the East Asia crisis of 1998, when it appeared that the aggregate exposure of European banks to debt from Asian, Latin American and East European countries stood at about €400 billion (end of 1997). This corresponded to 2 per cent of the total balance sheet of €19,636 billion of the European banking system, or about three times the €125 billion exposure of the North American banks (US and Canada). Moreover, lending by European banks to these regions had increased strongly in the three years up to the crisis, even after the first signs of trouble in the emerging markets became apparent in July 1997 (Bank for International Settlements 1998). That crisis also raised questions about internal risk management within European banks, and external control over lending policies.

In regard to the exposure from a national perspective, similar considerations apply a fortiori as to what extent a bank can be called national. German Landesbanken are by and large German, but British and Swiss commercial banks are internationally very active, especially in the US, and hence it is probable that they suffered losses in their international activities, and in particular in the US. The large losses by the German state-owned banks thus stand out as surprising. The combined write-downs of IKB, Bayerische Landesbank, West LB, LB Baden Württemberg and LB Sachsen stood at about $28.4 (€22) billion (on total assets of the German savings banks of €1,045 billion in 2007). Nevertheless, as the internationally active banks are headquartered and have their consolidated oversight in their home countries, it raises the question whether there is a certain analogy with a governance and supervision system. Also, from a national perspective, the combined write-downs of the two dominant Swiss banking groups of $54.2 (€42) billion (on a Swiss GDP of €309 billion in 2007), raises existential questions about the Swiss banking industry and the Swiss financial centre.

This observed difference in the impact on national banking systems can be traced in the profitability figures (Table 3.2), but not in the Basel tier 1 capital ratios data. On the basis of data published in the 2007 Annual Report of the BIS, profits of the major banks in Switzerland, Germany and France fell seriously and to a lesser extent in the UK. Spanish banks on the other hand saw an increase in pre-tax profits, even with a sizeable increase in loan-loss provisions, whereas Italian banks withstood the crisis well. The 'regulatory' capital ratios seemed to be much less affected, and certainly not yet a reason for concern, although the question can be raised whether they are sufficiently indicative. The (non-weighted) average tier 1 (Table 3.3) declined from 8.2 to 8 per cent in 2007. The same could be said for the loan-loss provisions, which has to take into account that the major losses of the banks discussed above were not on the banking book, but on the trading book.

As indicated below, the full cost of the crisis will only be known from the 2008 reporting season onwards. The year 2007 was the combination of a sparkling first half, and the start of the crisis and the write-downs in the second. The full impact of the crisis will thus only be reflected in the profitability and capital ratios from 2008 onwards. However, it is clear that 2007 will be a trend break of continuously rising profits in the banking sector since 2003. The post-crisis period will be a different era altogether.

Table 3.2 Profitability Ratios of Major Banks (as a parentage of total average assets)[1]

	Pre-tax profits			Loan-loss provisions			Net interest margin			Operating costs		
	2005	2006	2007	2005	2006	2007	2005	2006	2007	2005	2006	2007
Austria (3)	0.85	1.65	1.29	0.30	0.38	0.28	1.64	1.90	2.24	2.10	2.40	2.40
Australia (4)	1.52	1.62	1.67	0.14	0.13	0.15	1.92	1.96	2.01	1.70	1.64	1.63
Canada (5)	1.01	1.32	1.27	0.10	0.10	0.14	1.79	1.64	1.68	3.00	2.56	2.57
Switzerland (6)	0.66	0.87	0.31	0.00	0.00	0.01	0.63	0.53	0.45	1.67	1.73	1.70
Germany (7)[2]	0.38	0.55	0.28	0.06	0.07	0.04	0.65	0.68	0.52	0.96	1.32	0.98
Spain (5)	1.15	1.51	1.65	0.23	0.33	0.41	1.55	1.78	1.94	1.70	1.91	1.96
France (5)	0.76	0.87	0.41	0.06	0.06	0.09	0.93	0.76	0.47	1.47	1.43	1.28
UK (8)	0.87	0.97	0.67	0.23	0.27	0.23	1.23	1.26	0.94	1.59	1.70	1.36
Italy (4)	1.23	1.12	0.88	0.23	0.26	0.25	1.95	1.93	1.71	2.34	2.34	2.01
Japan (13)[2]	0.66	0.67	0.50	0.12	0.15	0.13	0.89	0.97	0.75	1.05	1.15	0.80
Netherlands (4)	0.58	0.57	0.38	0.05	0.10	0.10	1.09	1.17	0.99	1.29	1.48	1.37
Sweden (4)	0.90	1.06	0.98	0.01	-0.03	0.01	1.03	1.08	1.07	1.07	1.11	1.07
USA (11)	1.93	1.82	1.02	0.20	0.20	0.56	2.72	2.50	2.47	3.44	3.12	3.51

Notes: [1] All values are IFRS: the number of banks included is shown in parentheses

[2] Values are a mix of local and US GAAP

Source: Bankscope; FitchRatings.

Table 3.3 Capital and Liquidity Ratios of Major Banks[1]

	Tier 1 capital/risk-weighted assets			Non-performing loans/total assets			Net loan/total deposits		
	2005	2006	2007	2005	2006	2007	2005	2006	2007
Austria (3)	7.7	8.9	8.1	2.3	2.1	1.8	56.4	58.1	63.2
Australia (4)	7.5	7.2	6.8	0.1	0.2	0.2	88.3	89.8	85.1
Canada (5)	9.9	10.4	9.6	0.3	0.2	0.2	58.3	56.2	57.2
Switzerland (4)	11.7	11.7	9.8	0.2	0.2	0.1	25.2	26.1	27.3
Germany (7)	8.4	8.4	8.0	1.0	0.6	0.8	36.2	30.4	25.4
Spain (5)	7.9	7.6	7.9	0.5	0.5	0.6	69.9	76.7	76.1
France (4)	8.1	7.9	7.4	1.2	1.2	1.3	32.3	36.5	25.8
UK (7)	7.5	7.9	7.6	0.8	0.7	0.8	54.8	54.5	51.1
Italy (4)	4.7	5.0	6.6	4.0	3.2	3.1	42.7	49.6	70.9
Japan (10)	7.3	7.9	7.4	1.1	1.0	0.9	53.1	55.1	62.5
Netherlands (4)	10.4	9.4	10.0	0.6	0.6	0.4	54.1	55.8	55.1
Sweden (4)	7.1	7.2	7.1	0.4	0.4	0.3	71.7	74.2	74.9
United States (11)	8.4	8.6	8.0	0.3	0.3	0.6	63.4	63.6	61.5

Notes: [1] Weighted averages by banks' total assets, in per cent; the number included is shown in parentheses

Source: BIS (2008a).

The same disconnect between a fundamental decline in profitability figures and capital ratios can be observed in the US. Whereas the profitability of US commercial banks was cut in half, the capital ratios stayed almost at the same level. The write-downs since mid-2007 eliminated all of the profits made by the ten largest US banks over the period 2004–2007.[4]

The big difference between the EU and the US banking system, however, is the level of leverage, or the share of core capital on total assets. A rough comparison reveals that the level of leverage in the EU is almost double that in the US, or to say it the other way around, the level of own funds in the EU is half what it is in the US, with all the problems this can entail in a context of loss-taking. Table 3.4 below shows the size of total bank assets as a share of GDP of the top five banks based in a selected group of countries, the loan-to-deposit ratio, or the degree of underfunding and the leverage ratio.

Table 3.4 Core Bank Soundness Ratios in Selected EU Countries and the US, 2007

	Top 5 bank assets as % of GNP	Loans to deposits	Core capital ratio	Basel tier 1 ratio
Belgium	463	104	4	
France	293	101	3.5	7.4
Germany	165	94	2.6	8
Ireland	404	197	3.6	
Italy	131	161	7.4	6.6
Netherlands	521	125	3.8	10
Spain	184	250	7.2	7.9
UK	313	125	3.9	7.6
EU 27	237	133	4.3	
Switzerland	756	69	3.2	9.8
US	44	91	7.6	8

Sources: Bankscope, Eurostat, BIS.

The Basel tier 1 ratio is added as a point of comparison (based on BIS data referred to in the previous table). It shows worrying low levels of core capital, and an unclear relationship between the Basel tier 1 and the core capital ratio. For the EU, it also demonstrates marked differences in the average capital ratios between the southern and northern European countries.

The difference between the core capital ratios and the Basel ratios is even more pronounced in individual cases (Table 3.5). The Belgian bank

Dexia, an early casualty of the crisis, had a Basel tier 1 ratio of 11.4 per cent in June 2008, but a core capital ratio of only 1.6 per cent.

Table 3.5 Basel Tier 1 and Core Capital Ratios for Selected Banks

	Basel tier 1 ratio		Core capital ratio	
	End 2007	Jun-08	End 2007	Jun-08
Fortis	9.5	7.4	3.8	3
Dexia	9.1	11.4	2.4	1.6
ING	7.4	8.15	2.8	2.2

Sources: Annual and half-yearly reports of banks.

2.2 Impact on the European Insurance Sector: Less Discussed

The insurance sector is a much smaller actor in the financial system than are the banks. Total assets are about one-fifth of the banking sector in the EU. They are thus systemically much less important. Insurance companies are mostly liability-driven, meaning, as long as their risks on the liabilities side (life insurance, mass risk) are well controlled, and the assets to cover these risks are well diversified, they should not face too many problems. Unlike banks, insurance companies are less cyclical: demand for mass risk and life insurance should be fairly stable over time. The main risk in the context of this crisis should be related to bad investments, or overexposure to the real estate markets, as seems to have been the case with some companies. Notwithstanding this fundamental difference with the banking sector, it seems that markets have put the insurance sector in the same basket as the banks. Indexes have gone down almost to the same degree as banks.

The concern about the insurance sector increased as a result of the bailout of AIG in the US. However, this problem, together with the bankruptcy of Lehman, affected the banking sector more negatively, as it appeared that AIG had written coverage for over $300 billion of credit insurance for European banks. AIG itself explained these positions by commenting that they were 'for the purpose of providing them with regulatory capital relief rather than risk mitigation in exchange for a minimum guaranteed fee'.[5] A formal default of AIG would thus have had a devastating impact on banks in Europe, which explains why AIG's problems sent shock waves through the share prices of European banks.

One reason why the insurance sector has been less affected by the crisis is the limited transparency of the published accounts. There is no common method to date at European or international level to measure the minimum solvency requirements of insurance companies, which means that prudential supervision is conducted in different ways across the EU. The European Commission's Solvency II proposal would introduce a single method, but it is still under discussion in the EU Council and Parliament. In addition, the application of International Financial Regulatory Standards (IFRS) is also more limited as compared to the banking sector.[6] This has not prevented some groups from being exposed, and requesting participation in the state bailout plans, such as Aegon in the Netherlands or Ethias in Belgium.

2.3 Impact on Financial Market Activity

The impact on financial market activity was probably the severest, where the crisis broke a trend of growth in European capital markets. The hardest hit were the leveraged finance, asset-backed paper and securitisation markets, which became almost entirely frozen, whereas other segments remained stable, such as corporate bond issuance, at least from a European perspective. Issuance of corporate bonds and notes picked up in the second quarter of 2008, after having got off to a very low start in the first. Leveraged finance issuance, on the other hand, which includes leveraged loans and high-yield bonds, declined to €67.0 billion for the first three-quarters of 2008 compared to €243.3 billion over the same period in 2007.[7] Securitisation issuance declined over the same period from €309.2 for the first three quarters of 2007 to €26.3 billion over the same period in 2008.[8] IPO activity was still strong until the end of 2007, but declined sharply in the first half of 2008.

European mortgage-backed securities (MBS) issuance activity picked up during the second quarter of 2008 as compared to the previous quarter. By nationality, the largest increase was from UK borrowers, following the Bank of England's announcement in April 2008 of a Special Liquidity Scheme that enabled UK banks to swap illiquid assets, such as mortgage-backed securities, against UK Treasury bills (BIS 2008b). However, the activity is largely concentrated in the residential MBS segment, which will overtake 2007 in issuance volume, whereas other segments, including ABS (Asset-backed Security), CDOs (Collateralized Debt Obligations) and commercial MBS, were halved.[9]

The clearest market indicator of persistent stress is the interbank money market rate. Since the start of the credit crisis in August 2007, 3-month spreads of interbank (euribor) overnight rates have jumped from about 10 basic points before the crisis to about 50 in the early days of the turmoil and about 80 basic points until the end of the summer, to reach over 100 basic points in the aftermath of the Lehman bankruptcy. Throughout this period, central banks actively intervened to reduce tensions in the interbank markets, but apparently with limited success. It was only the government actions taken in the second half of October to guarantee interbank claims that managed to bring a halt to the widening spreads. Figure 3.1 shows the spread of the euribor over the eurepo rate, which is the rate at which one prime bank offers funds in euro to another prime bank in exchange for collateral – the spread of the unsecured over the secured lending. It shows the growing cost for unsecured lending since mid-2007.[10]

Spread EURIBOR vs. EUREPO - 1M and 3M

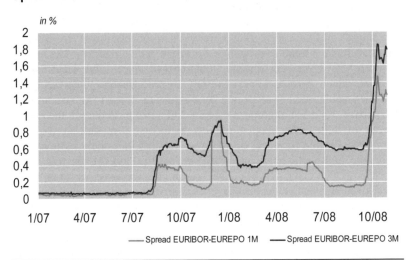

Figure 3.1 Spread of the Interbank Money Market Rate (Euribor) over Eurepo, January 2007–October 2008

3. THE POLICY RESPONSE

Policymakers reacted early on to the mounting problems in the financial sector, as well at the international, European and national levels. The question that arises is what went wrong to prevent this crisis from turning into a full-blown systemic crisis. More especially from a European perspective, the Ecofin (Economic and Financial Affairs Council) roadmap, put in place from October 2007 onwards, seems not to have been sufficient to stop financial instability from spreading and spiralling out of control. Were ministers underestimating the depth of the problem? Were they too complacent in the belief that it was an essentially US-grown problem? Or was it related to a policy coordination problem, as the inter-linkage between international, European and national policy levels gives rise to an unclear division of roles and confusing mandates?

In October 2007, the G7 Finance Ministers and Central Bank Governors asked the Financial Stability Forum to analyse the situation and make recommendations on how to improve the resilience of financial markets and institutions. At the European level, the Finance Ministers discussed the problems in financial markets at the informal Ecofin Council in September 2007, and came up with detailed conclusions during their October, December 2007, May and October 2008 meetings. But as these reactions seemed insufficient and the financial crisis became full-blown, heads of state and government stepped in and orchestrated the response within the Eurogroup and European Council.

But it is above all at the national level that the response was initiated, first as a debate about bank governance and supervision in those countries whose banks were badly hit. Once the crisis spilled out of control, one government after the other stepped in to prepare plans to re-capitalise its financial sector and unlock the interbank market, with differing degrees of conditionality.

One of the reasons why Europe disappeared from the scene is the non-existence of a 'European Treasury'. Although central banks played a dominant role in the first phase of the crisis, treasuries became the leading actors in the second. As banks had to be recapitalised, or interbank lending markets guaranteed, national treasuries had to step in. The 12 October Eurogroup meeting tried to give some coordination to these national plans, which was endorsed by the European Council three days later, but it did not come up with a European plan.

3.1 International Level

The lead in the reaction to the crisis was initially taken by the Financial Stability Forum (FSF), which issued its recommendations in April 2008, but it was overtaken in the second phase by the G20, convoked at the initiative of the French President. The G20 foresees a reform of the Bretton Wood institutions with a broader participation of countries and a central role for the International Monetary Fund (IMF) to detect financial system problems.

The FSF urges actions including strengthened prudential regulation and oversight, transparency in securitisation practices, limitations in the use of rating agents and better tools to detect stress, but it does not propose any fundamental shifts in the regulatory framework. Basel II and its three different pillars, with some adjustments, remain the basis for financial oversight. The capital requirements for the trading book remain largely unchanged, but liquidity regulation becomes a new objective. The report puts a considerable burden on the Basel Committee and national supervisors to improve things, but it is questionable whether they will be capable of coping, given the fatigue related to the long and protracted efforts which led to the Basel II Accord in 2006 and the huge oversight failures that were highlighted by the crisis. The immediate requirements for market participants on the other hand are limited, and essentially focused on more disclosure.

To improve the oversight of large internationally active groups, the FSF recommended the expanded use of international colleges of supervisors, as is also proposed by EU Finance Ministers. The FSF however stopped short of proposing any enhanced role for the IMF or BIS, or any other body in monitoring exposures in the financial system at large, or in allowing information from the colleges to be amalgamated and monitored more centrally.

The G20 meeting in Washington (15 November 2008) addressed the issue of strengthened international cooperation, but nothing concrete was decided. It proposed an enhanced role for the IMF to better identify vulnerabilities in the financial system and requested all G20 members to undertake Financial Sector Assessment Programmes (FSAPs) by the end of March 2009, to review the compatibility of the local regulatory systems with the international financial system. The FSAPs have been undertaken by the IMF since May 1999 to analyse financial systems across the globe, but it is unclear how, in the current global governance framework, their enforcement can be strengthened.[11]

What the role will be for the European Commission in this global governance framework remains to be seen. The Commission has over the last years been strongly involved in regulatory dialogues with the US and increasingly with other third countries, but was not represented in international bodies. Reporting lines from the G7 or G20 go directly to its member states, and the international organisations involved. Regional organisations, such as the EU, seem not to have a clear role.

3.2 European Level

The EU response was initially crystallised in the 'roadmap', adopted in October 2007, and further enhanced and updated in successive EU Council of Finance Ministers meetings. The roadmap moved to a second plan from October 2008 onwards, as the main concern became the national bailout plans and their implications for European integration.

3.2.1 The Ecofin roadmap and the 1st phase of the crisis
The 'roadmap' is an extensive action plan, with a long series of measures to be taken by certain target dates. It was an early indication of the EU's responsiveness to the crisis and its preparedness to make the adaptations in

the regulatory and supervisory framework. At the same time, however, it emphasised on several occasions that no deep structural change would be undertaken. On the contrary, the prevailing view was that the current institutional structure should suffice, which is entirely unrealistic, as the analysis below will show.

The October 2007 Ecofin Council, in response to the first signs of market stress, agreed on common principles for cross-border financial crisis management and on a roadmap to practically enhance supervisory cooperation. The common principles aim to protect the stability of the financial system and to minimise harmful impacts on the economy. Ministers insist that they will 'carefully cooperate' in the case of a cross-border crisis and will react 'based on common terminology and on a common analytical framework'. It built upon difficult work undertaken in recent years in the context of the Economic and Financial Committee (EFC) on financial crisis management and burden sharing.[12]

The December 2007 Ecofin Council spelled out the role of the EU regulatory and supervisory committees in this context. It asked the Commission to consider various options to strengthen the Level 3 Committees, but 'without unbalancing the current institutional structure', a sentence that was repeated by later Ecofin Councils. The Level 3 Committees, which have a mere consultative role, were requested to strengthen the national application of their guidelines 'without changing their legally non-binding nature', and to enhance their efficiency 'by introducing... qualified majority voting where necessary'. The Level 3 Committees were asked to analyse the options of 'voluntary delegation of supervisory competences'. To deal with the growing workload of the Level 3 Committees, the Commission was asked to consider more financial support under the EU budget.

In a letter to all his European colleagues dated 26 November 2007, the Italian Minister Tommaso Padoa Schioppa called for formal changes in EU legislation to entrust the Level 3 Committees with the powers to adopt binding decisions, and to endow them with adequate financial and human resources to perform their tasks.[13] He observed that, in view of the financial market turmoil, the European financial system was still unable to effectively respond to the challenges of a globally integrated market. Voluntary agreements, the Italian Minister remarked, proved incapable of ensuring an efficient area-wide supervisory teamwork during crisis episodes. The Level 3 Committees (L3C) should therefore be turned into agencies, with the power to set binding standards and to take decisions in a limited number of areas. The proposal however was hardly discussed in the Ecofin Council.

The debate on the appropriate governance structure accelerated in the run-up to the informal Ecofin Council which took place in Lublijana in

April 2008, with clearer positions from different member states. The British Chancellor Alistair Darling proposed to establish supervisory colleges by EU law and create cross-border stability groups to respond to financial crisis (3 March 2008). The Italian Minister reiterated his proposal to turn the Level 3 Committees into EU agencies. And the Hungarian Prime Minister proposed a uniform European financial supervisory authority, based on the model of the European System of Central Banks (ESCB) (21 February 2008). The informal Ecofin, to which Alexandre Lamfalussy was invited, discussed the EU dimension of supervision, but without coming to a concrete proposal.

The May 2008 Ecofin Council affirmed and increased the tasks assigned to the Level 3 Committees. In addition to the earlier tasks, these bodies were asked to develop a common European supervisory culture, to ensure efficient cooperation across financial sectors and to monitor financial stability and reporting risks to the EFC. On the latter task, the Council stressed 'that the EU Committees of supervisors should be able to gather aggregate information in order to assess these features within and across financial sectors and to alert the EFC on potential and imminent threats in the financial system'. One may wonder however whether the Council fully realised what it was asking of the Committees, with each of them employing only about 15 persons. Asking European Central Bank's (ECB) Banking Supervision Committee (BSC) to join forces with CEBS (Committee of European Banking Supervisors) and to 'ensure an efficient and appropriate division of labour amongst these two' is unrealistic, as the institutional contexts in which both bodies operate is entirely different and not comparable.[14]

On the supervision of EU-wide financial groups, the May 2008 Ecofin Council put its faith in the colleges of supervisors, as the FSF had also proposed. To allow these to function, a new memorandum of understanding on cross-border financial stability was signed amongst the supervisory authorities, central banks and finance ministries. It specifies a much clearer and more explicit division of responsibilities and tasks amongst the signatories than what had been in place so far.[15] It spells out common definitions and principles, rules on information exchange and cooperation agreements applicable in normal times and periods of crisis. No less than 113 authorities are signatories to the agreement, which is a very high number considering that close to one-half of the member states have a single FSA (Financial Service Authority), and that EEA (European Economic Area) countries are not included. In case of specific agreements pertinent to the supervision of financial groups, however, only those national authorities will be involved where a financial group has a presence. The agreement takes the form of an MoU, that is, it is not legally binding and cannot give rise to any legal claim, although it was, for the first time, made public in full.

3.2.2 A full-blown systemic crisis

Policymakers only started to realise the full scale of the financial crisis by the end of September 2008. Before that time, they continued to believe that this was essentially a US-grown problem, and that it would not affect the European financial system profoundly.[16] The succession of events in October 2008 dramatically brought home the message that Europe had an enormous problem of undercapitalisation in the banking sector, and that only a massive state-led recapitalisation would bring the systemic crisis to a halt. Calls for a European solution fell on deaf ears, and the reaction to the problems from Fortis onwards were entirely in national hands, with only an appearance of European coordination.

The state-led rescue of Fortis during the weekend of 27–28 September 2008 signalled the start of a series of bank bailouts across the EU, on a case-by-case basis, or as part of a general plan. The EU was absent during the earlier part of the crisis, and it was only the emergency Eurogroup meeting on 12 October in Paris, convoked at the initiative of President Sarkozy as President of the European Council, that provided some European coordination to the national rescue plans. A call for a European bailout fund, as informally discussed within the French Ministry of Finance, and also supported by a large group of European economists, was not withheld by the European G4, which met in an emergency meeting in Paris on 4 October, as Germany was said to be radically opposed to any such fund.[17] Two days later, the British Prime Minister was the first to formally announce a national bailout plan for a select group of large British banks, although he added explicitly that this should 'ideally be solved at the European level'.[18]

The main concern of the G4 meeting was to get the European Commission's flexibility in the approval of the national bailout plans, as well from a state aid and stability pact perspective, because of the exceptional circumstances. The meeting called for a new framework of financial supervision, and suggested an international meeting on financial sector governance. The meeting requested the Commission and the International Accounting Standards Board (IASB) to allow banks to reclassify trading book as banking book assets in order to embellish their balance sheets, on which a decision was taken by the Finance Ministers on 7 October.

The Eurogroup meeting on 12 October was the first to come up with a European response to the crisis, in the form of a concerted action plan of the eurozone to temporarily guarantee bank refinancing and keep important banks from failing. The meeting was convened at the level of heads of state and government, under the chairmanship of the French President. The ECB President and the British Prime Minister Gordon Brown were also invited. The Eurogroup decided that:

- governments can provide state guarantees to bank debt issues for up to five years under well-determined conditions, and can participate in these issues. All banks should be eligible for these operations, including foreign-owned banks; and
- governments can take equity stakes in financial institutions and recapitalise banks in trouble.

Moreover, the ECB was requested to ease its rules on collateral.

Governments were asked to avoid national measures that would negatively affect the functioning of the internal market and harm other member states. They committed to 'coordinate in providing these guarantees, as significant differences in national implementation could have a counter-productive effect, creating distortions in banking markets'. The support actions would be 'designed in order to avoid any distortion in the level-playing field and possible abuse at the expense of non-beneficiaries of these arrangements'.[19]

The Eurogroup decisions were endorsed by the European Council, which met a few days later in Brussels. In addition, the European Council decided to establish a 'financial crisis cell' to act in crisis situations. This mechanism will bring together representatives of the Presidency-in-office, the President of the Commission, the President of the ECB (in conjunction with the other European central banks), the President of the Eurogroup and the governments of the member states. The Council also welcomed the setting up of a high-level group by the Commission to strengthen the supervision of the financial sector.

The Ecofin Council had in the meantime decided to increase the minimum level of deposit protection to €50,000, leaving the possibility to the member states to increase it to €100,000. A formal Commission proposal on the subject was adopted a week later. The urgency of the review of the 1994 deposit guarantee directive (1994/19/EC) was widely acknowledged since the September 2007 Northern Rock bailout, but it took the EU more than one year to have a new directive in place. The Ecofin Council also adopted conclusions on executive pay and reiterated its call for a timely implementation of the roadmap.

3.3 The Local Debates and National Bailout Plans

Although the credit crisis is a global phenomenon, the debates remained largely national, with important nuances in the response. This must be kept in mind when considering an eventual European solution, as discussed in the next section. For some, the crisis has clearly demonstrated the limits of the current cooperative model of financial supervision, whereas for others, it has demonstrated the dangers of too much of a harmonised approach (as Franco Bruni stresses in Chapter 2). Some countries have already made adjustments to the supervisory framework. Most interesting from our perspective are the changes that were proposed in the institutional structure at the national level and how the roles of the different actors in financial supervision were altered.

The Paulson Report, published by the US Treasury (2008) a few days after the Bear Stearns collapse, is the most instructive. Although its drafting started well before the crisis broke, in the context of the debate on the competitiveness of the US financial markets, and its contents essentially concern the redesign of the US supervisory system, the report is also indicative for the EU debate. Not only does it demonstrate a willingness to embrace radical change, which many in the US thought to be almost impossible, it also has implications for the EU structure. US policy markets and officials have over the last few years been impressed by the EU's capacity to adapt its financial system in the Financial Services Action Plan, to implement the Lamfalussy proposals, and to create a more competitive financial market.[20]

The Paulson report sees the 'twin peaks' model, whereby supervision is organised by objective, that is prudential versus conduct of business supervision, as the long-term ambition for the US. Such an objective-based model of financial supervision is in place in the Netherlands and in Australia.[21] It recommends an enhanced regulatory and oversight role for the FED (Federal Reserve) as the central authority, with day-to-day supervision in the hands of a prudential and a conduct of business supervisor. Today, the FED is one of the four federal bank prudential supervisory authorities, and supervises about 15 per cent of the top 50 banks (Petschnigg 2005, p. 35), whereas prudential supervision of the (until recently) powerful investment banks was formally in the hands of the Securities and Exchange Commission (SEC), although it is debatable whether this was properly done.[22]

In the UK, the Northern Rock bank run, the first since Victorian times, and the losses incurred by several blue chip financial institutions led to broad debate about the adequacy of the structure of financial supervision. Although the FSA model was not called into question, the Bank of England was given a more important role. The UK Parliament report on Northern Rock criticised the lack of leadership in handling the bank failure and thus the non-functioning of the Tripartite Agreement between the FSA, the Bank and the Treasury. It proposed the creation of a new post of Deputy Governor of the Bank of England and Head of Financial Stability.[23] In his

Mansion speech on 18 June 2008, the Chancellor of the Exchequer, Alistair Darling, said the Government intended to provide a formal legal responsibility for financial stability to the bank as well, alongside its existing role in monetary policy. These proposals were confirmed in the Banking Bill of October 2008, which is expected to come into force in early 2009.

Further discussion on the structure of financial oversight was overtaken by the urgency of national bailout plans for the financial sector. At the same time, the acceptance that radical change was needed grew further during the month of October 2008. On the other hand, the need for financial assistance brought the discussion back to the member state level, as there is no European Treasury, and plans for a European fund were shelved by the German government. By 14 October, European governments had committed some €1,873 billion, or about 15 per cent of GDP of the EU-15, to national bailout plans in one form or another. This sum increased to over €2,170 billion by the end of November, but the crisis is not yet over.

The emergence of the national treasuries in dealing with the crisis raises some fundamental problems for the single market. While the European Commission recognised the urgency of the situation, it published guidance for state aid measures to banks in crisis.[24] The Commission stresses in this document that any measure taken should be exceptional, and that the situation in the financial sector should be reviewed every six months. They could otherwise 'generate harmful moral hazard'.[25] The European Commission specified several conditions that must be met:

- Non-discriminatory access, eligibility for support should not be based on nationality;
- State commitments to be limited in time and scope, while excluding unjustified benefits for shareholders;
- Adequate remuneration of the state financial support;
- Private sector contribution;
- Behavioural rules for beneficiaries that prevent an abuse of state support, such as expansion and aggressive market strategies on the back of a state guarantee;
- State aid should be followed by structural adjustment measures for the financial sector;
- Winding-up procedures should be open and take place on market terms.

It was added that observance of these principles, including in individual aid measures, is the responsibility of the member states, and subject to monitoring by the Commission.

A quick review of the measures adopted at member state level indicates that these rules have already been violated several times. Overall, most schemes are only open for domestic banks, without a clear definition of what this means, thus leaving much discretion in the hands of the Minister of Finance. The Dutch scheme for example is only open for systemically important Dutch banks.[26] State-sponsored subordinated debt schemes, which were used in the Dutch and Belgian context, are not permitted, according to the European Commission, as they protect the interests of shareholders.[27] And the Fortis liquidation procedure was not open. The European Commission has, under the state aid rules, been notified of and responded to most of the general national bailout plans, and also to some specific cases. It concerns so far the support schemes of 13 member states, in chronological order: Denmark, Ireland, the UK, Germany, Sweden, Portugal, the Netherlands, France, Spain, Finland, Italy, Greece and Belgium (the Austrian scheme is pending). It approved the cases of Bradford & Bingley, Hypo Real Estate, Roskilde Bank and IKB, and launched in-depth investigations into Northern Rock and WestLB.[28]

4. MODELS FOR A EUROPEAN REGULATORY AND SUPERVISORY REFORM

The debate on the reform of the European regulatory and supervisory structure has been running for at least a decade. It started in the wake of the start of monetary union, with the launch of the Financial Services Action Programme and the proposals of the Lamfalussy Committee. Until recently, the EU demonstrated that it was capable of adapting the supervisory structure and instituting a much greater degree of supervisory cooperation than had existed previously.

The reform, however, had not been subjected to a crisis situation, having been crafted during good weather conditions, not stormy ones. Discussions had been going on since 2005 over burden-sharing in the event of cross-border bank failures, but without much result.

The following discussion in section 4.1 should illustrate that we have probably reached the limits of what is possible under the current system, and that a quantum step needs to be taken. We review the shortcomings in the present regulatory and supervisory model, as the basis for formulating in section 4.2 a proposal for a European System of Financial Supervisors (EFSF).

4.1 Shortcomings in the Present Regulatory and Supervisory Model

Two proposals have been debated for quite some time concerning desirable changes to the present supervisory model: i) upgrading the Level 3 Committees and ii) strengthening the role of the supervisory colleges. In the context of European supervisory cooperation, two further issues need to be analysed: the functioning of memoranda of understanding and the role of the ECB, as elements of a possible future structure.

4.1.1 The role of the Level 3 Committees

The Level 3 Committees have managed to achieve a lot in a limited period of time, and with scarce resources. They can be credited with having eased the Commission's work on the implementing measures for framework directives and to have contributed to supervisory convergence and a European supervisory culture by continuously bringing together supervisors from the different member states on a wide variety of matters.[29] However, it rapidly appeared that their purely advisory role was hampering their drive. A discussion was kicked off in 2004 by the oldest of the Committees, the Committee of European Securities Regulators (CESR), with the Himalaya report (CESR 2004), which proposed an enhanced role for CESR in mediating between supervisory authorities and in delegating supervisory responsibilities.

Four years on, the issue is still on the table. Although the CEBS has taken sides with CESR, it seems that ministers are unwilling to change the role of the Committees, as is evident from the Ecofin Council deliberations in May 2008, referred to above. CESR, and also the former Italian Finance Minister, argued that it should not be difficult to turn the Committees into formal EU agencies, like the existing 28 European regulatory agencies. However, this would expand the mandate of the Level 3 Committees from essentially regulatory concerns to also include supervisory matters. This raises important legal, accountability and eventually fiscal issues. With formal mediation and delegation powers comes enforcement and the authority to sanction, which raises the sensitive matter of sovereignty. How will accountability be organised if the Committees have a more formal role? In addition, such changes touch upon, or could alter the allocation of, responsibilities between home and host supervisors as set out in the EU directives. And what if they incur formal responsibilities in the context of a troubled bank, as the coordinator of national authorities, which may raise financial issues?

A more formal role for the Committees could give them more clout in discussions with the member states, but this is possibly what some authorities are afraid of. So far, the Committees have acted more as an informal mediator, and often come up with the broadest possible consensus to come to an agreement between the member states. An example is the COREP (Common Reporting Framework) project of CEBS, which creates a common format for banks to use in reporting solvency ratios. Table 3.6 shows how many reporting cells for core (83 per cent) and detailed information (63 per cent) banks have to use on average in COREP. The maximum number of cells in which a bank could be asked to report is about 18,000, according to CEBS, as not all detailed information is applicable to all banks. This very high number is seen by bankers as the lowest common denominator, representing a totally unworkable compromise and a symptom of the lack of powers on the part of CEBS to impose a truly common (and integrated) reporting framework in the EU.

Table 3.6 Framework for Common Reporting of the New Solvency Ratio

	Number of Cells	Average Use % (non-weighted average)	Minimum Use %	Maximum Use %
Core	1,227	83% for all; 90% disregarding securitisation and market risk templates	20%	100%
Detailed	21,606	63%	5%	100%

Source: CEBS (2006).

The best example of the unwillingness of the May 2008 Ecofin Council to revisit the structural framework is the demand to the Committees to report to the EU Council on key developments, risks and vulnerabilities that could affect the stability of the financial system, as referred to above. This is not a core task of the Committees in the context of the Lamfalussy framework, nor do they have the means to undertake it. That the Council also involved the ECB's Banking Supervision Committee only emphasises the absence of realism of this request.

Another example of the unclear division of roles was the demand to banks by European Commission in reaction to the subprime crisis to provide more information on securitisation. The European Commission did not have up-to-date information on securitisation, and had to rely on sector organisations to provide insights into the size and functioning of these markets.

4.1.2 The model of colleges

The main means by which the EU Council deals with EU-wide financial groups are the supervisory colleges. Colleges are established in case a financial institution operates in another member state through one or more branches or subsidiaries. The college is chaired by the home supervisor of the group's parent and made up of authorities from all the countries in which the holding company has established a presence through subsidiaries or branches. Colleges function on the basis of mandatory written arrangements agreed upon 'ad hoc' by the competent authorities to allow the home country to carry out consolidated supervision of the group (art. 131 CRD, Directive 2006/48/EC).

In reaction to the financial crisis, the Ecofin Council requested that the role of the colleges should be strengthened and asked, again, that the EU Committees should play a role 'in giving operational guidelines to provide consistency in the working procedures of the different colleges and effectiveness of the decision-making process and provide reassurance to supervisors involved in the colleges, as well as monitoring the coherence of the practices of the different colleges of supervisors and sharing best practices'.[30] This demand was reiterated after the summer 2008, and also reflected at international level in the G20 conclusions. Amendments to the EU's capital requirements directive aimed at strengthening the role of colleges were proposed by the European Commission on 1 October 2008.[31]

The extensive reliance on colleges raises three major issues. Although supervisors work in a college, their statute, mandate, accountability, modus operandi and enforcement powers continue to differ importantly across the EU. EU legislation has introduced the single licence, and obliges supervisors to cooperate, but has not harmonised the national structures. Hence a home country authority may not have the same powers in the host country to enact certain disciplinary measures. The degree of independence and accountability of the supervisory authority differs. And the formal responsibility for financial stability is limited to the national boundaries. Although the same problem exists at a global level, the legal framework and the degree of market integration differ importantly, hence the question arises whether colleges are still appropriate in the EU context. From this perspective, colleges were the solution for the past and may be for the present, but not for the future.

The second issue raised by colleges is whether the information obtained is sufficiently shared and merged to have a broader picture on exposures in the interbank market and risks to stability of the European financial system. A basic problem is that the home country is supposed to have the full picture, not necessarily the host countries. The latter may in case of trouble rapidly feel badly informed, with the result that trust in the college disappears, and the college can no longer function as a college. This is related to a third problem, whether colleges effectively function as college in times of crisis. The information emerging from the rescue of Fortis in the weekend of 27–28 September 2008 is not reassuring in this context. The Belgian policymakers and supervisors contacted the two most important host countries, the Netherlands and Luxembourg, only after about 48 hours of discussions.[32]

Comparing the location and geographical presence of banking groups in the EU and Switzerland, 123 colleges should have been established in the EU (Figure 3.2). With 29, Germany chairs the highest number of colleges, followed by Switzerland (13), Italy (10), France (8) and the UK (7).[33] Taking into account the importance of groups that a country chairs, based upon the weighted average market shares of the countries in which the banks are active of which a certain country is the lead supervisors, the ranking is topped by Spain, followed by Belgium and the UK. The question can thus be raised whether these countries have the capabilities and the means to exercise the supervisory tasks as home country of globally active banking groups, and second, whether the information emerging from so many colleges gets sufficiently coordinated and amalgamated at European level.

Number of colleges of supervisors

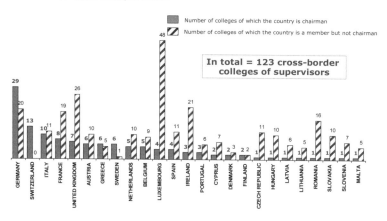

Figure 3.2 Colleges of Supervisors per EU Member State

4.2 Memoranda of Understanding: a Good Basis?

The legal basis for cooperation between colleges are memoranda of understanding (MoUs), which essentially have a bilateral nature. The recent capital requirements directive (2006/48/EC and 2006/49/EC) further harmonised the structure of cooperation between the home and host country authorities, and clarified the obligations on both sides.[34] It requires competent authorities to have written coordination and cooperation arrangements, or MoUs, in place for the supervision of banking groups. MoUs are not legally binding, however, and cannot give rise to any legal claim. The Northern Rock collapse demonstrated already how difficult it is for MoUs to work even at national level. At international level, the limited information available so far on the rescue of Fortis indicate that they are not effective, as discussed above.

MoUs are also used as a framework for information-sharing and coordination between authorities of different states to contribute to financial stability and crisis management. A first MoU was concluded by the ECB's Banking Supervision Committee in 2003, setting the specific principles and procedures for the responsible authorities in crisis management situations. This MoU was extended in 2005 to also include finance ministries, and recently radically upgraded (see above).

The core issue of MoUs, that is, information exchange, continues to be the Achilles heel of the single financial market. At a European Commission conference on the allocation of supervisory responsibilities, organised on 26 June 2007 just before the current financial crisis started, it was apparent just how little progress had been made on information exchange between supervisory authorities. The lack of information exchange had already been criticised in the 2001 EFC report (Brouwer II report), but had hardly been acted upon. This was also highlighted in an IMF report, published in May 2007, which found existing practices for supervisory cooperation and MoUs out of line with market developments. It called for much more ex-ante cooperation and information sharing than was the rule.[35]

The market turmoil, which started in August 2007, highlighted that the reach of the MoU between supervisors, central banks and finance ministries was insufficient. ECB officials have on several occasions complained about the lack of supervisory information to make financial stability assessments and monitor financial stress.[36] Supervisors are often hindered on professional secrecy grounds from exchanging this information with non-supervisory authorities in normal times. When they share the information in emergency situations, it is usually too late. It is highly questionable whether the new updated MoU will change this practice.

Even at the national level, it seemed that MoUs are precarious, as illustrated by the Northern Rock case, and the ensuing discussion between the Bank of England and FSA. After the extension of the Bank of England's powers, as was proposed by Alistair Darling, the discussion still revolves around who will have the formal power to pull the trigger for a bank in trouble.[37]

4.2.1 Role of the ECB: not clarified

Unlike the FED and the Bank of England, European authorities have not acted so far to clarify the mandate of the European Central Bank. The core task of the ECB is to maintain price stability, and then to establish its reputation as a new central bank for Europe. In 2002, Wim Duisenburg attempted to broaden the ECB's task to include banking supervision, but he was rebuked by the Finance Ministers.

According to the EU Treaty, the ECB is in charge of monetary policy and the smooth operation of payment systems, whereas financial supervision and stability remain the competence of the member states. Emergency liquidity assistance can be provided by national central banks in the Eurosystem to an institution operating in its jurisdiction, but at the costs to the central bank in question.[38] The ECB can contribute to the smooth conduct of policies pursued by the competent authorities relating to prudential supervision and financial stability (art. 105.5). Specific tasks concerning policies relating to prudential supervision of banks and other financial institutions, with the exception of insurance companies, could be conferred to the ECB, according to art. 105.6, but this is seen as a last resort and requires the unanimity of the member states.

Early on after its creation, the ECB attempted to enlarge its powers into the area of prudential supervision. In 2001, the ECB issued a paper on the role of central banks in prudential supervision, in which it argued strongly in favour of combining prudential supervision and central banking (ECB 2001). It even detected a trend in this direction and refuted the arguments against combining both: 'Arguments in favour of a separation of prudential supervision and central banking lose more of their force, while those in favour of combining become more prominent' (ECB 2001, p. 7). It concluded that 'when viewed from a Eurosystem perspective, the attribution of extensive supervisory responsibilities (that is, both macro- and micro-prudential) is likely to prove beneficial' (Ibidem p. 9).

The ECB attempts, however, led to a fierce reaction from the Finance Ministers in the Ecofin Council in 2002, with which the Ecofin until today may want to remain consistent. The May 2002 meeting (EFC 2002, p. 10) explicitly stated that the structure for financial regulation and supervision must be consistent with:

* The allocation of powers and responsibilities as set out in the Treaty;
* Appropriate accountability to EU institutions, in particular political accountability to the Ecofin Council;
* Subsidiarity, since supervisory tasks are best performed as close as possible to supervised entities and since financial crises may have implications for public finances;
* Neutrality with respect to models adopted at the national level.

Since that time, the ECB has kept a low profile on banking supervision matters. The ECB was part of the MoUs that were concluded on financial stability, but it did not make any political statements as it did in 2001. Only recently, it repeated on several occasions the need to have more supervisory information on financial institutions. As the ECB injects liquidity to the banking system based on appropriate collateral, it could suffer losses in case an illiquid bank appears to be insolvent. Hence the 'need of timely and exhaustive transmission of supervisory information at the European level'.[39] But the ECB was hardly in the scope of the discussions of the Ecofin Council during the first year of the crisis. Only its BSC was asked to step up the cooperation with CEBS.

4.3 A European System of Financial Supervisors

To respond to the shortcomings and inconsistencies discussed above, and to establish an effective supervisory system dealing with today's and tomorrow's supervisory challenges, EU policymakers will need to take a quantum step. With the reforms undertaken over the last years further to the Lamfalussy proposals, the limits of what can be done within the current EU supervisory structure have been reached, particularly when dealing with the cross-border banking crisis. 'It is only when the frameworks for regulation, supervision and crisis management match the actual structure of financial markets, that the negative externalities of financial crises can be managed properly', to quote the Swedish Central Bank Governor.[40] A further step forward will thus require deeper institutional changes. We propose to follow *mutatis mutandis* the roadmap that led to the creation of the ESCB in 1998. A European System of Financial Supervisors would bring all financial supervisory authorities in Europe under a single roof, while maintaining a plurality in the operational structure.

4.3.1 A roadmap
The roadmap would be composed of three parts: (1) the European Council formally mandates the High Level Expert Group on EU financial supervision to analyse the optimal structure of financial oversight and propose concrete steps leading to a European System of Financial Supervisors (de Larosière Committee); (2) the European Financial Institute is created to lay the groundwork for the establishment of a European System of Financial Supervisors; (3) the European System of Financial Supervisors starts at a certain target date.

Committees have been widely used in the European integration process, for broader political as well as for more technical issues. Not only are they apolitical in nature, but they also allow the pooling of the necessary technical expertise and knowledge. In addition, as a consensus has not yet emerged at

European policy level of the need for a radical change in the structure of European financial supervision, which is also caused by the lack of a European public debate (as opposed to national policy debates) on the subject, a Committee could contribute to creating the necessary consensus.

The Committee's mandate should be fourfold: (1) map the context; (2) analyse the different possible modalities in the institutional design of financial supervision and recommend the optimal structure for the EU; (3) outline in detail the objectives of the ESFS, its statute, primary tasks, administration, governance and financial resources; (4) assess the relationship between the ESFS and the deposit insurance and resolution authorities. The context should provide the rationale why the current structure is no longer sufficient, and to what extent the supervisory structure is no longer in line with market integration. The different possible responses should emerge from this. It should set out which tasks can be better executed at a centralised level, and which at a national or local level.

Depending upon the specific recommendations of the Committee, a European Financial Institute should be created soon after the delivery of the recommendations of the Committee. Its task should be preparatory and at the same time operational. It should do the operational work for the establishment of an integrated ESFS and the structures that are needed to perform these tasks. Pending an eventual Treaty change, it could function as an EU-wide agency, set up by the European Council, and already be empowered to act on certain matters, such as the collection and amalgamation of supervisory information, the execution of certain supervisory tasks such as mediation and delegation of tasks amongst national authorities, and performing a crisis cell function. It could at the same time continue to perform the regulatory tasks of the actual Level 3 Committees.

In a third phase, the ESFS would start to function under:

- common objectives for financial supervision;
- a single statute;
- a unified governance and accountability structure.

Objectives for financial supervision have so far never been formally harmonised at the EU level. Although the broad objectives are the same, safeguarding the stability of the financial system and protecting consumers/investors, important differences may exist in other objectives. The UK Financial Services Authority has as one of its objectives 'the promotion of public understanding of the financial system', which means that it needs to help users to understand what financial products they buy. To our knowledge, this is not necessarily an objective of other supervisory authorities in the EU. Acceptance of this objective would come to meet a growing need of financial literacy in a world with an increasing complexity of financial products.

Much inspiration for the format of the statute and the governance and accountability structure could be taken from the ESCB statute. The Governing Council of the ESFS should consist of an Executive Board and the Chairmen of the 27 national authorities, in the same way as the ESCB is governed. As with the ECB President, the chairman should report periodically to the Ecofin Council and the European Parliament on financial stability issues.

The Committee should analyse two specific issues carefully in more detail:

1. To what extent should a functional approach be followed to financial regulation, or should a more objective-based model be followed?
2. How will subsidiarity be applied to financial supervision, that is, which tasks can be more efficiently exercised centrally as compared to locally?

The answer to the latter question could ease the response to the first, in the sense that conduct of business supervision will by and large remain at a local level, which implies that, from that perspective, a more objective-based approach would be easier. The current crisis has also indicated that one of the reasons for separation between banking and insurance (and investment banking) supervision, that is, the likelihood of systemic effects, is no longer tenable. As demonstrated above, the insurance sector can also be regarded as systemically important, which supports an objective-based approach.

The Committee should also analyse how the links between the ESFS and the ECB will be worked out. This crisis has amply demonstrated that well developed communication lines between central banks and supervisors are extremely important, as are also clear divisions of responsibilities. We would strongly support a clarification of the financial stability role of the ECB and the ESCB, while maintaining supervision outside their mandate.

Another tricky issue to analyse is the maintenance of the home country control. We would argue in favour of a two-tier system, whereby supervisory responsibilities for systemically important EU-wide groups are shared between the home country and the ESFS. The core supervisory responsibilities would be delegated to a supervisory board in the ESFS, with day-to-day monitoring placed in the hands of the local supervisors.[41]

4.3.2 Other possible scenarios
Several other possible scenarios discussed above could be considered for moving forward:

The upgrading of the Level 3 Committees into EU agencies
The upgrading of the Level 3 Committees is more of a short-term, interim solution that raises more difficulties than it solves. It gives more powers to the Committees without addressing the differences of statutes and powers of the national authorities, and the related issues of accountability and control. It does not solve the supervisory problems discussed above.

More generally, turning the Level 3 Committees into EU agencies would create three new regulatory agencies, in addition to the 28 that already exist at the EU level. In the aftermath of the financial crisis, financial supervision issues could be better dealt under a single roof, and the institutional structure put in place as the result of a proper political process, rather than rapidly turning the existing Committees into agencies, and in this way circumventing a deeper discussion about the proper supervisory structure Europe needs.

The use of art. 105.6 of the EU Treaty and giving more powers to the ECB for banking supervision
The Treaty article is limited to banking supervision, and to 'specific tasks' as related to banking supervision. The fact that insurance companies could not be part of it and that it is limited to specific tasks means that it poses too many constraints to be used as a long-term solution. In addition, the question remains whether it would be appropriate for the ECB to exercise banking supervision within the ECB, whose main mandate is ensuring price stability.

The report of the High Level Expert Group on EU financial supervision (de Larosière Group) would be of utmost importance in analysing the trends globally in this domain, and summarising the pros and cons of the different institutional models, to come to an optimal structure for the EU, also including the degree of cooperation with the central bank.

A European FSA, or single prudential and single conduct of business supervisor
A fully-fledged single FSA, or single supervisors-by-objective, would not be adapted to the state of European market integration, and not pass the subsidiarity test.

4.4 A European Resolution Trust

A necessary corollary to an ESFS should be a European Resolution Trust, as a safety net for short-term financial problems of EU-based financial institutions. The European Central Bank can only provide liquidity against collateral to keep the money market functioning, but has no powers to resolve a solvency crisis. A European Resolution Trust could be managed by the European Investment Bank (EIB) (Gros and Micossi 2008b). Appeals for its funds would be decided by the Governing Council of the ESFS. The EIB is a public agency and issues guaranteed bonds to finance its operations. Its Board of Governors is made up of the Ministers of Finance of the member states. At present, the EIB has capital and reserves of €30 billion, upon a total balance sheet of €300 billion. In addition, it can call upon an additional capital of €156 billion, which is currently uncalled for. Its capital is subscribed for on a proportional basis by the different member states.

A European Resolution Trust could take equity stakes in or provide guaranteed loans to financial institutions in trouble. Support by the Trust would be based on adequate remuneration, to preserve the value of the public investment and to make sure that those who mismanaged would pay for the consequences. Losses could be distributed across member countries according to where they arose.

A European Resolution Trust would be a much more appropriate safety net for European-wide active banks than having to rely on national solutions. It would be more neutral, as it would come from an EU-wide institution and do away with distortions created by national bailout plans. It would be more efficient, as it would provide guarantees to depositors on a European-wide basis. And it would be more appropriate, certainly for those banks that have outgrown their national boundaries. The Trust would apply to troubled financial institutions of a certain size that have a Community dimension, based on a minimum share of their total EU assets outside their home country. The thresholds of the EU merger control regulation could function as a benchmark to distinguish between Community and national competence.[42]

In this context, one could also consider creating a federal deposit protection fund in the EU. Rather than attempting to further harmonise the different national deposit protection schemes, as the European Commission did in its proposal of 15 October 2008, it may be easier and probably more efficient to create an EU-wide deposit protection fund from the beginning.[43] Although the minimum level of deposit protection was increased, the Commission proposal continues to leave a large degree of discretion to the member states, and does not solve the home-host problem. As with the Icelandic banks, citizens cannot be expected to know whether a foreign bank in a given country is a branch or subsidiary, and the different implications this distinction may have on the insurance of their deposits under the host or home deposit protection scheme.

5. THE GLOBAL DIMENSION

EU policymakers have rapidly brought the debate about the reform of financial regulation and supervision to the global stage by launching a debate for the reform of the Bretton Woods institutions and calling for a

G20 meeting. While there rightly are certain issues that should also be discussed at global level, this should not stop the EU from bringing its own house in order. This is even more important since the EU represents more than 50 per cent, on some accounts even more than 55 per cent, of global bank assets. Seen from the perspective of developing countries, calling for concerted action on bank governance, supervision and oversight, means that those who are principally hosting these markets have to take the lead in controlling them.

By taking a clear initiative along the lines outlined above, the EU could demonstrate to the outside world that it is assessing the full policy implications of the crisis and aligning its structure of financial oversight along lines similar to that used for monetary policy. It would at the same time be a clear indication globally that it is taking the lead in reforming the structure of financial oversight.

Asking the IMF to take a more important role in financial oversight, by undertaking Financial Sector Assessment Programmes, is noteworthy, but nothing dramatic. The IMF has been undertaking these assessments since 1999, and the outcome has been used by besieged supervisors in EU countries to claim that they had high ratings. In addition, the enforcement powers of the IMF are limited. But should not the EU start to undertake its own assessments? Regulatory compliance can be enforced by the EU, but this is not so easily achieved in the area of supervision. The creation of an ESFS could fill this void.

Table 3.7 Main Indicators of the Size of the EU's Financial Markets*

2007 bn €	World	EU	EU%	US	US%
GDP	37,461.57	10,775.07	29	13,682.43	37
Gross national savings	8,647.60	2,344.96	27	1,053.74	12
Domestic stock market capitalisation	44,714.11	10,116.56	23	13,682.43	31
Total bank assets	58,229.99	29,632.88	51	7,688.11	13

Notes: *According to the ECB, total EU bank assets are €41,072 billion, meaning that the EU percentage of global bank assets could well exceed 51 per cent. As the ECB does not offer statistics on bank assets at global level, it is not possible to use ECB data for purposes of comparison.

Sources: IMF, *Global Financial Stability Report*, IMF International Financial Statistics, September 2008.

6. CONCLUSIONS

A quantum step needs to be taken to upgrade and adapt the structure of financial oversight in the EU. The financial crisis exposed dangerous weaknesses in the regulatory and oversight structure that need to be urgently corrected to restore confidence in the financial system and to keep the single market alive. To date, EU policymakers have not been sufficiently willing to consider changes in the institutional structure. We believe that this position is no longer tenable, for the following reasons:

- The EU Council of Finance Ministers has increased the number and magnitude of tasks assigned to the supervisory (Level 3 or Lamfalussy) committees – CESR, CEBS and CEIOPS (Committee of European Insurance and Occupational Pensions Supervisors) – to absurd levels, tasks that far exceed their mandate, capabilities or competences.
- Supervisory opinion-sharing and information consolidation remain the Achilles heel of the single financial market. A common data pool, a succinct number of common supervisory data formats and data-sharing with non-supervisory authorities simply do not exist.
- Placing trust in colleges of supervisors is a provisional solution for the present, not a sustainable one for the long-term. Colleges strengthen the bilateral spaghetti model of European supervision, at the expense of a truly integrated and consolidated oversight. In addition, colleges need to work in a context of non-harmonised statutes, mandates and powers of national supervisors, which greatly undermines their effectiveness.
- The basis for cooperation between national treasuries, central banks and supervisors are Memoranda of Understanding. The total number of authorities involved in such MoUs and their non-binding nature make these instruments almost entirely unworkable in an EU context, and all the more so in times of crisis.

Certain conditions are of critical importance during a financial crisis: a clear hierarchy in the decision-making structure, up-to-date supervisory information and competence to act. As events have demonstrated, with a multitude of supervisory authorities in charge, these conditions are not in place in the EU today. On the contrary, the asymmetries in the supervisory systems in the EU are widespread, rapidly causing confusion, misunderstandings, and even mistrust and ring-fencing in times of trouble.

The creation of a European System of Financial Supervisors, modelled upon the ESCB, is the way to overcome these weaknesses. Under an ESFS, EU supervisors would work under a single umbrella, a single institutional structure, on the basis of harmonised principles and statutes, but with full application of the subsidiarity principle.

Against this background, this chapter puts forward three recommendations:

1. The European Council should formally mandate the High-Level Expert Group on EU financial supervision to analyse the optimal structure of financial oversight and propose concrete steps leading to a European System of Financial Supervisors;
2. A European Financial Institute should be created to lay the groundwork for the establishment of the European System of Financial Supervisors;
3. The European System of Financial Supervisors should be given definitive target date to commence operations.

The intention of the ESFS would not be to create a single European Financial Services Authority. Rather, it would follow the 'twin peaks' or objective-based model of supervision, based on the subsidiarity principle. Only those tasks that can be better performed at the European level would be centralised, namely crisis management, data-sharing and macro-prudential oversight, pooling of expertise in the supervision of large systemically important financial institutions, mediation amongst supervisors and supervisory decision-making. In this spirit, conduct of business control would largely remain at national level.

A European Resolution Trust should be created to work in tandem with the ESFS as a mechanism to deal with systemically important European-wide financial institutions. The European Resolution Trust would be managed by the European Investment Bank.

These moves should be widely communicated to European citizens to restore confidence in the financial system and in the single financial market.

Table 3A.1 Key Financial Indicators of the Top Five Banks in the EU and Selected Other Countries

Country	Total assets (mil €)	Total equity (mil €)	Loans to customers (mil €)	Deposits from customers (mil €)	Asset/ GDP (%)	Loans/ deposits (%)	Equity/ assets (%)
Austria	698,475	44,722	392,763	299,996	257.9	130.9	6.4
Belgium	1,550,751	62,342	621,514	598,792	463.0	103.8	4.0
Bulgaria	17,080	1,976	11,259	11,126	59.1	101.2	11.6
Cyprus	83,675	6,623	44,702	55,020	535.1	81.2	7.9
Czech Rep.	105,850	7,276	51,718	74,986	83.3	69.0	6.9
Denmark	625,020	20,960	373,771	187,028	274.5	199.8	3.4
Estonia	34,665	2,653	27,278	14,662	227.0	186.0	7.7
Finland	274,996	21,561	140,087	91,409	153.0	153.3	7.8
France	5,550,460	196,302	1,593,553	1,580,763	293.3	100.8	3.5
Germany	3,990,498	104,581	931,919	988,265	164.7	94.3	2.6
Greece	287,210	22,754	196,660	165,573	125.9	118.8	7.9
Hungary	69,416	6,359	49,255	38,481	68.6	128.0	9.2
Ireland	769,816	27,508	480,773	244,336	403.9	196.8	3.6
Italy	2,006,529	147,987	1,221,732	758,484	130.7	161.1	7.4
Latvia	21,620	1,797	14,315	9,899	108.4	144.6	8.3
Lithuania	23,035	1,540	17,047	10,418	82.2	163.6	6.7
Luxembourg	309,875	15,998	103,668	104,238	854.2	99.5	5.2
Malta	14,010	1,698	6,421	8,981	258.7	71.5	12.1
Netherlands	2,954,809	113,227	1,500,757	1,197,983	521.1	125.3	3.8
Poland	106,567	10,756	62,595	79,588	34.5	78.6	10.1
Portugal	317,520	18,585	221,113	144,597	194.7	152.9	5.9
Romania	40,746	3,247	25,360	23,951	33.6	105.9	8.0
Slovakia	31,029	2,320	16,240	22,151	56.6	73.3	7.5
Slovenia	31,719	2,140	21,896	16,114	92.0	135.9	6.7
Spain	1,934,416	138,873	1,838,315	734,621	184.1	250.2	7.2
Sweden	1,013,630	40,785	623,086	327,833	305.4	190.1	4.0
UK	6,406,952	248,052	2,846,061	2,280,745	312.9	124.8	3.9
EU	29,270,369	1,272,622	13,433,858	10,070,040	237.2	133.4	4.3
Iceland	129,934	8,228	82,684	39,809	890.0	207.7	6.3
Norway	243,316	13,004	195,088	110,360	85.7	176.8	5.3
Switzerland	2,357,865	74,747	557,616	807,249	756.3	69.1	3.2
USA	4,474,314	339,328	1,966,141	2,156,126	44.4	91.2	7.6

Source: Bankscope, Eurostat.

NOTES

1. This chapter is an abridged version of a task force report which was published by CEPS in December 2008.
2. See proposed amendments to the Capital Requirements Directive (CRD) in the area of securitisation, in which the European Commission proposes that banks should hold capital for at least 10 per cent of their securitised exposures (see http://ec.europa.eu/internal_market/bank/regcapital/).
3. Data until 17 November 2008 (source: Bloomberg).
4. 'Vanished profits', *New York Times*, 17 October 2008.
5. K-10 annex of AIG annual report, quoted in Gros and Micossi (2008a).
6. See for example the announcement by Allianz of the valuation of its stake in Commerzbank at double the market price, 10 November 2008.
7. European Third Quarterly High Yield and Leveraged Loan Report for 2008 (available from www.ehya.com).
8. 2008 Q3 Securitisation Data Report (www.europeansecuritisation.com).
9. Ibid.
10. Drawn from Nowotny (2008).
11. See http://www.imf.org/external/NP/fsap/fsap.asp for hundreds of FSAP country reports.
12. Work on crisis management and burden-sharing started in the EFC in 2004, but was the subject of deep controversy between the member states on the need for a formal agreement on these matters. Cross-border crisis management exercises and simulations have been conducted on a regular basis in recent years.
13. The letter was published on 11 December 2007 in abridged form in the *Financial Times*.
14. 2866th Council Meeting, Economic and Financial Affairs, Bruxelles, 14 May 2008, Council Conclusions, p. 13.
15. In March 2003, the ECB initiated a memorandum of understanding on 'high-level principles of co-operation between the banking supervisors and central banks of the European Union in crisis management situations', which was updated in 2005.
16. This was the main message of the historic press briefing given by the German Minister of Foreign Affairs Frank Walter Steinmeyer in front of the NYSE building, on 25 September 2008, in the margins of his participation in the UN annual meeting. Two weeks later, the German government announced a €500 billion support plan for the financial sector.
17. 'European banking crisis, A call to action's *Financial Times*, 2 October 2008, (available from www.voxeu.org).
18. Gordon Brown on BBC News, 6 October 2008.
19. Eurogroup Summit, 12 October 2008, Press Release, pp. 2–3.
20. See, for example, the report by the General Accountability Office (US GAO, 2004) as well as the Paulson Report.
21. The Paulson Report came out clearly against the FSA (Financial Services Association) model: 'An objectives-based approach also allows for a clearer focus on particular goals in comparison to a structure that consolidates all types of regulation in one regulatory body' (p. 14).
22. According to Calomiris (2008), the Basel II rules were effectively applied by the SEC to investment banks.
23. 'There is a need for "creative tension" within the regulatory system, and so these powers and responsibilities should not be granted to the Financial Services Authority. We propose the creation of a new post of Deputy Governor of the Bank of England and Head of Financial Stability'. See UK House of Commons Treasury Committee (2008, p. 4).
24. See State aid: Commission gives guidance to member states on measures for banks in crisis, 13 October 2008 (http://ec.europa.eu/comm/competition).
25. European Commission (2008b, p. 10).

26. For a bank to qualify as an Eligible Bank under the Dutch scheme, it must satisfy the Bank Eligibility Criteria: (1) be a bank as defined by the Dutch Financial Markets Supervision Act; (2) have a corporate domicile in the Netherlands; (3) have substantial business in the Netherlands; (4) have an acceptable solvency ratio.
27. European Commission (2008b), p. 3, art. 23.
28. See http://ec.europa.eu/comm/competition/state_aid/what_is_new/news.cfm.
29. See Casey and Lannoo (2005), for a more extensive discussion on this issue.
30. 2866th Council Meeting, Economic and Financial Affairs, Bruxelles, 14 May 2008, Council Conclusions, p. 13.
31. Proposal for a directive of the European Parliament and of the Council amending Directives 2006/48/EC and 2006/49/EC as regards banks affiliated to central institutions, certain own funds items, large exposures, supervisory arrangements, and crisis management, Bruxelles, COM(2008) 602/3
32. According to an article by Pascale Den Dooven, a journalist for *De Standaard*, 15 November 2008, the Belgian authorities only called their Dutch counterpart on midday on Sunday, inquiring why the Dutch had not taken contact, whereas the Dutch replied that they were waiting for a call. This anecdote is highly revealing about the efficacy of colleges, home-host relations and memoranda of understanding.
33. Data collected by the Italian Bankers Association (ABI), April 2008.
34. A proposal for amendment of this directive was recently made by the European Commission.
35. See IMF (2007).
36. See for example Bini-Smaghi (2008b).
37. 'FSA should have sole right over bank rescues', *Daily Telegraph*, 17 September 2008.
38. This happened for example with Fortis bank, when the Belgian Central Bank provided €45 bn emergency liquidity in the weekend of 28–29 September 2008. The provisions applicable to these operations within the Eurosystem were clarified by ECB in its 1999 Annual Report, see ECB (2000), p. 98.
39. Bini-Smaghi (2008a).
40. As remarked by the Swedish Governor Stefan Ingves, 'Regulatory challenges of cross-border banking: Possible ways forward', Conference on the Financial System, Reserve Bank of Australia, Sydney, 21 August 2007, http://www.riksbank.com/pagefolders/ 31131/070821e.pdf. The Governor referred to the concrete challenges posed for supervisors by a bank like Nordea and called in this speech for a European Organisation for Financial Supervision (EOFS), a variant of the proposal discussed above. The Governor had already made this proposal in a speech in October 2006, in which he emphasised that upgrading CEBS was not the solution, as it would not make it a supervisor.
41. See Schoenmaker and Oosterloo (2008) for a more detailed elaboration on this issue.
42. Council Regulation (EC) No 139/2004. In addition, the merger control has two exceptions in the application: the 'Dutch clause' (article 22) and the 'German clause' (article 9), which add more flexibility to the system to decide whether a merger is Community or national competence.
43. The Commission proposal (art. 12) requests the Commission to report on the possible introduction of a Community deposit-guarantee scheme, together with any appropriate proposals by the end of 2009, Proposal for a Directive of the European Parliament and of the Council amending Directive 94/19/EC on Deposit Guarantee Schemes as regards the coverage level and the payout delay, COM(2008) 661 final.

BIBLIOGRAPHY

Andoura, Sami and Peter Timmerman (2008), *Governance of the EU: the Reform Debate on European Agencies Reignited*, Working Paper no. 19, Bruxelles: EPIN, European Policy Institutes Network, October.

Bank for International Settlements (BIS) (2008a), *2007 Annual Report*, Basel (http://www.bis.org).

Bank for International Settlements (BIS) (2008b), *Quarterly Review*, September.

Bank for International Settlements (BIS) (1998), *International Banking and Financial Market Developments*, August.

Bini-Smaghi, Lorenzo (2008a), Slides from his presentation at the Conference on the ECB and its watchers, 5 September.

Bini-Smaghi, Lorenzo (2008b), 'Supervision and central banking: improving the exchange of information', Conference speech, Milan, 12 June.

Bjerre-Nielsen, Henrik (2007), 'Governance systems of financial regulatory and supervisory authorities in a European perspective', speech for the SUERF seminar, Nicosia, March.

BNP Paribas (2008a), 'Banks in the financial crisis, act II', *Conjuncture*, October–November.

BNP Paribas (2008b), 'British banks and the subprime crisis', *Conjuncture*, July.

Borio, Claudio E.V. (2008), *The Financial Turmoil of 2007–?: a Preliminary Assessment and Some Policy Implications*, BIS Working Papers, no. 251, Bank of International Settlements.

Calomiris, Charles W. (2008), *Another 'Deregulation' Myth*, Washington, D.C.: American Enterprise Institute, http://www.aei.org/publication28801.

Casey, Jean-Pierre and Karel Lannoo (2005), *Financial Regulation and Supervision Beyond 2005*, CEPS Task Force Report, Bruxelles: Centre for European Policy Studies, February.

Committee European Banking Supervisors (CEBS) (2006), *Framework for Common Reporting of the New Solvency Ratio*, Cover Note, 13 January.

Committee of European Securities Regulators (CESR) (2004), *The Role of CESR at 'Level 3' under the Lamfalussy Process (Himalaya Report)*, CESR/04-527, Paris, 28 October.

Di Giorgio, Giorgio and Carmine Di Noia (2001), *Financial Regulation and Supervision in the Euro Area: a Four-Peak Proposal*, Wharton Financial Institution Center, Working Paper no. 2 (published also as 'Financial market regulation and supervision: how many peaks for the Euro area', *Brooklyn Journal of International Law*, no. 2, 2003).

Di Noia, Carmine (2008), 'A proposal on financial regulation in Europe for the next European Council', *Vox EU*, http://www.voxeu.org/index.php? q=node/2462.

Economic and Financial Committee (EFC) (2001), *Report on Financial Crisis Management* (Brouwer II report), 17 April.

European Central Bank (2000), *Annual Report 1999*.

European Central Bank (2001), *The Role of Central Banks in Prudential Supervision*.

European Central Bank (2008), *Financial Stability Review*, June.

European Commission (2008a), Communication from the Commission: the application of State aid rules in relation to financial institutions in the context of the current financial crisis, 2008/C270/02 of 25 October.

European Commission (2008b), Public consultation paper on amendments to commission decisions establishing CESR, CEBS & CEIOPS, May.

Financial Stability Forum (2008), *Enhancing Market and Institutional Resilience*, April.

Gros, Daniel (2007), *Bubbles in Real Estate? A Longer-term Comparative Analysis of Housing Prices in Europe and the US*, Working Document no. 276, Bruxelles: CEPS, Centre for European Policy Studies, October.

Gros, Daniel and Stefano Micossi (2008a), 'The beginning of the end game', *CEPS Commentary*, Bruxelles: Centre for European Policy Studies, September.

Gros, Daniel and Stefano Micossi (2008b), 'Crisis management tools for the Euro area', *CEPS Commentary*, Bruxelles: Centre for European Policy Studies, September.

Gros, Daniel and Niels Thygesen (1990), 'Concrete steps towards monetary union', in *Governing Europe: the Single Market and Economic and Monetary Union*, 1989 Annual Conference Proceedings, vol. I, Bruxelles: Centre for European Policy Studies.

International Monetary Fund (2007), *Mission Report on Euro-area Policies*, 30 May.

JPMorgan (2008), 'How will the crisis change markets?', Asset Allocation and Alternative Investments JP Morgan Research, 14 April.

Lannoo, Karel (2006), *European Financial System Governance*, Policy Brief no. 106, Bruxelles: CEPS, Centre for European Policy Studies, July (also published in Passarelli Francesco (ed.), *Unione Europea: Governance e Regolamentazione*, Bologna: Il Mulino, 2006).

Nowotny, Ewald (2008), 'Towards supervisory convergence in Europe: a national perspective', conference speech, Belgian Financial Forum, Bruxelles, 13 November.

Padoa Schioppa, Tommaso (2007), Letter to fellow EU Finance Ministers published in *The Financial Times*, 11 December.

Petschnigg, Reinhard (2005), *The Institutional Framework for Financial Market Policy in the USA seen from an EU Perspective*, Occasional Paper no. 35, Frankfurt: ECB, European Central Bank, September.

Schoenmaker, Dirk and Sander Oosterloo (2008), *Financial Supervision in Europe: a Proposal for a New Architecture*, in L. Jonung, C. Walkner and M. Watson (eds), *Building the Financial Foundations of the Euro: Experiences and Challenges*, London: Routledge, pp. 337–354.

Speyer, Bernhard and Norbert Walter (2007), *Towards a New Structure for EU Financial Supervision*, Deutsche Bank Research, August.

UK House of Commons (2008), *The Run on the Rock*, Treasury Committee, HC 56–I.

US Department of the Treasury (2008), *Blueprint for a Modernized Financial Regulatory Structure*, Paulson Report, March.

US Government Accountability Office (GAO) (2004), *Financial Regulation: Industry Changes Prompt Need to Reconsider U.S. Regulatory Structure*, GAO-05-61, Washington, D.C.: GAO, November.

Véron, Nicolas (2007), *Is Europe Ready for a Major Banking Crisis?*, Bruxelles: Bruegel, August.

4. Institutional and Policy Dynamics in the EMU's Internal Governance and External Representation

Daniela Schwarzer

1. INTRODUCTION

The consequences of the global financial and economic crisis clearly do not stop short of the Economic and Monetary Union (EMU). On its tenth anniversary, EMU for the first time has slipped into recession resulting in a massive increase in unemployment and pressure on public finances.

Like the previous economic downturn in the years 2002–2003, the current crisis is unlikely to hit all members of EMU with the same impact. Economic divergence will most probably increase. As a consequence, diverging political preferences with regard to economic policy making, are likely to put the governance of the EMU to its first severe test.

Meanwhile, on the international scene, the euro has gained attractivity, both for potential future members, as well as in the global financial markets. Nevertheless, a particular challenge consists in affirming the euro's international role in a changing economic world order.

In the euro's first decade, economic developments and the first political experiences made with the historically unique setting of EMU have led to creeping and explicit modifications of the governance set-up of EMU. The first part of this chapter addresses fundamental economic developments in the EMU and, against this background, turns to the question, in how far internal governance rules and mechanisms have been modified in order to accommodate previously unexpected developments and circumstances. It suggests that some changes in economic thinking are part of the explanation why the internal governance set-up of the EMU has slowly but surely evolved. While the core of the ordo-liberal model, the European Central Bank, has not been touched in its independence or policy orientation, the views on the function of fiscal policy as the second pillar of macroeconomic policymaking, and the necessary control mechanisms have undergone some dynamics. A further evolution of EMU governance, also as a result of the current crisis, is probable.

The second part of this chapter addresses EMU's international dimension, that is the evolution of the global role of the European currency and of its attractiveness to non-EMU members as well as the dynamics of its external political representation. In both Section 2 on internal governance and Section 3 on the international dimension, specific attention is paid to the consequences of the current financial market and economic crisis which is already now reshaping certain parameters of economic governance in the EMU.

2. THE INTERNAL GOVERNANCE DIMENSION

2.1 The Economic Record after Ten Years

2.1.1 Growth, inflation and employment 1999–2008

For the first decade of EMU, the European Central Bank has delivered solid monetary policy results. With an average of 2.0 per cent (1999–2007), inflation in the eurozone was low, both in international and historical comparison (US inflation was 2.7 per cent in the same period). As the ECB quickly gained credibility in the markets and inflation expectations were revised downwards, interest rates in the money and capital markets sank. The year 2008, however, became the year of inflation with an estimated price increase of 3.4 per cent in the euro-area (Commerzbank 2009, p. 6) which was mainly due to rising prices in the energy and food sector, as well as rising wages.

The initial fear that EMU could become an inflation community have proved to date to be unfounded. For the year 2009, inflation rates well below 2 per cent have been forecasted. The question now is rather whether the EMU is about to slip into a recession. The growth performance of the eurozone has caused concern well before the current crisis and the resulting recession as it ran below the EMU average. From 1999 to 2007, the GDP of the EMU countries only grew by 2.2 per cent (in the same period, the US GDP grew by 2.8 per cent, the EU GDP by 2.5 per cent). The years 2002 (0.9 GDP growth in the eurozone) and 2003 (0.8 per cent GDP growth) had been particularly weak. For the year 2008, GDP growth is also estimated to be 0.9 per cent only, and forecasts for 2009 are even worse. The unemployment rate which had stabilized around 7 per cent on EMU average is likely to climb over 8 per cent given the economic downturn and will probably only fall in 2010 at the earliest (ibid.).

In times of economic crisis, the disappearance of exchange rates among the EMU countries has proven highly beneficial. The now 16 member states – just like in the sharp U-turn following the end of the New Economy boom – profit from the fact that the downturn is not aggravated by additional costs due to currency movements among the participating member countries.

2.1.2 Economic integration under the conditions of EMU

The expectation that the euro would reinforce economic integration in the EMU has been proven right. The share of intra-EMU trade had risen from 27 per cent in the year 1999 to 32 per cent in the year 2006. Among other factors (liberalization, harmonization of financial market rules, progress in the field of information and communication technology etc.), the euro contributed to the integration of European financial markets. Nevertheless, further progress remains to be made (becker 2008, p. 10).

As far as the markets for goods and services are concerned, further integration needs to be achieved if someday the common currency zone were to be underpinned by a truly integrated economy. Furthermore, labour markets remain fragmented: a high degree of cross-border labour mobility is unlikely to occur within the EMU while wage bargaining and social security systems maintain their historically grown national specificities. As long as these fragmentations persist in the EMU, markets only function insufficiently. As a consequence, asymmetric shocks will not be compensated effectively, resulting in a reinforcement of regional economic cycles (Dullien and Schwarzer 2005).

2.1.3 Economic divergence and political responses

The reasonably good EMU average data for inflation, interest rates and – with some reservations – economic growth indeed hides considerable imbalances and divergence between the EMU member states. An important indicator for this is the development of current account balances. Germany or the Netherlands for instance have a net surplus vis-à-vis their EU partners. After recording a deficit from 1999 to 2007, Germany jumped to a surplus of 6.7 per cent of GDP in 2008. Meanwhile, countries like Spain, Portugal or Italy recorded comparatively strong deficits. In addition, France's surplus at the beginning of the EMU turned into a foreign trade deficit of 2.5 per cent of GDP.

These current account deficits indicate a loss of competitiveness. As they go along with external debt, growing account deficits can cause longer-term problems. Paying back the debt may imply constraints for the development of domestic demand (see Chapter 6).

The development of unit labour costs is the major reason for the loss of competitiveness. Since the start of EMU, unit labour costs increased by roughly 20 per cent in Italy and Spain, and by about 15 per cent in France. Repeated exaggerated wage increases have reduced the competitiveness of some countries (Dullien and Fritsche 2007, pp. 56–76). In Germany, unit labour costs have remained stable due to moderate wage agreements and successes in restructuring and reforming the economy. The wage constraint has led to very low inflation rates and hence a real devaluation.

The developments in inflation rates and competitiveness continued to diverge strongly even during the short economic recovery of the years 2007 and 2008. In times of recession, these developments are likely to become even more visible. Even without new EMU member states, it is expected that the divergence in growth, inflation and employment is going to increase (BNP Paribas 2008). As a consequence, the 'One-Size-Fits-All' monetary policy which is based on EMU average data combined with the fact that markets only function insufficiently across borders and hence do not absorb asymmetric shocks satisfyingly, has intensified cyclical developments in some regions or member states. Prolonged and deepened low growth periods can yet have negative consequences for companies' willingness to invest, for the development of employment, and for economic growth in general.[1]

These market imperfections – and the result that the EMU is not evolving towards an Optimum Currency Area (OCA) with the speed that was initially expected – are increasingly taken into account both in the political debate and in the academic analysis of the EMU. Economists have pointed out that the cost–benefit calculations (with regard to their EMU membership) of countries in a situation of strong overvaluation and consequently low growth might change. A lively debate on adaptation costs and whether single countries can and might leave the EMU at some point has developed among bank economists, thinktankers and academics. The topic of growing tensions in the EMU has been picked up by some politicians. Former (and new) Italian Prime Minister Silvio Berlusconi in 2005 or new French President Nicolas Sarkozy in 2006–2007 underlined the problems of national policymaking in the EMU. What has not yet been formulated and implemented is a consistent policy to respond to this analysis.

Also public finances are likely to diverge in the EMU countries, especially after the billions of euros spent on national stimulation programmes in the current economic downturn and for the stabilization of the financial sector. The possible consequences should not be underestimated (see, for example, Fels 2008). The massive pressure on the budgets and the expected deficits can trigger new dispute over the fiscal rules of the European Monetary Union.

Unsolid public finances and renewed debates on the costs of EMU membership and an eventual leaving of the EMU can trigger speculative reactions in the financial markets, which can increase the interest rates on state bonds. This can eventually make the refinancing of bonds and of the public deficit impossible for some member states.

Even today, without an acute political debate on single countries possibly leaving the EMU, the markets for the first time since the introduction of the euro distinctly evaluate and sanction single member countries. The interest on public bonds varies up to 2 per cent between some countries (3.25 per cent for Germany, 4.96 per cent for Italy, 6.21 per cent for Greece).[2]

2.2 Constitutional Stability, but Dynamic Practices Below Treaty Law

The first ten years of the EMU have been characterized by a high degree of constitutional stability. Ever since the Maastricht Treaty defined the parameters of EMU, the legal bases of EMU have remained mostly unchanged, although the European treaties have been revised on several occasions.[3] The European Central Bank still represents the 'institutional core'[4] of the eurozone without a political counterweight on the EMU level. Furthermore, the division of tasks between the European and the national level with regard to economic policymaking has remained unchanged in the EU Treaty ever since the EMU was created. But below the level of Treaty law, institutional and political dynamics have unfolded in the EMU's first decade thanks to which the existing governance mechanisms in the EMU have evolved. For most cases, the economic situation and an evolving understanding of the functioning of the EMU economy can be identified as triggers.

2.2.1 The reform of the Stability and Growth Pact
The rules for fiscal policy coordination have been modified twice since the Maastricht Treaty (see, for example, Schwarzer 2007). Firstly, in 1997, the Stability and Growth Pact was adopted. Even before the start of EMU, the Pact added details and hardened the rules of the Maastricht Treaty and spelled out the terms for a more speedy procedure leading to sanctions. At the time, the Pact was widely seen as being one key guarantor of stability for the single currency and the designers of the Pact, notably the German government, did not expect the sanction mechanism to be applied. The deterring character of the Pact was expected to be sufficient to ensure sound fiscal policies which underpin the ordo-liberal orientation of the Maastricht Treaty.

In 2005, the Pact itself was reformed in order to enable more political discretion in its application, in particular with the objective to allow governments to take into account cyclical conditions in single member states in the Pact's application as the stabilizing role of fiscal policy had become a concern. Prior to the reform, countries like Germany, France, Portugal and Italy had repeatedly breached the deficit rules in the years of low economic growth (2002–2004) and were about to face sanctions. In particular the German and French government pressured the Ecofin (Economic and Financial Affairs Council) to temporarily postpone the application of the Pact's sanctioning procedures, pointing to the need to grant national fiscal policies a sufficient stabilizing role, and a subsequent ruling of the European Court of Justice declared part of the Ecofin decision to be illegal. This reinforced the political dynamics towards a reform of the Pact.

Germany is probably the most interesting country case the EMU has to offer to illustrate a certain rethinking on the stabilizing role of fiscal policy. During the Maastricht negotiations, the German government was the strongest proponent of the institutionalization of New Classical ideas, and in the mid-1990s pushed through the Stability and Growth Pact further cementing this logic. In 2000, the then Minister of Finance, Hans Eichel, argued in a speech on 'Fiscal policy for a new decade' along with New Classical economists that fiscal policy is ineffective (Eichel 2005). At this time, there was little acceptance of the argument that one should allow for deficits due to the working of automatic stabilizers. In the years following the New Economy crisis of 2001, Germany tried to close the growing budget deficit by new taxes and cuts in expenditure. According to European Commission data, the cyclically adjusted German budget deficit only increased by 0.1 percentage points in 2002 and quickly was brought back down even though the German economy was still trapped in stagnation and unemployment was rising, reaching its peak only in 2005. This restrictive policy did not allow automatic stabilizers to work fully and negatively affected real activity. But in 2005, Eichel accepted that deficits increase in a downturn and have thus to be decreased in a boom: 'We will always have a deficit in a downturn as then tax revenue will be weak and expenditure for unemployment increases. We have to get rid of these deficits in good times'. He hence accepted the notion of automatic stabilizers – but only after Germany had gone through months of public debate in which, firstly, mostly international commentators (academics but also financial journalists) criticized pro-cyclical fiscal restraint in the low growth period. They were later joined by the German research institutes and academics, and Finance Ministry officials, who increasingly argued that the costs of pro-cyclical consolidation might be more significant that initially expected. Later, in 2006, the German government endorsed the strategy to stimulate economic growth in order to get a solid upswing under way and then consolidate the budget in 2007.

In parallel, the approach toward the Stability and Growth Pact changed. Its strict application had been seen for a long time as a precondition for the stability of the common currency, not only because of the possibly negative effects of lax fiscal policies, but also because the credibility of the EMU was felt to be endangered if its rules were not applied rigorously. The German government tried to prevent breaking the Pact or its reform for some time even after it had already come into conflict with these rules precisely because it was clinging on to the normative consensus that lead to its creation (Schwarzer 2007). But seeing the problematic effect of procyclical restrictive fiscal policy, Germany redefined its position on the stabilizing role of fiscal policies and in parallel requested more flexibility in the application of the Pact. It found allies in France, Portugal and Italy which shaped a coalition of member states pushing for the reform of the Pact.

2.2.2 The Lisbon Agenda and the Broad Economic Policy Guidelines

The Lisbon Agenda was streamlined in the year 2005. The objective to create the most competitive economy until the year 2010 was abandoned, and measures strengthening employment and growth have been emphasized. The Broad Economic Policy Guidelines (BEPG), that is the core document of economic policy coordination in the EU, and the Employment Guidelines were merged upon the decision of the European Council in spring 2005 to become the 'Integrated Guidelines for Employment and Growth' and closely linked to the Lisbon Agenda. This new core document of economic policy coordination in the EU and the EMU is now written in a three year horizon and devotes a specific chapter to the specificities of the eurozone.

More important than the consolidation of several documents into one key publication is the fact that this reform has created a more consistent policy coordination process which interlinks coordination efforts which were previously running in parallel in highly interdependent policy areas. Moreover, European coordination processes are now more coordinated with national policy cycles in order to increase the chance to actually influence national policy outcomes. The stronger focus on growth and employment in the Lisbon Agenda and the Integrated Policy Guidelines is in line with the shifting focus in fiscal policy coordination.

2.2.3 New economic thinking in fiscal and monetary policy

Before the launch of EMU and during its first years of existence, the dominant question was how national fiscal policy could be controlled in such a way that deficits are kept low and that the fiscal environment is favourable to low inflation. But the economic decline in the EMU together with new findings of economic research on the fiscal dimension of macro-economic stabilization contributed to raising interest in the question of what kind of fiscal policy would enhance sustainable growth. The reform of the Stability Pact builds upon the presumption that enforceability can mainly be achieved by enhancing the economic rational of the fiscal rules in order to increase ownership by national policymakers. Consequently, the academic and political debate surrounding the reform of the Stability Pact shifted away from the question how fiscal discipline and low inflation could be ensured, and evolved towards welfare considerations and growth enhancing policy coordination, yet also discussing measures to improve long-term sustainability (Fischer et al. 2006). This wider discussion about the role and control of national fiscal policy in the EMU is still evolving to date.

The discussion about automatic stabilizers hence gained importance within the Broad Economic Policy Guidelines,[5] that is the core document of economic policy coordination in the EU. Furthermore, the long-term sustainability of public finances has become a matter of intensified debate, as the member states had stopped short of consolidating sufficiently in the boom years 2000 and 2002. The role of discretionary fiscal stabilization policy, on the contrary, was only very occasionally evoked in the time of the reform of the Stability and Growth Pact. But under the impact of the global economic crisis 2008 it became the most important focus of the European debate.

The renewed interest in stabilization policy also gained ground in the monetary policy debate.[6] The New Keynesian approach recommends central banks to run a strategy of flexible inflation targeting: by using a host of forecasts on the economic outlook and exogenous price shocks, central banks use their interest rate to keep inflation on target over the medium term. As long as inflation expectations are well anchored, this implies that a central bank cuts interest rates if the economic outlooks weakens and increases interest rates if the economy starts to grow faster. Hence, inflation targeting implies a countercyclical stabilization policy by the central bank – in contrast to the prescriptions of New Classical thinking of the 1980s and early 1990s.

While the ECB originally gave a 'prominent role for money, as signalled by the announcement of a quantitative reference value for the growth rate of a broad monetary aggregate' (ECB 1999, p. 39) and made the monetary analysis its first pillar of monetary policy strategy, it reformed its strategy in 2003. It degraded growth of monetary aggregates to the second pillar and put a number of indicators usually related to a standard inflation targeting into the first pillar of its monetary policy. The loss in relevance of this approach is also reflected in the fact that it has ceased to review the monetary reference value on an annual basis. Moreover, in the ECB's press statements, the analysis of monetary aggregates now only follows after the analysis of the economic outlook (ECB 2003, p. 79). Economists have interpreted this change as an adjustment towards the changed thinking in economics and current international standards (Svensson 2003).

2.2.4 Institutional innovation: the Eurogroup at the core of coordination

Not only did policies evolve, but also the fora for economic policy coordination developed once the euro was adopted.

The most important institutional innovation of the eurozone is the Eurogroup. This is an informal forum of the Ministers of Finance and the Economy of the EMU member states and so far constitutes the only exclusive EMU-forum on the government level.[20] The Eurogroup was not anchored in the EU Treaties or secondary law. It is not part of the Council system, although its sessions are prepared by the Economic and Financial Committee which likewise supports the work of the Ecofin. The Eurogroup has no decision-making power and no defined mandate. Its interaction with the ECB, the European Commission or the European Parliament is not formally regulated.

France had already during the Maastricht negotiations pushed for a stronger political counterweight to the ECB. When the negotiations on the Stability and Growth Pact promoted by Germany were about to come to its term at the end of 1996, beginning of 1997, France once again claimed a 'gouvernement économique' to complement the ordo-liberal model of EMU which largely followed German proposals.

Germany and France traditionally pursue diverging preferences over the set up of the EMU, especially over the role of the European Central Bank and the question of economic governance (see, for example, Pisani-Ferry 2006). These divergences were not entirely solved by the Maastricht Treaty but still regularly surface today.

Given the first experience with practical coordination under conditions of the EMU, not only the French government but also other actors had come to the conclusion that the institutions and processes laid out in the Maastricht Treaty were probably insufficient for a single currency zone (Pütter 2006, p. 58). In August 1997 the informal Ecofin meeting in Mondorf-Luxembourg and the Franco-German Economic Council on 14 October, 1997 helped to sketch a compromise: an informal meeting of the Ministers of Finance and the Economy with a clearly stated mission. Germany did not want an institutionalized economic government, partly because it sought to avoid any doubt about the institutional and political independence of the European Central Bank in view of a difficult domestic discussion on EMU (Collignon and Schwarzer 2003). The creation of the Eurogroup was based on a European Council decision of 12 December 1997 in Luxembourg. According to the Council decision, the European Commission and the ECB should be invited to participate in these meetings. This ensured the support by the small member states which hence saw their chance to participate in a dialogue with the European Central Bank.

The practical work of the Eurogroup evolved over time in close interaction with the EU organs, in particular the Ecofin and the European Council. In several of its Conclusions since 1998, the European Council detailed aspects of the practical work of the Eurogroup, for instance on the external representation of the eurozone (see below), on the internal coordination of economic policy or on the introduction of a two year Presidency of the Eurogroup. With every new year of EMU, the importance of the Eurogroup became more evident for the participating member states, in particular for creating trust among the partners, for a smooth exchange of information and views and for formulating common positions. The difficult economic situation in the years 2002 and 2003 and the political tensions over the application of the Stability and Growth Pact underlined the importance of the Eurogroup for the discussion over the content and rules of fiscal and economic policy coordination in the EMU.

The informal character of the Eurogroup is not only a concession to Germany, but also a reaction to the fact that the institutions of the EU and the EMU are designed for different groups of countries: while the ECB is responsible for currently 16 member countries, the Ecofin as the decision-taking organ for economic policy in the EU assembles all 27 EU members. The rules concerning the Ecofin in the Maastricht Treaty had been designed under the assumption, that there would only be a rather short transition period during which not all EU members are EMU members and that the institutional unity of the Ecofin should be maintained. Decisions related to EMU only are hence also taken in the Ecofin, but in some cases only EMU countries have a voting right.[8]

The decision of Denmark, the UK and later also Sweden not to take part in the EMU changed the picture: the question arose whether the Ecofin was indeed the right forum for economic policy discussions and decisions relevant to the EMU. The accession of ten new states to the European Union on 1 May 2004 reinforced the quest for an exclusive forum for EMU members, especially as the convergence process is less dynamic than had been initially expected. With its informal character, the Eurogroup also corresponds to the concerns of those EU member states which are not (yet) part of the EMU and which are highly interested in avoiding an institutional and political decoupling of the EMU from the non-EMU member states.

The Lisbon Treaty signed on 13 December 2007 would – if ratified – for the first time provide the Eurogroup with a legal basis in an EU Treaty. The corresponding protocol[9] mostly codifies the 'modus vivendi' which has evolved ever since the introduction of euro.

Despite – or even thanks to – its informal character, the Eurogroup has become the key forum for the member states to forge an economic policy consensus and to pre-agree important decisions which are later on formally agreed by the Ecofin Council (for instance the reform of the Stability Pact) (see Pütter 2006).

2.3 Managing the Economic Crisis

In the second half of 2008, the eurozone was confronted with a particular governance challenge when possible bankruptcies in the banking sector, the massive economic decline and the problems of liquidity for some member states neighbouring the EMU announced political tensions and further political and economic instabilities. The pressure of the crisis led to further adaptations of policies and institutional mechanisms, which yet follow the logic of the modifications that were implemented prior to the crisis.

2.3.1 The first eurozone summit

On 12 October, 2008, the then acting EU Council President Nicolas Sarkozy summoned the first eurozone summit. The then 15 EMU member states for the first time met on the level of Heads of State and Government (though with the participation of the opt-out country Great Britain) in order to discuss eurozone matters against the backdrop of the intensifying financial crisis. They agreed on a joint plan to back the banking sector and on coordination of the initiatives. Furthermore, work on improved surveillance structures should be coordinated. The first eurozone summit confirms the usefulness of an EMU format on the governmental level, as is the Eurogroup. There is to date no indication that a eurozone summit will become a permanent forum. But it could be re-used as an ad hoc crisis management pool.

Prior to the summit, Franco-German tensions over the necessity of an intensified coordination in the eurozone had developed; it involved arguments over economic governance as old as the debate over EMU prior to the Maastricht Treaty. The French government and President Sarkozy had initially evoked the future development of the EMU as one potential priority for its EU Presidency in the second half of 2008 and had repeatedly claimed the introduction of a 'gouvernement économique'. But no concrete initiatives were put forward. In January 2008, Prime Minister François Fillon suggested summoning the eurozone Heads of State and Government for a eurozone summit in order to discuss the functioning of the eurozone in the first half of 2008 upon the presentation of a report by the European Commission on the functioning of the eurozone. In particular matters of economic coordination and of the external representation should be put on the agenda (Ehrlich and Proissl 2008). But the reluctance of the German government in particular to support this initiative made the French side abandon it.

The deepening of the international financial market crisis in autumn 2008 caused the acting EU President Sarkozy to set up a series of international summits, among which was the first eurozone summit. Once again, Franco-German differences caused difficulties, for instance during the G4 meeting with Italy and the UK, when Germany blocked the initiative to create a common European bailout fund for the banking sector and refused to engage in discussions over strengthening EMU governance, while setting up its own deposit guarantees without consulting its partners.

2.3.2 Monetary and fiscal policy reactions

Under the pressure of the financial market crisis, the ECB swiftly adopted its role as a 'Lender of last Resort'. This included some adaptations of its instruments (such as of the timing of the provision of liquidity; Becker 2008b). It furthermore engaged in international cooperation, for instance with the US Federal Reserve.

Once it was discovered that the monetary policy reactions to the crisis only had a limited impact, a consensus evolved that the European Union and the member states should react to the crisis with fiscal means. Most member states unilaterally developed first fiscal stimulus programmes. The European Commission then took the initiative to coordinate the national packages and to design complementary European measures. This initiative takes into account the fact that in open economies, cyclical stabilization can no longer be effectively achieved in the national context, as the impulse spreads across the national borders. A demand stabilizing fiscal policy should hence be conducted on the EMU level which not only has a single currency, but also strongly integrated markets and a comparatively low degree of economic openness (22.6 per cent of GDP) (ECB 2008).

For years, the European Commission had argued against discretionary fiscal stabilization policies and had criticized such measures within its surveillance of national fiscal policies. Now, discretionary fiscal policy is acknowledged as a possible way out of the crisis. But there is no consensus as to how the costs for such measures should be shared in the EMU. For instance the German government was pushed by its EU partners, by the European Commission and by the International Monetary Fund (IMF) to engage more strongly in fiscal stabilization, given the importance of the largest EMU economy for a general recovery and the sound public finances of Germany.

The conflict between the initial German position and the request by the EU partners reveal two structural problems: firstly, at the end of 2008, there was still no economic policy consensus (in particular between France and Germany) in this case about the question which degree of fiscal stabilization would be adequate. Given national responsibility for budgetary policy and given the comparatively small volume of the EU budget and its multiannual structure, the European scope to act is small if governments disagree. Secondly, there is a discrepancy between the integrated eurozone economy and the political willingness to share the costs for economic stabilization in a truly European way (see, for example, Münchau 2008).

The necessity to stabilize the European economy in the recession may have further-reaching consequences for the governance mechanisms of the eurozone. The Stability and Growth Pact will probably only be applied loosely: the European Commission and the two largest eurozone economies Germany and France have advocated the possibility that member states are allowed to break the 3 per cent ceiling for the deficit without having to fear sanctions (see Chapter 5 for further details) (Merkel and Satkozy 2008). If more short-term margin of manoeuvre is granted to the member states, some EU countries such as Germany or the Netherlands are likely to put other issues on the European policy agenda, that is the quality of public finances and the long-term sustainability of public debt (as Zuleeg and Martens suggest in Chapter 6).

2.3.3 Loans to financially support EU members

It cannot be excluded that increasing pressure exerted by financial market actors makes it inevitable that the European Union stabilizes further member countries which are not yet part of the EMU. This would considerably increase the EU's need for capital as such loans could not be paid from the EU budget.

Based on art. 119 ECT (European Communities Treaty)[10] the Ecofin Council has granted a three year credit to Hungary which amounts to €6.5bn on 4 November, 2008 in order to alleviate the balance of payment problems of the country and in order to prevent a collapse of the national banking system. Latvia is likely to get the same kind of support. In order to pay these stabilizations on the periphery of the eurozone, the European Commission issues eurobonds to raise money which goes into the balance of payment loans accredited according to art. 119 ECT – an instrument which has not been used since the 1990s. The possibility for the Commission to raise balance of payment loans was limited to €12bn, before this ceiling was raised to €25bn by an Ecofin Decision in December 2008. One reasons for this is that a collapse of the financial sector in some EU countries would entail serious risks for the EMU. Its consequences would spill into the EMU as it is mostly banking corporations from EU or EMU countries that have bought themselves into the banking and insurance sectors for instance in Central and Eastern European countries.

The President of the Eurogroup, Jean-Claude Juncker, has furthermore suggested that the European Union should issue bonds in order to finance infrastructure projects. The current crisis hence – in parallel to the running debate on the review of the EU budget – not only fuels discussions about the financing of EU policies and about the necessary autonomy the EU should have, but likewise raises the question whether it would make sense to provide the EU with the possibility to indebt itself.

2.3.4 OCA revisited: responding to cyclical divergence and longer business cycles

The acknowledgement of market imperfections (see above) in the EMU has re-animated the debate on possible answers to tensions building up within the currency zone. If economic fluctuations are more lasting than thought and have larger costs than expected, then the assumption that one can just forego all national stabilization arguments has to be rethought, as has happened with regard to fiscal policy. Three possible policy conclusions regarding the problems of EMU not becoming an OCA and increasing cyclical divergences have been brought up.

Firstly, a country could seriously consider leaving the EMU in order to regain national monetary autonomy to alleviate some of the problems. Yet, the costs of leaving the EMU and re-establishing a new national monetary order would be extremely high, economically and politically. This is why playing around with the blame on the euro may be a strategy some national politicians will use, but they are unlikely to seriously consider leaving the EMU. Furthermore, legally, this option would first have to be designed with the EU-27 as the EU Treaty does not provide for this case.

Secondly, as the assumptions that the EMU would transform itself into an OCA have proven wrong, governments could put an increasing effort on cross-border market liberalizations (especially labour, capital and services, which from an EMU point of view should integrate further). The Lisbon Process was partly designed to increase market liberalization and integration, but is not deemed to have delivered the expected success. As national adaptation costs may in some cases be high, the Open Method of Co-ordination seems insufficient. The European Commission (2008), in line with the new insight that EMU does not automatically transform itself into an OCA, has proposed to improve the structures to deal with implementing reforms at the eurozone level, acknowledging explicitly that there are euro-area-specific, rather than EU-specific, externalities in economic reforms.

A third possible view which builds on the insights of OCA theory is that a currency union needs a fiscal stabilization mechanism at the highest level. For the time being, this debate which touches on the question whether the EMU needs political union is still mostly held in the academic and thinktank community and has not spilled over into the policymaking community. Not even governments like France, which for decades have claimed a 'gouvernement économique' for the EMU, have come forward with concrete suggestions. The only exception was probably the former Belgian Prime Minister Guy Verhofstadt (2006), who claimed a political union to complement the single currency.

For the time being a growing unease about economic divergence in the EMU can be observed in the political debate on the national and the EU level. Growing attention is devoted to the academic debate on prolonged cyclical divergences and potential remedies. No policy strategy is yet defined for the EMU to counter these developments, but the debate is likely to become more dynamic.

3. THE EXTERNAL DIMENSION

3.1 The International Success of the Euro

3.1.1 New attraction of the euro for the opt-out countries
Despite certain doubts about the eurozone's ability to tackle the crisis, the attraction of the euro as a 'safe haven' in an era of turbulence has risen considerably for the non-participating EU countries as well as for Iceland. Denmark and the United Kingdom, which have negotiated an opt-out in the Maastricht Treaty, debate a possible EMU membership. Denmark experienced an attack on the Crown in October 2008 which led to a devaluation of the currency and to an increase in central bank interest rates to 5.5 per cent (while the Danish Central Bank had previously roughly followed the ECB interest rate policy and had participated in the European Monetary System II (EMS II). Under the impression of market turbulences and concerns about the stability of the national banking sector, public opinion has changed in such a way that Prime Minister Anders Fogh Rasmussen may even consider holding a referendum on Danish EMU membership soon. Also in Sweden, which has opted not to fulfil the convergence criteria for political reasons, discussions have developed on a possible change of strategy with regard to EMU membership. Further market turbulence and speculation against the currency can lead to a situation in which the cost–benefit analysis with regard to an EMU membership might change.

3.1.2 A safe haven for Central and Eastern Europe
In 2007, Poland openly questioned its EMU membership perspective and the Kaczynski government at the time announced a referendum on EMU membership which would have been incompatible with the EU Treaty.[11] Under the impression of the crisis, the government of Prime Minister Tusk seeks to join the EMU until 2012 and wants to become a member of the

EMS II in June 2009 (Runner 2008). A strong devaluation of the Zloty has caused concern in Poland whether pressure on the Polish currency and the Polish financial markets could increase. Also the Czech Republic and Hungary have recently abandoned their EMU-sceptical stance. Similarly to the Baltic States, which seem to seek EMU membership as early as 2011, these two countries have increased their preparation in order to be ready for a convergence test soon. In most Central and Eastern European member states the benefits of an EMU membership under the impression of the financial market and economic crisis, suddenly seem to clearly outweigh the maintenance of the national currency and the national monetary and exchange rate policy. EMU promises lower interest rates, lower risk premiums (which currently price-in the risks of devaluation for the Central and Eastern European currencies) and more stability due to lower exchange rate fluctuations and higher credibility for the national banking sectors. Especially the fact that Slovakia (which became an EMU member on 1 January 2009) has experienced lower pressure from the financial markets than the other Central and Eastern European member states, has led to increased interest from those member states in the EMU (Economist Intelligence Unit 2008).

These developments do not automatically imply that the Eastern enlargement of the European Monetary Union will speed up. The lower interest rates and the reduced commodity prices have a positive effect on lower inflation in the candidate countries and make monetary convergence easier to obtain. But fiscal convergence and the need to stabilize exchange rates vis-à-vis the euro may turn out to be more difficult. Meanwhile, a softening of the convergence criteria in the Maastricht Treaty is unlikely. The reason is not only that the ECT is difficult to change, but also that a too high degree of heterogeneity, for instance regarding unit labour costs or inflation as is the case for Italy, Portugal and Greece, imposes high costs on the concerned countries and creates political tension in the EMU. A restrictive application of the convergence criteria (as was the case with the refusal to let Lithuania into EMU in 2006) meanwhile maximizes the potential of the European Commission and the ECB to maintain the 'top-down' reform pressure on the EMU candidate countries (Dyson 2008, p. 409).

3.2 Exchange Rates and Exchange Rate Policies

3.2.1 External value of the euro
In the ten years of the euro's existence, its external value has, on several occasions, provoked controversial political debates. After the introduction of the new currency on 1 January 1999 the value of the euro for some time declined vis-à-vis the main international currencies and reached its lowest value of \$0.85 against the US\$ in June 2001. Reasons for this decline were

interest rate differentials between the euro and the US$, and also the comparatively high growth expectations in the USA at the time of the Dot-Com boom. In the newly created EMU a debate evolved whether the euro was failing to gain sufficient confidence among investors and whether the ECB should intervene to support the European currency.

Mid-2002, the euro recovered from its previous weakness when the US-Dot-Com bubble collapsed, the interest differential between Europe and the US turned around and the US current account deficit grew larger.[12] At the same time, the eurozone economy recovered. As of 2005, the euro soared vis-à-vis the US$.

The euro reached its peak vis-à-vis the US$ on 15 July 2008 (1 euro = 1.59 US$) but then declined by over 20 per cent in the course of the second half of 2008. The outflow of capital from the eurozone can be explained by several variables, for instance that investors estimate that the security of US bonds is higher and markets are more liquid in the US than in the eurozone with its bond markets divided along national borders (Gros and Micossi 2008). In addition, the so-called Carry-Trade (Flassbeck 2008) sharply reduced for the euro. Furthermore, market participants may have some doubts as to how far the European Union is able to react effectively to the financial and economic crisis.

3.2.2 The functioning of euro exchange rate policy

Exchange rate policies for the euro involve both the ECB and the finance ministers. Both yet pursue distinct objectives: while the ECB has the prime objective of ensuring price stability, the finance ministers pursue broader fiscal and economic policy objectives which may or may not be compatible with the aim of ensuring low inflation. The Maastricht Treaty had to strike a balance between both, but leaves some ambiguities over the organization of exchange rate policies. These were the result of the fundamental conflict over price-stability orientation and the independence of the ECB on the one hand, and other objectives and means for economic policymaking.[13]

The Treaty rules were decided as follows: according to art. 111 TEU (Treaty on European Union), the eurozone can enter a system of fixed exchange rates with countries outside the EU and it can formulate general orientations for exchange rate policy which however must not endanger the ECB's objective of price stability. Formal agreements have to be decided with unanimity by the Council upon proposal by the ECB or the Commission and after consultation with the European Parliament. As only members of the eurozone can vote on exchange rate matters, the Eurogroup de facto decides, as is the case in other matters such as the implementation of the Stability and Growth Pact.

General orientations for exchange rate policy are understood to cover informal agreements with partners outside the eurozone, as well as unilateral position-taking by the eurozone (European Commission 2008). In this latter case, the Council acts with qualified majority, either on a recommendation from the ECB, or on a recommendation from the Commission and after consulting the ECB. The Eurosystem (the system of national central banks of the euro area and the ECB) holds the eurozone's foreign exchange reserves and carries out interventions.

The European Council meeting in Luxembourg 12–13 December 1997 (OJ C 35, 2 February 1998, p. 1) limited the formulation of exchange-rate orientations to exceptional circumstances, such as clear misalignments. Moreover, it invited the Ecofin to regularly monitor the euro exchange rate in order to assess whether exchange rate developments are consistent with the underlying economic situation. These deliberations also take place in the Eurogroup which has considerably strengthened its role since the start of the EMU (see above). As exchange rate policies and other economic policies are so closely interlinked, the Eurogroup provides a forum for the dialogue between the relevant players in the game: the President of the ECB takes part in the Eurogroup meetings, while the Eurogroup President as well as the Commissioner for Economic and Monetary Affairs are invited as observers to the meetings of the ECB Governing Council.

Like many other governance practices in the EMU, the conduct of exchange rate policy has also evolved in an informal manner. So far, the formal instruments such as the general orientations on the basis of art. 111 have not been applied. Even when preparing the ground for the foreign exchange interventions in autumn 2000 in order to counter the weakness of the euro, the Eurogroup commented on the exchange rates in a *communiqué*. The coordinated interventions in September 2000 followed an agreement at Eurogroup level, after which the Eurosystem carried the interventions out together with G7 partners.

In November 2000, the Eurosystem intervened unilaterally, without another specific agreement as the 'green light' to intervene had been provided by the Eurogroup in September (Henning 2007).

Nevertheless, and despite the nomination of a two-year President of the Eurogroup, the Eurogroup still does not systemically formulate a common view on exchange rate developments and policies. This became particularly clear in spring–summer 2008, when the euro appreciated strongly against the US$ and other important currencies. Among others, the two largest EMU member states, Germany and France, for some time publicly disagreed over the question as to whether there was a need to intervene in order to weaken the euro (a French quest) or whether the strong euro was no problem for the European economy (for a long time the view of the German Finance Minister). More consistency in opinions and public statements would yet be an important prerequisite for a common exchange rate policy and for the Eurogroup-Ecofin to reclaim authority from the

ECB which has practically taken the dominant role in the EMU's first
decade (ibid., p. 335). Alternatively, a majority vote on exchange rate
issues would enable the Eurogroup to act more decidedly. This step of
integration yet is unlikely to happen soon. Rather, conflicting interests
between the member states and the ECB or among the member states may
cause instability and/or paralysis. The problem of economic divergence in
the EMU, which risks being aggravated by the current crisis (see above),
may increase the dissent within the EMU over exchange rate levels and the
perceived costs of exchange rate fluctuations. If economic developments
continue to diverge strongly, so probably will the positions of the member
states on the 'right' exchange rate policy for the euro.

3.3 The Challenge of External Representation

3.3.1 The case for strengthening external representation
Since the introduction of the euro, the case for a single European voice on
international financial matters has been strengthened considerably.[14]
Sharing a single monetary and exchange rate policy makes it logical for the
participating member states also to defend a common position in
international fora dealing with macroeconomic matters such as the IMF and
the G7–G8. This is especially so as the eurozone has become more exposed
to international portfolio shifts due to the substitutability between assets
denominated in euros or in US dollars. Furthermore, a consolidated
representation of the euro-area in international fora would strengthen the
euro-area's negotiating power and could increase its gains from
international policy coordination. The rise of new economic powers
notably China, India and Brazil, reduces the relative weight of the
eurozone. Pooling the external representation in international financial
institutions may hence become necessary to maintain influence. Long-term
growth projections expect the eurozone's quota share in the IMF to decline
from 23 per cent in early 2008 to 12 per cent by 2050. Furthermore, the
European members in the G7 will continue to lose share in the world
economy.

In addition, many partners of the EU would prefer dealing with a single
interlocutor, rather than with a multitude of different actors – consolidating
the external representation would not only enable the EMU to better defend
its interest, but could also increase the interest of other players in
cooperating with the eurozone.

3.3.2 Representation in the Bretton Woods institutions and
the 'G-Groups'
But despite the strong arguments for a consolidation of a single eurozone
representation, the efforts of the member countries to speak with one voice

on international financial matters have not yet led to a coherent external representation of the eurozone. While the ECB represents the monetary side coherently in the most important international financial fora and vis-à-vis key partners such as the US or China, the 'economic side' still remains fragmented: there is the Eurogroup President, the acting Council Presidency which chairs the Ecofin, the Commissioner for Economic and Monetary Affairs and for some issues also the Commissioner for Trade, and of course, from case to case, different EU member states. It is hence very difficult for the eurozone to convey a consistent view for example of exchange rate issues and coordination among the different parties involved is necessary (and may be time-consuming).

In several regards, efforts have been made to improve the EU-EMU's ability to speak with a single voice in international fora. On the political level, the appointment of the Eurogroup President for a two-year-term was an important move, especially as he participates in G7 meetings. On the administrative side, cooperation on the Committee level has been improved in the sense that the Economic and Financial Committee (EFC) and the Eurogroup Working Group (EWG) elaborate joint positions which are then presented at IMF meetings by the EU Presidency and by the Eurogroup in G7 meetings. Furthermore, the Presidents of the ECB and the Eurogroup and the Commissioner for Economic and Monetary Affairs now hold joint press conferences after G7 meetings. Specialized committees (including representatives of the member states, the ECB and the Commission) meet regularly in Brussels and Washington in order to coordinate the EU-EMU's positions in the IMF board. A chairman with a two-year term presents EU-EMU positions to the Board of Directors of the IMF.[15]

Despite these and further coordination efforts, Europe's coordination in the IMF is not sufficient: 'Not only do the topics on which coordination takes place remain limited, but there have also been occasional problems to fully translate the common lines agreed in Brussels into the statements of EU executive directors in Washington'.[16] Although the EU countries have the largest aggregate share in the Bretton Woods Institutions, the EU is less influential in them than the US – which has about half the aggregate quota.[17] This is all the more problematic, as the perception has evolved that the EU is from time to time criticized for being over-represented in the Bretton Woods Institutions in terms of seats and aggregate voting power.

Some EU countries do not support the idea of having a single chair at the IMF for the eurozone in order not to lose influence if they give up their national chair.

Regarding the 'G-groups' (G7, G20) and the OECD (Organisation for Economic and Co-operation Development), the eurozone's representation is also far from optimal. There are proposals to consolidate European representation, not only because this would improve the representation of the EU or EMU, but also because this would allow the entry of some systemically important emerging market economies more easily, in order to obtain a more relevant global forum.

The consolidation of the EU's or the EMU's representation in these fora would help to form a 'G-group' that is both efficient and has a wide coverage of relevant players. There is as yet no sufficient support among the EMU member states.

3.3.3 Relations with key strategic partners

Most EU member states hold bilateral relationships with key strategic partners such as the US, India, China, Russia, Brazil, Japan or South Africa. In addition, the EU has developed regular bilateral fora with the world's key economic powers dealing with macroeconomic and financial issues. The bilateral dialogues between the EU and its key strategic partners are a useful complement to the multilateral fora.

So far, most of these dialogues are held by the EU-27, and not by the eurozone, although the ECB is generally invited to participate. The notable exception of a eurozone initiative was the Troika trip to China in November 2007: the eurozone for the first time engaged in a bilateral dialogue with China in a troika format: the EMU was represented by the Eurogroup President Juncker, European Commissioner Joaquín Almunia and ECB President Jean-Claude Trichet. Together with the Chinese side, they agreed to explore ways to further enhance the dialogue between China and the EU. This first EMU troika trip was a sign of a cooperative approach by all parties involved on the EU-EMU side (Aghion, Ahearne, Belka, Heikensten, Pisani-Ferry, Sapir, von Hagen 2008, p. 89).

4. CONCLUSIONS

4.1 A Gradual Adaptation of the Rules, the Institutions and   Underlying Ideas

In the first decade of the EMU's existence, the governance mechanisms have been spelled out and have been considerably adapted to the new political and economic environment. The analysis shows that major adaptations were implemented especially whenever economic pressure was high. A first series of reforms was decided upon in the context of the economic downturn in the years 2002–2003 (notably the reform of the Stability and Growth Pact, the reform of the BEPG and the Lisbon Process). The current financial market and economic crisis has once again fuelled the debate on the economic governance set-up of the EMU and has led to decisions such as to hold a eurozone summit, to step up discretionary fiscal policy and soften the application of the reformed Stability and Growth Pact, to move forward towards better coordinated European and international banking, and financial market supervision and regulation etc.

This chapter has further argued that the thinking about the functioning of the EMU has considerably evolved since the euro was launched on 1 January 1999. Policies and coordination mechanisms are now in place which represent a certain evolution of the framework of the Maastricht Treaty based on the neo-classical economic paradigm. Today, a different view is taken on the role of discretionary and non-discretionary fiscal policy in the EMU especially as it has turned out that the EMU is not evolving towards an Optimum Currency Area as quickly as was expected when the Maastricht Treaty was drafted. As has been argued above, the view on monetary policy has also slightly changed. However, the primacy of monetary stability and the independence of the ECB are not questioned and it is highly unlikely that reforms touching on the monetary pillar of the EMU will occur.

If policies and coordination mechanisms have evolved in the way described in this chapter, this was possible due to a combination of different factors: the economic (and resulting fiscal) pressure to act, new economic thinking (in general but also in particular for EMU), new learnings about the functioning of the coordination framework (which is historically unique and has hence never been tested before it was put in place in the EMU) and an improved understanding of the degree of cooperation and communication between the different actors involved in economic policymaking in the EMU that was needed.

So far, all reforms have been implemented below Treaty law. Some of them took the form of Council resolutions, others (such as the Stability and Growth Pact and its reform) were legislative procedures and led to Regulations. The example of the successful establishment of the Eurogroup illustrates the potential and the flexibility in the EU and EMU to establish and develop institutions step by step in cooperation with the essential actors of EMU. As early as the times of the Constitutional Convention, the Eurogroup had already developed a stable 'modus vivendi' and was widely considered the core political forum of the EMU. Not only had the Ministers of Finance and the Economy recognized their interest in the meeting, but also the ECB, the European Commission, the Ecofin and the European Parliament had acknowledged the necessity of this forum (and the European Parliament in an input to the Convention formulated very clear ideas about its future cooperation with the Eurogroup). The upcoming enlargement of the EU (and prospectively of the EMU) may also have served as an accelerator to consolidate the Eurogroup as part of the EMU coordination set-up, as the new members which acceded to the EU on 1

May 2004 shifted the balance of EMU members and non-EMU-members at least temporarily from 12:15 to 12:25. The relatively falling share of EMU members in the Ecofin emphasized the need for an EMU-exclusive forum.

4.2 Future Challenges for the Eurozone

The up-coming Eastern enlargements of the eurozone will further challenge the set-up of the EMU. The sheer number of member states, reflected for instance in an increasing number of participants in the Eurogroup, will have an impact on the atmosphere (the confidentiality of which has been identified as one of the key factors for the Eurogroup's success) and the working methods. With 20 and more members, the intimate character of the Eurogroup and its consensus-building power is likely to change. Further, with the accession of more Central and Eastern European Countries (CEECs) to the EMU, the divergence of national interests is likely to increase as the CEECs define their preferences against the background of a structural and cyclical setting, which from case to case may diverge from the to-date mostly Western European members of the EMU. Furthermore, some CEECs have traditionally taken a rather reserved stance on integration and close policy coordination.

Growing economic divergence and the possibly diverging political preferences with regard to economic and monetary policy in the EMU are not solely a result of the current crisis, but will very probably be enhanced in the current recession. So far, no coherent policy response has been given to the cyclical divergences which have built up in the EMU since the last economic dip in 2002–2003 and which – under less critical economic circumstances than are present today – had already caused debates on a possible EMU exit of selected EMU countries. The current crisis will probably aggravate the problem that market mechanisms are not able to counterbalance regionally diverging economic developments. This would raise the question which other instruments could be developed.

The power with which the crisis hits some EU countries could in the worst case seriously increase financial market pressure on EMU members such as Greece, Italy, Spain or Portugal. European bond spreads have widened to records, as rating agencies have downgraded or have threatened to downgrade some EMU members due to worsening public finances. High risk primes on government bonds could put public finances under serious pressure, if not even cause payment problems. If this case does occur, the No-Bail-Out-Clause (art. 113 ECT), according to which neither the EU nor any of its members would bail out another member state, could de facto be abandoned. The current Treaty law only provides for 'balance of payment loans' for non-EMU countries experiencing liquidity problems. Politically, it seems unacceptable not to support EMU members which may encounter similar problems, especially as a destabilization of the banking sector in EMU countries could have serious repercussions for the rest of the eurozone.

4.3 The Impact of the Lisbon Treaty

In case of its ratification, the implementation of the Lisbon Treaty could trigger further institutional dynamics. The Treaty's protocol would strengthen the Eurogroup's ability to further increase its role in the institutional set-up of the EMU and in its international representation.

In addition, there are two institutional innovations relevant to the EMU: the Commission, which according to the protocol should prepare the Eurogroup meetings, now has a legal basis to exert the role it plays in EU economic policy also in EMU matters as long as the member states agree with unanimity. Furthermore, the protocol establishes a 2.5 year term for future Eurogroup Presidents. This not only gives the work of the President more continuity as it adds 25 per cent to the term, but the longer mandate could also be used to synchronize the legislature of the European Parliament with the eurozone Presidency.

According to the Lisbon Treaty, the European Council would in the future decide on the evaluation of member states' economic policies in view of the Broad Economic Policy Guidelines with a qualified majority vote. The concerned member state hence has no veto. Furthermore, the EMU member states can decide with a qualified majority vote to reinforce the surveillance of national budgetary policies and that they seek to establish EMU-focused Economic Policy Guidelines which have to be in line with the Broad Economic Policy Guidelines for the whole EU. The new mandate for the European Council Presidency will probably enhance cooperation among the following partners: the new Council President, the Trio-team Presidency and the new President of the Eurogroup. Coordination with the European Commission will also be strengthened, especially as its role in the implementation of the Stability and Growth Pact has become more influential.

But beyond these innovations, the future role of the Eurogroup will decisively depend on how the participating member countries and in particular the President of the group will assume their tasks in practice and how relationships and interaction with the other relevant institutional partners, the ECB, the European Commission, the Ecofin Council and increasingly also the European Parliament, will evolve.

Irrespective of the question whether the Lisbon Treaty enters into force or not, the member states of the EMU and the EU face the challenge of developing and defending a common position in the emerging debate on the reform of the global economic system. While it seems unrealistic today that a new exchange rate system à la Bretton Woods will be installed, other topics such as the future of the Bretton Woods Institutions and the creation of stronger European and transcontinental surveillance structures for financial market actors are on the agenda and merit a European input. An important question the EMU members have to solve prior to any further reform proposals is whether they are willing to pool their membership in the Bretton Woods Institutions. Further progress also remains to be made as far as bilateral relationships with key partners such as the US or China are concerned. Regarding the future of global exchange rate policies, the eurozone first of all had to engage in consensus-building processes: political debates over euro exchange rate developments since the start of the EMU have shown that the member states often diverge in their views of the need and degree of intervention which will make any further reaching step rather difficult. The underlying problem is a fundamentally different view of exchange rate policies: while for example Germany sees monetary policy as a by-product of a monetary policy, France tends to see it as an instrument that one should use (Pisani-Ferry 2006).

In the ten years since the euro's creation, the member states of EMU have step by step adapted the internal governance set-up and – less importantly – also the international representation of the EMU to the existing circumstances. The reaction to the current financial market crisis has shown that the eurozone's willingness to act together has increased under the existing pressure and that – despite the complex decision-making mechanisms – it has been able to formulate policy responses rather swiftly. But it has also become obvious that the existing economic interdependencies in the EMU have not entirely translated into European political action. The second largest economy of the world to date does not dispose of the instruments that habitually any truly integrated economy has at its disposal. This can create economic policy incoherence. The evaluation of risks and benefits of any cooperation still run along national lines and not in view of EMU aggregates – despite the obvious interdependencies which, in the long run, will make unilateral action less and less impactful.

NOTES

1. For a detailed argumentation see Dullien and Schwarzer (2009).
2. Ten year government bond spreads, 23 January, Thomson Reuters, www. markets.ft.com.
3. See Amsterdam Treaty, in Official Journal of the EU, C 340, 10 November 1997; Nice Treaty in Official Journal of the EU, C 80, 10 March 2001. The Treaty establishing a Constitution for Europe, in Official Journal of the EU, C 310, 16 December 2004, and the Lisbon Treaty, in Official Journal of the EU, C 306, 17 December 2007, allude only marginally to the EMU's institutional framework (see below). An overview of the

moderate modifications is provided by Umbach and Wessels (2008, in particular pp. 54–57).

4. Ibid., p. 58.
5. Schwarzer (2007) has traced this process since the Irish case in 2001.
6. This argument is taken from the paper of Dullien and Schwarzer (2008).
7. The macroeconomic dialogue (also referred to as 'Cologne Process') brings together – in two yearly meetings – government representatives of the eurozone with social partners as well as representatives of the Commission and ECB. However, these meetings take place at a political level only once a year (the second meeting takes place at a technical level). Due to the higher number of participants and the lack of regular meetings, the exchange is less continuous and integrated than in the Eurogroup. For a general description of the Cologne Process see Niechoj (2005).
8. The so-called 'Outs' do not have voting rights regarding art. 104, para. 9, 11; art. 106, para. 2; art. 111; art. 112, para. 2b; art. 123, para. 4 and para. 5 (ECT) and regarding exchange rate policy, staffing of ECB posts as well as specific measures of implementation of the Stability and Growth Pact.
9. Protocol no. 14 concerning the Eurogroup, attached to the consolidated version of the Treaty on European Union and the Treaty on the Functioning of the European Union, in Official Journal of the EU, C 115, 9 May 2008, p. 283. This protocol corresponds to protocol no. 12 (concerning the Eurogroup) of the Treaty establishing a Constitution for Europe, in Official Journal of the EU, C 310, 16 December 2004, p. 341.
10. Specified by Council Regulation (EC) no. 332/2002 of 18 February 2002 establishing a facility providing medium-term financial assistance for Member States' balances of payments, in Official Journal of the EU, L 53, 23 February 2002, pp. 1–3.
11. The EC Treaty provides for an automatic EMU membership as soon as the convergence criteria are met.
12. For a detailed discussion of the development until 2008 see European Commission (2008, pp. 41f).
13. For this conflict, see for instance Randall Henning (2007, pp. 317f).
14. A good summary of the arguments for a consolidated external representation is given by European Commission (2008, pp. 281ff).
15. More details on the consolidation on the administrative level are given by European Commission (2008, pp. 114–144).
16. Ibid., p. 141.
17. Ibid.

BIBLIOGRAPHY

Becker, Werner (2008a), *Der Euro Wird Zehn. Den Kinderschuhen entwachsen*, Deutsche Bank Research: EU-Monitor no. 57.

Becker, Werner (2008b), *Die Währungsunion im Reifetest der Finanzkrise*, Deutsche Bank Research, Aktueller Kommentar, 29 October.

BNP Paribas Market Economics (2008), *Eurozone: Internal Imbalance*, April.

Collignon, Stefan and Daniela Schwarzer (2003), *Private Sector Involvement in the Euro: the Power of Ideas*, London: Routledge, pp. 159–170.

Commerzbank (2009), *AG: Konjunktur, Zinsen und Wechselkurse – International. Economic Research*, Annual Issue, December–January.

Dullien, Sebastian and Ulrich Fritsche (2007), 'Anhaltende Divergenz bei Inflations – und Lohnentwicklung in der Eurozone: Gefahr für die Währungsunion?', *Vierteljahreshefte zur Wirtschaftsforschung*, no. 4, 56–76.

Dullien, Sebastian and Daniela Schwarzer (2005), *The Eurozone under Serious Pressure. Regional Economic Cycles in the Monetary Union Need to be Stabilised,* , SWP Comment, C 22, Berlin: Stiftung Wissenschaft Politik.

Dullien, Sebastian and Daniela Schwarzer (2008), *Building on Shifting Sand: Political Science and the Economic Consensus of EMU,* Paper presented at the Workshop '10 Years of the European Monetary Union', Hertie School of Governance, Berlin, 24–25 April.

Dullien, Sebastian and Daniela Schwarzer (2009), 'Bringing macro-economics into the EU budget debate: why and how', *Journal of Common Market Studies,* **47** (1), 153–174.

Dyson, Kenneth (2008), *European States and the Euro Area: Clustering and Covariance in Patterns of Change,* in K. Dyson (ed.), *The Euro at 10: Europeanization, Power, and Convergence,* Oxford: Oxford University Press, pp. 378–413.

Economist Intelligence Unit, The (2008), *European Economy: an Unattainable Safe Haven?,* 17 November.

Ehrlich, Peter and Wolfgang Proissl (2008), 'Sarkozy wagt neuen Anlauf für EU-"Wirtschaftsregierung"', *Financial Times Deutschland,* 15 January.

Eichel, Hans (2005), interview with the *Süddeutsche Zeitung,* 15 January, http://archiv.bundesregierung.de/bpaexport/interview/70/774970/multi.htm.

European Central Bank (1999), 'The stability-oriented monetary policy strategy of the Eurosystem', *ECB Monthly Bulletin,* Frankfurt, January, 39–50.

European Central Bank (2003), 'The outcome of the ECB's evaluation of its monetary policy strategy', *ECB Monthly Bulletin,* Frankfurt, July, 79–91.

European Central Bank (2008), *Monthly Bulletin. 10th Anniversary of the ECB. 1998–2008,* Frankfurt am Main.

European Commission (2008), *The Euro@ten, Successes and Challenges after Ten Years of Economic and Monetary Union,* European Economy 2.

Fels, Joachim (2008), *Euro Wreckage? A Remix,* Morgan Stanley, Global Economic Forum, 7 November.

Fischer, Jonas, Lars Jonung, and Martin Larch (2006), *101 Proposals To Reform the Stability and Growth Pact. Why so many? A Survey,* Economic Papers no. 267, European Economy, Economic and Financial Affairs DG, European Commission.

Flassbeck, Heiner (2008), 'Carry trade – der devisenmarkt führt die ökonomie ad absurdum und die ökonomen schweigen', *Financial Times Deutschland,* 8 February.

Gros, Daniel and Stefano Micossi (2008), *A Call for a European Financial Stability Fund,* Centre for European Policy, Studies Commentary, 30 October.

Henning, C. Randall (2007), 'Organizing foreign exchange intervention in the Euro area', *Journal of Common Market Studies,* **45** (2), 315–342.

Merkel, Angela and Nicolas Sarkozy (2008), 'Nous ne pouvons pas attendre', *Le Figaro,* 26 November.

Münchau, Wolfgang (2008), 'German complacency poses a serious threat', *Financial Times,* 30 November.

Niechoj, Torsten (2005), 'Koordinierung à la Keynes? Der Makroökonomische Dialog des Kölner Prozesses', *Integration,* no. 1, 68–80.

Pisani-Ferry, Jean (2006), 'Only one bed for two dreams: a critical retrospective on the debate over the economic governance of the euro area', *Journal of Common Market Studies*, **44** (4), 823–844.

Pisani-Ferry, Jean, Aghion Philippe, Marek Belka, Jürgen von Hagen, Lars Heikensten and André Sapir (2008), *Coming of Age: Report on the Euro Area*, Bruxelles: Bruegel, 15 January, p. 89.

Pütter, Uwe (2006), *The Eurogroup: How a Secretive Circle of Finance Ministers Shape European Economic Governance*, Manchester: Manchester University Press, p. 58.

Runner, Philippa (2008), *Financial Crisis Builds Polish Euro-entry Momentum*, www.euobserver.com, 28 October.

Schwarzer, Daniela (2007), *Fiscal Policy Co-ordination in the EMU: a Prefence-Based Explanation of Institutional Change*, Baden-Baden: Nomos.

Svensson, Lars E.O. (2003), *In the Right Direction, But Not Enough: the Modification of the Monetary-policy Strategy of the ECB*, Briefing Paper for the Committee on Economic and Monetary Affairs of the European Parliament for the Dialogue with ECB, Princeton University.

Umbach, Gaby and Wolfgang Wessels (2008), *The Changing European Context of Economic and Monetary Union: Deepening, Widening, and Stability*, in K. Dyson (ed.), *The Euro at 10: Europeanization, Power, and Convergence*, Oxford: Oxford University Press, 54–68.

Verhofstadt, Guy (2006), *The United States of Europe*, London: Federal Trust for Education & Research.

5. EU Fiscal Policy in the Age of Turbulence: Will the Lisbon Strategy Survive It?

Carlo Altomonte, Francesco Passarelli and Carlo Secchi

'Exceptional times call for exceptional measures'. These are the words used by the EU Commission President in November 2008 to launch a comprehensive plan to drive Europe's recovery from the economic crisis. The 'Recovery Plan', as it has been called, is the largest coordinated manoeuvre of countercyclical fiscal policy attempted at the EU level. In fact, overall the Plan calls for a fiscal stimulus of more than €200 billion or 1.5 per cent of EU GDP (Gross Domestic Product), to be mobilised within national budgets (in excess of €170 billion, 1.2 per cent of GDP) and EU and European Investment Bank budgets (around €30 billion, 0.3 per cent of GDP).

In the short term, the plan calls for measures to boost demand, save jobs and help restore confidence. In terms of the centralised EU's contribution to the Plan, that comes from accelerating payments of up to €6.3 billion under the structural and social funds within the EU Budget. In particular, the Commission has simplified the criteria for the use of the European Social Fund, re-programmed some spending and stepped up advance payments from early 2009, so that member states have earlier access to up to €1.8 billion in order to reinforce active labour market policies, and where necessary opt for full Community financing of projects during this period. Up to €4.5 billion of cohesion funding is being brought forward, alongside other measures to accelerate the implementation of major investment projects. The Commission is also mobilising a further €5 billion for the period 2009–2010 to improve energy interconnections and broadband infrastructure.[1] The European Investment Bank is instead increasing its yearly interventions in the EU by some €15 billion in 2009 with a similar figure in 2010.

Over the medium term, the plan foresees a 'smart investment' strategy by member states, in order to preserve and possibly improve on the progress achieved with the Lisbon Strategy in terms of economic growth and sustainable prosperity, in particular with respect to climate change. More specifically, the plan calls for a greater focus of investments in education and (re-)training, to help people retain their jobs and get back into the labour market, whilst raising productivity. The plan also calls for investment in infrastructure and energy efficiency, in order to keep people in the construction industry in work, save energy and improve efficiency.

Notwithstanding the large effort at bay, the outcome of the Plan in terms of its ability to achieve an effective 'recovery' of the EU economy is highly controversial. The main reason is that the bulk of the plan (some 85 per cent of all the available resources) is entirely in the hands of the (decentralised) fiscal policy decisions of the member states. Such a model of governance raises a number of critical issues, which we discuss throughout the remaining of the chapter: the timeliness of the concerted action and the effectiveness of discretionary fiscal policy decisions to actually boost demand, and hence growth, in the EU; the effects of the decisions on the short-term status of public finances in Europe and, as a consequence, the running of monetary policy by the European Central Bank (ECB);[2] the management of the spillover effects these actions might generates across member states; and the consistency of the actions undertaken with the general goal of the Lisbon Strategy of achieving a structurally higher potential growth rate for the EU economy.

Before discussing these critical issues, it is nevertheless useful to place fiscal policy in the context of the broad economic policy framework of the Economic and Monetary Union (EMU) as stemming from the prescriptions of the Maastricht Treaty.

1. THE TRADITIONAL GOVERNANCE OF FISCAL POLICY UNDER EMU

The extent of the extraordinary fiscal stimulus 'sponsored' by the European Commission can be understood if we look at the prevailing view within Europe until early 2008. The conventional wisdom behind the monetary union has maintained that discretionary fiscal policy should *not* be used as a tool to stabilize output over the cycle. The stabilisation role is normally left to the monetary policy over the entire euro area, under the conditions that price stability is not endangered; in case of asymmetric shocks eventually hitting member states, stabilisation should be achieved via the work of the automatic stabilisers (see below and the chapter by Zuleeg and Martens in this volume for a discussion).

The latter is the policy framework ultimately enshrined in the Maastricht Treaty, a framework certainly different from the traditional Keynesian paradigm, according to which the private economy is inherently unstable and output volatility involves significant economic costs. As a result of this paradigm, over the 1970s and partly the 1980s the governance of economic policy was run under the idea that a bigger government could generate microeconomic inefficiencies, but the latter were regarded as a collateral damage of the much larger and positive role the government had in terms of contribution to stability (Blinder and Solow 1974). Moreover, it was postulated that the larger the government size (in terms of public expenditure), the larger its ability to cushion the negative effects of output volatility.

In the 1980s the economic literature developed instead a different perspective: real business cycle models started to show that fluctuations could be originating on the supply side rather than the demand side, a case in which little could be done by government intervention. Moreover, the same welfare costs of macroeconomic fluctuations were questioned, since they were thought to be very small for consumers (original estimates by Lucas found that the utility gain from eliminating fluctuations in consumption was equivalent to the gain from a permanent increase in the consumption level by 0.1 per cent only).[3]

As a result of these debates, the Maastricht Treaty still puts a great deal of emphasis on stability as one of the ultimate goals the EU wants to achieve, but the definition of stability is clearly more oriented toward prices rather than output, since the former is (correctly) seen as a pre-condition, together with public finance close to balance, for long-run growth, another important EU goal. In particular, the latter view derives from the observation that, in the period 1970–1990, budgetary policies in Europe have been asymmetric over the cycle, thus violating the tax-smoothing rule:[4] deficits increased during recessions, but never reversed to a position of surplus during expansionary phases, as shown by Figure 5.1 below, originally proposed by Buti and Sapir (1998). As a result, governments have experienced an upward trend in the national public debt as a share of GDP.

Various economic theories have been put forward to explain this apparently myopic behaviour of Governments:[5] the existence of 'fiscal illusion', according to which voters typically overestimate the benefits of current government spending and underestimate the costs of future taxation, leading to a political business cycle (governments tend to adopt expansionary policies during election years); the incentive for a government in charge, with scant chances of being re-elected, to accumulate debt in order to limit the budgetary options available to its successor; the underlying features of political institutions, with weak coalition governments and parliamentary systems normally associated with a tendency to debt accumulation. Considering the presence across Europe of many of these features, it is therefore not surprising to observe a general deterioration of public finances in the 1970–1990 period.

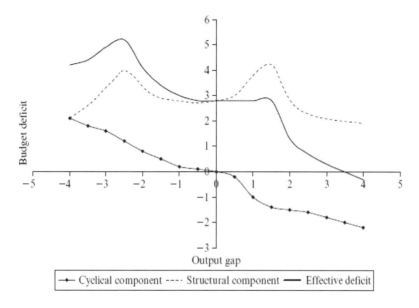

Figure 5.1 Output Gap and Budget Balance, EU Countries, 1970–1990

Taking into account this myopic behaviour of Governments, the provisions of the Economic and Monetary Union have thus been set up in order to fully encompass the link existing between fiscal and monetary policy via the intertemporal budget constraint: in the long run, the discounted sum of a government's expected expenditures cannot exceed the discounted sum of its expected revenues, that is, sooner or later governments' public debts have to be repaid (Sargent and Wallace 1981). Since among the expected revenues for a government there are not only taxes, but also seignorage, that is, the ability of a government to finance its deficits through the creation of money,[6] as soon as there are public deficits to be closed, there is an incentive for governments to try to increase money growth and generate inflation: recognising this, rational agents would raise their expectations of inflation. Therefore, in an economy which experiences significant budget deficits, inflation rates tend to be relatively higher. The latter clearly goes against one of the main tenets of the EMU, that is, to ensure price stability. Therefore, the European authorities have always called for public finances to be balanced in the medium run. Sound public finances are also necessary since high public deficits tend to crowd out resources to the detriment of private investments, thus hampering growth. Low public deficits and debt, instead, contribute to growth, since they contribute to maintaining both interest rates and the tax burden under control.

The previously discussed effects are all strong cases for budgetary discipline in any context, in particular from a national point of view. In a context of monetary union with decentralised fiscal policies, however, there are two other additional channels which call for a stricter joint control of public finances (Altomonte and Nava 2005). Suppose that a government, once a single currency has been created, starts to increase its public spending: in this case it will experience a larger internal demand, associated with higher interest rates. However, since monetary policy is common, part of the increase in the interest rates spreads out to other countries, generating a negative spillover for everyone. There is therefore an incentive to agree on common rules that discipline public finance. A second channel is related to the possible moral hazard a single government faces as soon as it is part of the EMU: once the monetary policy is common and the financial markets become progressively integrated, it is in the ultimate interest of the central bank not to let any single country go bankrupt, since an insolvency would negatively affect all the member states. Anticipating this result, governments, if left free to set their public deficits, will opt for looser attitudes in the running of their public finances. Lacking explicit rules that prevent such a behaviour, as soon as the budgetary positions deteriorate the central bank will be expected to either set lower than needed interest rates, in order not to worsen the budgetary position of governments, or to monetise the public debt. In all cases, the lack of an explicit deficit rule will hinder price stability.[7]

With a view to securing the benefits of union-wide financial stability, in the Maastricht Treaty countries reached therefore a consensus on the design of a supranational fiscal policy co-ordination framework at the EU level. The rules were adapted to the institutional characteristics of EMU at the time and designed to encourage sound budgetary policies by the member states, while allowing sufficient margins for national budgetary flexibility. Reference values for government deficit and debt were agreed at 3 per cent and 60 per cent of GDP, respectively, and a set of generic procedures (the 'Excessive Deficit Procedure' in art. 104 of the Treaty) was agreed, with the idea of foreseeing political and financial sanctions, in case a member state over a longer period started to generate significant deviations from the reference values. However, the excessive deficit procedure was deemed not completely adequate to guarantee the fiscal discipline of member states, once the 'carrot' of EMU entry would no longer be available, especially in light of the negative records in terms of public deficits and debt achieved in the past. As a result, in 1997 the excessive deficit procedure was complemented by the Stability and Growth Pact (SGP).

The core elements of the Pact, which originally did not deal with the debt criterion, but only with the deficit one, include a strengthening of the surveillance of budgetary positions (the so-called 'preventive' arm of the pact), setting time limits by which the various steps of the excessive deficit procedure of art. 104 have to be put in place by the competent institutions. The Pact also specifies in detail the exceptions according to which a member state can exceed the deficit threshold. While TEC (Treaty establishing the European Community) art. 104, par 2a states that the excess has to be 'exceptional and temporary', the SGP translates this situation into a recession in a member state of more than 2 per cent of GDP in a given year. In any case, however, the excess of the deficit over 3 per cent of GDP has to be temporary. Therefore, in order to avoid sanctions, the deficit has to move back below the reference value in the year following the one during which these 'exceptional' circumstances occurred. In addition, the Pact contains also a dissuasive arm, formalising the amount of the sanctions (foreseen by art. 104, para. 11) accruing to a member states failing to take appropriate actions against an excessive deficit. In terms of economic policy, the substantial novel requirement of the Pact with respect to the Maastricht Treaty was that EU countries are obliged to set country-specific medium-term objectives of budgetary positions 'close to balance or in surplus'. In other words, the mere respect of the 3 per cent ceiling of budget deficit foreseen by the Maastricht criteria is not enough. Rather, member states have to achieve a zero per cent deficit in the medium run, or even a budget surplus.

Hence, as it can be seen in this brief synopsis of the last fifteen years of EU economic policymaking, the idea enshrined in the EMU policy framework has always been that fiscal policy should not be discretionary, because the latter by and large would result in procyclical behaviour, especially in good phases of the cycle: to this extent, its scope is limited by the excessive deficit procedure.

Therefore, given these constraints, the EMU has always been considered as a market in which a negative shock symmetrically affecting all countries (such as a global economic crisis) should find an optimal response in the common monetary policy of the European Central Bank. Fiscal policy should instead be used when an asymmetric shock, hitting only one or few member states, would take place. Moreover, such fiscal correction should be enforced via the use of automatic stabilisers rather than discretionary fiscal decisions: the requirement for budget balances to be close to zero or in surplus would then guarantee that the full exploitation of automatic stabilisers can take place in a picture of overall stability for public finances.[8]

Given this overall framework of economic policy, it is easy to see how the 2008–2009 Recovery Plan, that is, a set of common discretionary fiscal policy actions suggested by the very same European Commission, seems to represent a veritable 'revolution' in the traditional economic set-up of EMU. The reasons behind such a dramatic change are explored in the next subsection.

1.1 The Recovery Plan in the Context of the EU Fiscal Policy

The word 'extraordinary' seems well considered when assessing the 2008–2009 Recovery Plan, if not for the size of the effort, at least for the very same nature of the policy under consideration, which, calling for discretionary fiscal actions by the member states, seems to go against the commonly accepted policy framework of EMU as stemming from the Maastricht Treaty. Why then such a dramatic change in the conduct of economic policies across the Continent? The answer has to be sought in the extraordinary nature of the crisis: the slow-down induced on the economic cycle originates from a liquidity crisis in the financial sector then transformed into a solvency crisis of the banking industry, with the ensuing consequences for the real economy in terms of drying up of credit for new investment, lack of consumers' confidence, and hence lower growth in the medium run (Altomonte and Nava 2008). As a result, the 2008–2009 economic crisis is a quite unique situation in which the traditional transmission channel of monetary policy onto the real business cycle is not effective, because the greater liquidity provided does not translate into higher investments of firms. Such an unprecedented consequence makes monetary policy virtually useless in trying to provide a real stimulus for the economy.

As a consequence, we now have a reversal of circumstances with respect to the 'Maastricht' set-up: rather than being subject to a 'monetary' paradigm in which price stability plays a central role, the needs of fiscal policy now dictate the agenda for the central banks in the world, and the EU is no exception: lower interest rates are not sought after in order to allow firms to invest (since the greater liquidity available is imperfectly mediated by the banking sector), but rather are used to keep low the burden of the growing debt induced by an expansionary (and discretionary) fiscal expenditure, the only component which is thought to properly stimulate the cycle in this contingency.

Once that is assessed, given the nature of the crisis the only possible answer seems therefore to be a discretionary fiscal policy. Clearly, all the limits of such an economic policy tool remain, however, and should be minimised.

In particular, it is well known that a discretionary fiscal policy suffers from at least three lags: a lag of information, in that not governments' decisions not necessarily pick the best, most effective plans for the economy; a lag of decision, since agreeing on a fiscal bill is often time-consuming and open to many sort of compromises; and a lag of implementation, in that the 'time to market' of fiscal policy decisions is, more often than not, too late in displaying their effects with respect to the actual critical phases of the cycle. This is why the economic literature (and the same Maastricht Treaty), tend to attribute a general positive role to automatic stabilisers, since they tend not to be subject to the typical lags undermining the effectiveness of discretionary stabilisation measures. Moreover, in the current phase of economic downturn, any expansionary fiscal policy (discretionary or via the automatic stabilisers) entails a deterioration of budget balances by the member states, and hence some form of infringement of the Growth and Stability Pact that should be dealt with. Finally, there is an issue of coordination: in the growingly integrated EU Single Market, member states might decide to play a dangerous free-riding game in order to benefit from the positive spillovers accruing to them from fiscal expansions abroad, without having to pay the costs in terms of budget balances, which remain national.

We now turn to discuss these issues.

1.1.1 Managing the lags of fiscal policy

In order to cope with the well-known lags of discretionary fiscal policy, the EU Recovery plan stresses three characteristics of the actions undertaken, which should be:

* *timely* so that they quickly support economic activity during the period of low demand, as delays in implementation could mean that the fiscal impulse only comes when the recovery is underway;
* *targeted* towards the source of the economic challenge (increasing unemployment, credit constrained firms/households, etc. and supporting structural reforms) as this maximises the stabilisation impact of limited budgetary resources;
* *co-ordinated* so that they multiply the positive impact and ensure long-term budgetary sustainability.

The joint respect of these criteria for fiscal action should be such to minimise the possible lags typical of any discretionary action of fiscal policy. As acknowledged by Debrun et al. (2008), in fact, countries with relatively lean public sectors like Japan and the United States have a consistent record of enacting discretionary fiscal packages explicitly aimed at stabilising the economy, with some degrees of success. Even in their case, the challenge is to make sure that such actions are timely, targeted and co-ordinated, and that they are symmetric over the cycle, that is, any stimulus should be reversed during the upturn.

To this extent, the same EU Commission has actually called for a fourth characteristic in the fiscal policy, namely the fact that actions are *temporary*, so as to avoid a permanent deterioration in budgetary positions which would undermine sustainability and eventually require financing through sustained future tax increases (see Chapter 6 in this volume for an extensive discussion of this issue). Clearly, in the short term the deterioration of the budgetary position has to be accommodated within the rules of the Stability and Growth Pact: this is where the issue of flexibility in the assessment of the budgetary position steps in.

1.1.2 Flexibility in budget balances

An expansionary fiscal policy action in a phase of downturn is possible thanks to the elements of flexibility introduced in the reformed SGP. In particular, the application of the excessive deficit procedure foreseen in TEC, art. 104 was revised in 2005. The Council has clearly stated that the excessive deficit procedure has to be engaged when there is an overshooting of the 3 per cent deficit criterion. However, the exceptions to this rule already foreseen in the Treaty, as well as the timing of the application of the procedure, have been significantly amended in order not to hinder structural reforms of public finances and avoid a procyclical behaviour of the SGP. In particular, the Council has redefined the exception foreseen in TEC, art. 104, para. 2a: any (temporary) excess over the reference value which results from a period of negative growth rate (thus no longer a recession of at least 2 per cent, or 0.75 per cent), or even from the accumulated loss of output during a protracted period of very low growth relative to potential growth, should be considered as exceptional, and therefore not sanctioned, thus correcting one of the major criticisms of the Pact, namely its procyclical attitude.

Moreover, the Council has stated that 'all other relevant factors' foreseen by TEC, art. 104, para. 3 in assessing a 'safe' budgetary position should be better taken into account with respect to the past implementation of the Pact, without prejudice, however, to the overarching principle that, before other relevant factors are taken into account, the excess over the reference value is temporary and the deficit remains close to the reference value. In particular, to foster the implementation of structural reforms, the Council has proposed that the Commission's report under TEC, art. 104, para. 3 should 'appropriately reflect developments in the medium-term economic position (in particular potential growth, prevailing cyclical conditions, the implementation of policies in the context of the Lisbon agenda and policies to foster R&D and innovation) as well as developments in the medium term budgetary position (in particular, fiscal consolidation efforts in "good times", debt sustainability, public investment and the overall quality of public finances)'. Furthermore, the Council has also stated that 'due consideration has to be given to any other factors which, in the opinion of the concerned member state, are relevant in order to comprehensively assess in qualitative terms the excess over the reference value. In that context, special consideration has to be given to budgetary efforts towards increasing or maintaining at a high level financial contributions to fostering international solidarity and to achieving European policy goals, notably the unification of Europe, if those have a detrimental effect on the growth and fiscal burden of a member state'.

Finally, the deadlines for the various procedures foreseen under TEC, art. 104 have been extended. In particular, the standard deadline for correcting an excessive deficit has been maintained as the year after its identification and thus, normally, the second year after its occurrence. The Council has agreed, however, that the overall assessment of 'all other relevant factors' foreseen by TEC, art. 104, para. 3 should be taken into account in setting the initial deadline for the correction of an excessive deficit. As a result, while as a benchmark countries in excessive deficit are required to achieve within one year a minimum fiscal effort of at least 0.5 per cent of GDP in cyclically adjusted terms (net of one-off measures), in case of special circumstances resulting from the previously discussed assessment, the initial deadline for correcting an excessive deficit could be set one year later, that is, the second year after its identification and thus normally the third year after its occurrence. Moreover, these deadlines for correcting the excessive deficit could be further revised and extended if unexpected adverse economic events with major unfavourable budgetary effects occur during the excessive deficit procedure.

It then follows that, at least in the short term, the budgetary policy rules in the EU are flexible enough to allow the fiscal stimulus plan to be deployed by the member states. Furthermore, another element of flexibility which has been introduced alongside the 2008–2009 recovery plan is related to the application of state aid rules (especially in the banking sector) in a way that achieves maximum flexibility for tackling the crisis, while maintaining a level playing field in the internal market. These new steps include a simplification package to speed up decision making, a temporary increase in the 'safe harbour threshold' for risk capital to €2.5 million and, also temporarily, further scope for member states to guarantee loans to businesses.

Provided that the exceptional circumstances leading to the flexible interpretation of the rules are reverted once the economic crisis is over, the current approach undertaken by the European Commission should allow the EU to organise for 2009 and 2010 an important stimulus to its economy, without endangering the overall stability of EMU.

1.1.3 Coordination of the fiscal policy stimulus

As we have seen, the fiscal stimulus engineered by the EU stays within the Stability and Growth Pact, while making use of the full flexibility offered by the Pact. However, de facto member states who launch stimulus packages benefit in two ways: they stimulate demand in their own economies; and they stimulate demand in other member states so giving a major boost to their own exporters. To the extent that actions are co-ordinated, they can thus generate multiplier effects and avoid the problems which can result from a piecemeal approach. The latter is a well-known characteristic of EMU, in which members share a large amount of 'club goods', including monetary stability, interest rates and the external exchange rate (Cohen and Wyplosz 1989; Jacquet and Pisani-Ferry 2001; von Hagen and Mundschenk 2001). The existence of such 'club goods', however, raises an issue of free-riding behaviour, which manifests itself in an incentive to ignore fiscal spillovers (see, for example, Beetsma 2001). In other words, recognising that it will benefit in any case by a fiscal stimulus undertaken by a neighbouring country, a member State might take a free ride attitude and provide an action of fiscal policy of a sub-optimal level. The potential generalisation of this behaviour would then lead to a second best scenario of fiscal policy action in Europe.

Given the centrality of the issue of coordination in providing an effective outcome for the fiscal policy stimulus under way, let us be more detailed on these points, and let us attempt to connect them to the institutional architecture that provides governance within the EU.

As stated above, in the internal market, any fiscal expansion provided by a member substantially increases the demand for imports from other members. This represents a positive spillover which comes to the other members at zero costs. In fact, only the member who increases the public deficit will pay for the full cost of the expansion, whereas the others will only enjoy the benefits of a positive effect on the demand for national products. The more integrated the market, the larger this asymmetry between private costs, which are concentrated on one member, and public benefits, which spread over the single market members. Intuitively, with the asymmetry, on the one hand, members will be reluctant to be the 'payers'; on the other hand, they will try to get the benefits from 'free riding' the expansion carried out by others. In other words, within the single market there is a high risk of underprovision of fiscal expansion efforts. Thus, there is a coordination problem, that is a result of a typical 'prisoner dilemma' situation.

This kind of problem arises any time the policy implemented by some member generates a positive or a negative externality on other members.

To counter these effects, the EU thus needs a substantial amount of positive coordination, which of course does not mean that all member states should adopt the same approach, but rather that they should move in the same direction in terms of fiscal stimulus. It also mean that a large amount of monitoring and control must be done by central institutions at the EU level.

However, the latter is easier to be said than done in the EU, since, even if affected by generalised recessionary conditions and thus willing to implement some coordinated policy actions, member states might be hindered by the heterogeneous status of their specific macroeconomic conditions. For example, growth rates in 2009 vary from around +2 per cent in Slovakia, Bulgaria, Romania and Poland, to contractions of –5 per cent or more in Estonia, Ireland or Latvia. The EU Commission figures for government deficits in 2009 also vary from nearly –11 per cent in Ireland to a surplus of +2 per cent in Finland, while on average the euro-area sees its public deficit double from 2 to 4 per cent. Moreover, some economists in some member states have expressed concern about deflation unless a fiscal stimulus is quickly injected, while there is double digit inflation in others (for example Bulgaria). The heterogeneity of the situation is also clear in the fiscal policy packages approved by the major member states during 2008–2009, and reported in Table 5.1.

Table 5.1 Fiscal Policy Packages Approved by Member States, 2008–2009

Country	Size of package	Period covered
Germany	€81 billion	2008–2009
France	€26 billion	2009
Italy	€6 billion	2009
Spain	€38 billion	2008–2009
UK	€21 billion	2009

Source: National governments as of February 2009.

Apart from the reported heterogeneity in member states' initial conditions, in the case of the current economic crisis two other kind of externality arises which potentially exacerbate the problem. First, every country in the world is now actively using fiscal policy as a tool to soften the effects of the crisis. As a result, markets are 'flooded' with a very large supply of government bonds, especially by prime emitters, such as the US or the United Kingdom. As a consequence, countries suffering from a worse credit record due to the particularly negative effect of the crisis (for example Spain) or their status of public finances (for example Italy) see a significant increase in the cost of debt with respect to their historical benchmark. Hence, they are relatively more reluctant to fully cooperate with the fiscal expansion. Second, one has to consider the stability effect induced by the recovery policy. Suppose the policy is effective in giving the financial markets more stability; given the nature of the crisis, stemming from highly integrated credit markets, the higher stability quickly spreads over the system and presumably is enjoyed by all members. Also in this case, countries will enjoy an immediate positive spillover, and thus also in this case the problem of underprovision of efforts and free riding in stabilisation policies arises.

Hence, it is clear the EU is facing an important coordination problem. Sovereign members have an incentive to let the others pay the bill. In this situation is likely that markets have anticipated that the total stabilization effort is not optimal. Financial institutions have not received enough support from governments, and internal demand has not been sufficiently boosted by additional public demand. In other words, the deficit of governance at the EU level is reflected by a higher bill paid by the EU citizens, which means either a lower activism of fiscal policy or higher costs of financing the same fiscal expansion.

Summing up, there is a general lack of confidence about the ability of overcoming the crisis with adequate policy measures by the members of the EU. As a consequence, the effects of the crisis are higher, in particular for the member states whose fiscal policies are rather disconnected.

What to do? Of course the benchmark is full integration in fiscal policy and in the measures that face financial instability. The US, for example, does not have such a coordination problem. The full cost of recovery policies has been paid by the federal budget, and distributed across states by federal taxation and subsidies. Stability plans and fiscal expansions have been decided within a federal context, with democratic foundations and, to a certain extent, with decisional efficiency. This has made polices more credible and predictable for markets.

Arguably, higher credibility means that the same effort produces larger effects, or the same effects can be reached with a smaller effort. For example, in the case where the government announces its availability to recover a domestic financial institution with public funding, credibility increases the value of the government's insurance. As a consequence, after the announcement, the institution's risk of failure is perceived to be low, and no instability will actually occur. No instability means no outflow for the public budget. In one word, the effect of the government's insurance on the system's stability might come at zero (or at a very low) cost. At the basis of this virtuous situation there is credibility. Part of credibility is due to efficiency in policymaking. Also the demand boosting of fiscal expansion is higher when there is a credible central government. In many cases, expansion occurs just because of a credible announcement of the fiscal measures. Summing up, fiscal policies and support plans are more credible and effective in federal contexts; in general, effectiveness and credibility are positively related to the degree of policy integration among partners.

Coming back to Europe, to some extent the crisis has thus increased the demand for more political integration within the EU. However, full coordination via the central government is impossible under the current institutional setting, since the EU does not have a federal political system and the ability to generate consistent deficits on the Union's budget. An important role in ensuring coordination within this particular phase of the economic crisis has thus been played by the Commission: recall, however, that the Commission has only the powers attributed to it by member states under the Treaties. The main legal and budgetary instruments for stimulating demand and employment are in the hands of the member states. The Commission cannot replace their actions or attribute further funds to itself. Its own budget is of great strategic importance but at around 1 per cent of EU GDP it is a tiny fraction of the EU public spending as a whole and around half the government budget of the Netherlands or one eighth that of France! But the Commission can propose modifications to EU law and budgets, and works with the European Parliament and member states to adopt and implement those changes. It has made proposals on, for example, deposit guarantees, capital requirements, credit ratings agencies and in the context of the Strategic Energy Review. Under the Recovery Plan it has proposed further measures on among other things structural funding, greener taxation and energy efficiency. Third, the Commission monitors the implementation of both new measures and existing EU law to ensure that member states meet their commitments and that a level playing field is maintained. It has approved key state aids in record time, sometimes within 24 hours. Finally the Commission represents the EU as a whole in international negotiations, both in established fora like the WTO (World Trade Organisation) and the G8 and in specific crisis meetings like the Washington summit and those that will follow it.

The Commission has shown the ability of full understanding the severity of this crisis. Within the limits of the current institutional setting, it has provided any possible effort to increase the manoeuvre space of the member states and to coordinate their measures.

The current EU institutional setting, however, is tightening, not just on the executive side, but rather on the legislative side. Currently, the Union's competencies on fiscal policy are rather limited and concern 'light' measures, such as guidelines, coordination, recommendations. As discussed above, the most effective European rule is of course the SGP, that is however designed to inhibit fiscal deficits, rather to promote joint expansionary fiscal policies. Beyond the Stability Pact, no specific fiscal initiative that impacts on the members' deficits can be taken at the central EU level. This means that any possible fiscal action that the countries take together is based on unanimity and voluntary participation. No enforcement device exists. Thus, free riding is always an option. As a consequence, loose coordination comes as a possible result of the EU decisional mechanisms. In fact, with unanimity any decision is self-enforcing, and possibly unanimity does not help in reducing the chance of free-riding substantially.

In this situation, the risk of prevailing national egoisms and blocking vetoes in economic policymaking is still strong. Then, the next questions are: what has triggered the Recovery Plan? Has it been optimally framed?

First, the Plan represents an outstanding result, under the current institutional setting and the current level of policy integration. The members have been able to reach a very high level of coordination because the crisis is exceptionally severe. But still the doubt is that something more could have been done if the EU had more power with respect to the national governments. Given all the problems previously analysed, this form of coordination is clearly weaker than full centralisation. As a consequence, also credibility is lower, and costs are higher.

A related argument concerns the limited EU ability of promoting transfers across countries. Again, as illustrated above, fiscal recovery measures are costly. Costs, not only benefits, can be different across countries. For example, costs are particularly high for highly indebted countries. When the costs of the same policy are different across members, but the benefits are equally shared, a certain degree of redistribution is needed. Redistribution can be done in different ways. Taxation is one of them, and probably it is the most efficient one. In the EU, however, there is no possibility to tax the members who gain more or who pay less, in order to compensate the others. As a consequence, if no other efficient transfer methods are available, the countries might be unwilling to provide the right effort. In synthesis, our counterfactual argument is the following: in the presence of an efficient redistribution mechanism across member states, the chance of designing an optimal Plan of national stimuli is higher. Again, the deficit of EU governance raises the expected costs of economic policies for the EU citizens.

So far we have not distinguished between members of the euro-area and non-members. If we make that distinction, the asymmetry among countries is even stronger. Namely, fiscal expansion may generate the risk of instability in public finances. For some EU members outside the euro-area, this has triggered expectations of depreciation of the national currency. Interest rates have increased for those countries, making the provision of capital more difficult and costly. This has reduced the benefits of the fiscal expansion. Then, it is not surprising that some small members of the EU who have not adopted the single currency have been, other things being equal, more reluctant to provide high efforts. This argument suggests that the euro-area should be more open to new accessions, and the new entries should be speeded up credibly, in order to dissipate the risk of any speculative attack.

Once having assessed all the different aspects related to the efficacy with which an unprecedented, discretionary fiscal policy stimulus has been undertaken at the EU level, let us now turn to a different perspective, and namely the consistency of such a fiscal policy, assuming it has been correctly implemented, with respect to the medium-term growth goals set by the EU within its Lisbon strategy.

1.2 The Recovery Plan and the Lisbon Strategy

According to the European Commission, the Recovery Plan is an extensive reinforcement of the Lisbon Strategy for Growth and Jobs in both the short and longer term. In particular, in the idea of the EU institutions, the Recovery Plan should be a comprehensive response to the current crisis, with measures to boost demand and protect citizens from unemployment complemented by measures to step up investment in strategic areas where jobs can be created, which will also contribute to Europe's competitiveness and sustainable prosperity in the long term. To that extent, the same Commission postulates that, within fiscal policy actions, member states strengthen the instruments to ensure their commitments under the Lisbon Growth and Jobs Strategy.

However, looking at the issue from an analytical perspective based on the evidence available insofar, the critical areas of implementation of the Lisbon Strategy traditionally reside in the working of product markets, still affected by cumbersome regulations and not enough innovation and competition, especially in services (Mandl et al. 2008); it then follows that any credible solution to the long-run competitiveness problem consistent with the Lisbon Strategy is likely to generate short-term costs in terms of job losses. That is not consistent with the current priorities of the member states, and thus the idea that the Recovery Plan is just another step within a serious implementation of the Lisbon Strategy (that is, a strategy aimed at restoring competitiveness for the EU economy) seems insofar to be nothing more than wishful thinking.

The inconsistency is also evident in the approach of the same Commission, which espouses the idea that the top priority of the Recovery

Plan should be to protect Europe's citizens from the worst effects of the financial crisis: 'they are the first to be hit whether as workers, households, or as entrepreneurs'. If one has to judge the Plan in view of the necessary steps needed to fulfil the EU competitive gap (the Lisbon Strategy), the latter is an ill-conceived priority. We argue instead that protecting jobs today is not necessarily the best way to protect workers tomorrow, because these policies are likely to hamper the speed of the recovery after the crisis; or, put it in another way, a wrong focus in the policy response within the current turmoil can actually endanger the benefits that Europe can achieve within the Lisbon Strategy for Growth and Jobs.

Figure 5.2 shows the effects of the Lisbon strategy over the last seven years, decomposing the growth rate of each country into growth rate of productivity and growth rates of hours worked (what we refer to as employment growth), the two most important indicators at the basis of long-run growth of countries.

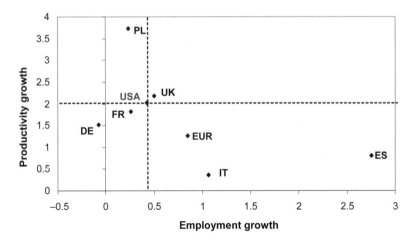

Source: OECD Productivity Database.

Figure 5.2 Lisbon Progresses, 2000–2007

Looking at these data, we can see that the EU growth potential has increased to almost 2.5 per cent per year in the last years,[9] vs. less than 2 per cent at the start of the decade. However the growth rate has been achieved with a certain bias towards adjusting growth via raising the employment rate, that is, a labour market adjustment which has hindered an equal growth in productivity, leading some economists to talk of a 'productivity-employment' paradox.

The political economy argument behind this evolution is quite clear: since the mid 1990s a certain degree of consensus has prevailed in Europe on policies aimed at reforming the labour markets towards greater flexibility, an action which has brought about a reduction of unemployment to historically low levels across all countries (see Figure 5.3). The political benefits of reforming the product markets in order to foster higher productivity are instead less clear cut, due to the action of powerful interest groups in societies, especially in services sectors, often characterised by the presence of a strong incumbent player. Thus, to the extent that governments face a trade-off in spending their political capital, it is not surprising that most of the policy actions undertaken in the last years to achieve the Lisbon targets have been relatively biased in favour of reforming the labour, rather than the product market.

Clearly, in the long run the latter is not an optimal strategy. In particular, it is interesting to look at the evolution of the two drivers of growth over the two periods 2000–2003 and 2004–2007, since we get the reactions of countries to two different distinct phases of the cycle: the period 2000–2003, characterised by a marked phase of slowing down of the cycle, with mini-recessions present in a number of countries (Italy, Germany, US); and the period 2004–2007, characterised instead by positive cyclical conditions, reaching their peak in 2007, when the US started to slow down.

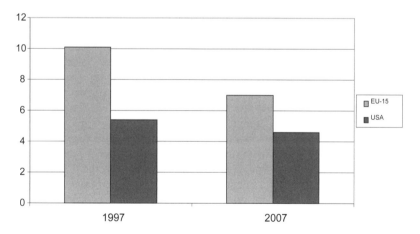

Figure 5.3 Unemployment Rate in EU vs. USA, 1997–2007

Table 5.2 shows how the USA tend to adjust their cycle through changes in the labour market to a greater extent (from –0.43 to 1.27), while the EU has kept the labour market growing even in the downturn of the early 2000s, consistently with the 'bias' towards labour previously detected.

Table 5.2 Lisbon Decomposed

	2000–2003		2004–2007	
	Employm grw	LabProd grw	Employm grw	LabProd grw
France	−0.25	2.2	0.775	1.425
Germany	−0.73	1.8	0.575	1.25
Italy	1.10	0.4	1.025	0.35
Poland	−2.25	4.9	2.725	2.625
Spain	3.00	0.6	2.5	1.05
UK	0.25	2.4	0.75	1.95
USA	−0.43	2.6	1.275	1.5
EU	0.58	1.4	1.125	1.175

The latter tendency for Europe is also confirmed if we look at the volatility of the growth rates of employment and productivity over the two business cycles of the 1990s and the 2000s. Figure 5.4 measures volatility as the standard deviation of quarterly GDP growth rates over eleven quarters, which allows us to compare results obtained with country characteristics over the same periods. A decline in output volatility is a clear trend, with the decline more pronounced in the more volatile economies, so that the variance diminished dramatically from the 1960s to the 2000s, a phenomenon often referred to as 'great moderation'.

Within this general trend, which puts the US in a comparable general perspective with the EU, we can again decompose the volatility of the growth rates over the cycle for each component of growth. Carrying such an exercise, we see that the reduction in US volatility derives from a drop in volatility of both productivity and the labour market.

However, when compared to the EU, the US maintains a relatively higher volatility of labour markets adjustment both with respect to their productivity, and with respect to the EU-15 (see Figure 5.5 below). The latter confirms that adjustments to cyclical conditions in the US are likely to pass through the labour markets, at least to a higher extent than with respect to the EU-15. The recent evidence of the impressive surge of unemployment in the US as a reaction to the 2008–2009 crisis confirms this structural characteristic of the US economy.

Conversely, given the political economy bias previously mentioned, the Euro-area has kept an 'artificially' low volatility of its labour markets for both decades, with a worrying increase in the volatility of the productivity component, coupled with growth rates of productivity in the second part of the Lisbon period decreasing rather than increasing (from 1.4 to 1.17 for the euro-area).

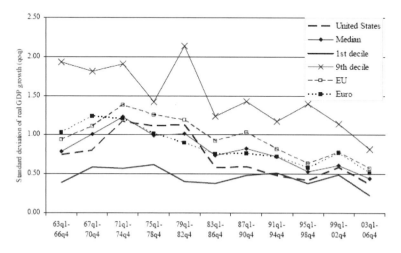

Source: Debrun et al. (2008).

Figure 5.4 Volatility of Output, Different Countries, 1960–2000

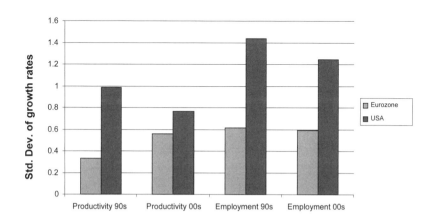

Figure 5.5 Volatility of Growth Components, EU and US

There is therefore the clear risk that the cyclical adjustment to the economic downturn in Europe takes place through investments, rather than the labour markets, with further depression of productivity growth rates, and dire implications for the future prospects of growth. Upgrading the capital stock might in fact be more costly than reabsorbing unemployment, due to the need to finance it at the (presumably) higher interest rates associated with the economic recovery. The emphasis the EU Commission is putting on preserving jobs is thus a perfectly understandable signal from a social and political point of view, not a good one if one aims at a speedy recovery of the EU economy.

On a more optimistic note, however, another political economy argument regarding the relationships between the Lisbon Strategy and the Recovery Plan can be made. In essence, provided that good reforms can be identified, as discussed above, it is likely that the current financial and economic crisis can achieve a higher effectiveness of the same reforms.

The central role in our argument is the status quo effect. In general, status quo in politics is a big obstacle to good reforms, due to the general reluctance of people to abandon current status for changes that are intrinsically uncertain, in the sense that they may lead to improvements, but also to losses. In other words, people are usually risk averse, as far as political reforms are concerned.

As a consequence of this reluctance to changes, policymakers are used to preserve the status quo, even when this is not the right thing to do. For example, protection of mature and low productive sectors is politically preferred to strategic reconversion to new, dynamic and more productive industries. In this case, the cost of the change is mainly represented by the cost of moving labour force from the old industries to the new ones. At the microeconomic level, this is the cost of dismissing a low productive worker in a declining industry, retraining him and re-hiring him in a new and more productive sector. One could call this the cost of abandoning the status quo. Our argument is that, in a situation of economic crisis, this cost is lower because a certain amount of dismissals is going to occur in any case.

Thus, the cost of changing the status quo for implementing good reforms is lower in crisis situations. This lowers the political cost of the change consistently, and paradoxically, this makes feasible the implementation of ambitious strategies for improving the productivity of the entire economic system. Therefore, as odd as it may seem, this is the period in which the reforms of the Lisbon Strategy are more viable from a political viewpoint.

2. CONCLUSION: A MULTI-LEVEL GOVERNANCE FOR THE EU FISCAL POLICY

We have seen that the extraordinary crisis the world economy has gone through in 2008 and 2009 has called for extraordinary actions in economic policy at the EU level, and namely the resurrection of a discretionary fiscal policy on a continental basis as the only viable response to the current phase of economic turbulence. Such a policy however still suffers from a number of well-known drawbacks: a coordination problem, induced by the possibility of free riding by member states on the fiscal policy actions; and a consistency problem, since the expenditures undertaken by countries are not necessarily the first-best solutions to the long-run prescriptions foreseen within the Lisbon Strategy for Growth and Jobs.

Interestingly, both problems arise from political economy considerations, to the extent that the structure of national incentives for national governments is not in line with EU-wide needs. As has already been discussed, an ideal solution to this problem would be a federal, centrally managed set-up for fiscal policies, with the ability of the EU to generate consistent deficits on the Union's budget. However, we are all aware that such a set-up is not possible within the current institutional framework, since the EU does not have a federal political system.

Therefore, the EU might try to overcome the problem in the effective use of fiscal tools through some forms of coordination at the various stages of the economic policy decisions, a concept well-known to political scientist as 'multi-level' planning. First of all, since as already discussed the Commission has a limited role in influencing member states' actions on fiscal issues, the crisis has shown the important role played to this extent by the Eurogroup. As it is known, since not all EU members participate in the euro-area, the Eurogroup has been created at the Council level to deal with co-ordination at the euro-area level.[10] In October 2008, under the French Presidency, the Eurogroup (for the occasion enlarged to the UK) has been instrumental in engineering a coordinated response to the financial crisis that has greatly contributed to resurrecting financial markets, stopping the panic on the market and paving the way for more structural actions then undertaken by each member state in the form of banks' recapitalisation. The Commission has then stepped in providing the necessary guidelines, under competition rules, for such actions.

The coordinated response, involving different levels of governance and different competences, has been insofar appropriate to constitute a minimal set of responses to the current crisis. However, other steps can be undertaken.

At the member states' level, and for the reasons previously stated, the fiscal policy actions undertaken should be clearly and more directly linked to the annual monitoring exercise of the Lisbon Action Plans undertaken by the Commission. A greater ability to enforce eventual changes in the direction of these plans might be envisaged to this extent. We have pointed out that during crisis periods, the political cost of implementing good reforms tends to be low. Reforms are more feasible, and citizens are less reluctant to change the status quo. Thus, policymakers may try to be more strategic and ambitious while supporting recovery, avoiding to generate a trade-off between actions aimed at protecting employment and the necessary support of private firms' investments.

At the Council level, the Eurogroup should be used more frequently, and eventually at the level of Heads of State and Governments, as for the case under the French Presidency, to ensure a first nucleus of coordinated fiscal policy at the continental level, thus extending the scope of the reinforced cooperation already constituted by the euro.

Finally, within the governance of this strengthened Eurogroup, some explicit form of centralisation of fiscal policy at the EU level could be designed via specific tools, and namely the possibility to raise EU-level debt managed directly by the EU institutions.

One possibility in this direction is represented by the so-called *Eurobonds*. These, in the community jargon, are additional sources of funding outside the budget of the member states (that is, outside the requirements of the Growth and Stability Pact) that can finance initiatives of a strategic trans-European interest, for example transport networks or the initiatives under the national plans for the implementation of the Lisbon Strategy. Unlike all other sources of funding (VAT resource, GNP – Gross National Product – etc.) they do not have a clear 'national' identification, and therefore they are likely not to be included in the usual battles on the net balances within the EU budget. Rather, since the subscription of Eurobonds would be voluntary, they would constitute a sort of market test of the European initiatives that Eurobonds are earmarked to fund.

More specifically, the Eurobonds could be generated in two ways:

- Guarantee instruments for financing private venture capital, dedicated to specific initiatives which would repay the investment with income, like the already approved Instrument for Loan Guarantee of the Trans-European Transport network projects (LGTT), funded with €1 billion from the EIB (European International Bank) and the EU Budget (50 per cent each). One might think of an extension of such instruments within the budget structure, and equal spending commitments, that is, dedicating to Chapter 1a (Competitiveness and Growth) the savings possibly achieved by the reform of Chapter 1b (cohesion) of the budget, at least for the part of funds still going to the EU-15.

- Proper debt instruments, and namely bonds officially emitted by the EU institutions. The maturity of the bonds could then be equal to the period of financial programming, namely seven years, with bonds emitted at the beginning of each programming period.

In the latter case, and in general once these instruments become part of the EU budget, their use should be reconciled with art. 268 of the Treaty, which explicitly foresees equal annual revenues and expenditures. To this extent, one could take advantage of the provision embedded in the new Lisbon Treaty which 'institutionalises' the multi-annual financial perspectives, and accordingly extend the interpretation of art. 268, in the sense that a zero net budget balance has to be achieved not yearly, but within the seven-year horizon. Alternatively, if these instruments are placed outside the EU budget, contributions to member states as security-repayment of principal and debt service should be clearly recorded outside the rules of the Growth and Stability Pact, requiring a specific intergovernmental agreement as for the division of the financial charges and their beneficiaries.

NOTES

1. The Commission is transferring resources not required under the ceiling of heading 2 (Agriculture) in respect of the year 2008 to heading 1A (Competiveness), in order to fund €3.5 billion between 2009 and 2010 for energy and broadband infrastructural projects. The remaining €1.5 billion will remain under heading 2 to finance infrastructures in rural areas.
2. Zuleeg and Martens in Chapter 6 of this volume discuss the long-run implications of fiscal policy in terms of sustainability for the EU budgets.
3. These extreme views are however controversial in the literature, with a debate still ongoing on the extent to which volatility matters for welfare and the long-run growth of an economy.
4. The tax-smoothing optimal rule of public finance maintains that since it is not optimal to continuously change the tax rate in order to balance the budget, deteriorations and improvements in budget balances are used as a buffer to accommodate the effect of cyclical fluctuations of economic activity.
5. See Alesina and Perotti (1995) and Persson and Tabellini (2004) for a more detailed discussion.
6. When a government is able to print money (for example because it influences the central bank), it is in essence borrowing interest-free, since it receives goods today in exchange for the money, and must accept the money in return (when the consumers use the money for their transactions) only at some future time. In addition, the government gains further if in issuing new money it creates inflation, since the latter reduces the real value of its debts.
7. See Beetsma (2001) and Canzoneri and Diba (1996), as reported in Sapir et al. (2004).

8. See Zuleeg and Martens in Chapter 6 of this volume for a discussion of the long-run sustainability of public finances and the role played by automatic stabilizers.
9. The potential growth rate can be obtained by the simple sum of the employment growth (1.5 per cent) and the productivity growth (1 per cent) rates.
10. The Eurogroup consists of the Ministers of Finance of the euro-area member states alongside the Commissioner for Economic and Monetary Affairs and the President of the ECB. The Eurogroup has no role in the conduct of monetary policy, which is in the remit of the ECB. From the outset, the Eurogroup has had an informal status in the sense that it does not venture into voting on policy, but rather prepares such voting by the Ecofin (Economic and Financial Affair Council).

BIBLIOGRAPHY

Alesina, Albert and Roberto Perotti (1995), *The Political Economy of Budget Deficits*, IMF Staff Papers, no. 42, 1–31.

Altomonte, Carlo and Mario Nava (2005), *Economics and Policies of an Enlarged Europe*, Cheltenham, UK and Northampton, MA, USA: Edward Elgar Publishing.

Altomonte, Carlo and Mario Nava (2008), *Bruxelles Salva Wall Street? La Governance dell'Economia Europea e la Crisi Finanziaria*, ISPI Policy Brief no. 99, Milano.

Beetsma, Roel (2001), *Does EMU Need a Stability Pact?* in A., Brunila, M. Buti and D. Franco (eds), *The Stability and Growth Pact*, Palgrave: Houndsmills.

Blinder, Alan S. and Robert M. Solow (1974), *Analytical Foundation of Fiscal Policy* in Blinder A. et al., *The Economics of Public Finance*, The Brookings Institution.

Buti, Marco and André Sapir (1998), *Economic Policy in EMU*, Oxford: Oxford University Press.

Cohen, Daniel and Charles Wyplosz (1989), *European Monetary Union: An Agnostic Evaluation*, CEPR Discussion Paper, no. 306, London.

Debrun, Xavier, Jean Pisani-Ferry and André Sapir (2008), *Government Size and Output Volatility: Should we Forsake Automatic Stabilization?*, European Economy, Economic Papers no. 316, Bruxelles.

Hagen, Jürgen von and Suzanne Mundschenk (2001), *The Functioning of Economic Policy Coordination*, Bonn: Center for European Integration Studies (ZEI).

Jacquet, Pierre and Jean Pisani-Ferry (2001), *Economic Policy Coordination in the Eurozone: What Has Been Achieved? What Should Be Done?*, London: Centre for European Reform.

Larch, Martin and Alessandro Turrini (2008), *Received Wisdom and Beyond: Lessons from Fiscal Consolidation in the EU*, European Economy, Economic Papers no. 320, Bruxelles.

Mandl Ulrike, Adriaan Dierx and Fabienne Ilzkovitz (2008), *The Effectiveness and Efficiency of Public Spending*, European Economy, Economic Papers no. 301, Bruxelles.

Persson, Torsten and Guido Tabellini (2004), 'Constitutional rules and fiscal policy outcomes', *American Economic Review*, **94** (1), 25–45.

Sapir, André et al. (2004), *An Agenda for a Growing Europe: the Sapir Report*, Oxford: Oxford University Press (better known as the *Sapir Report*).

Sargent, Thomas J. and Neill Wallace (1981), 'Some unpleasant Monetarist arithmetic', *Federal Reserve Bank of Minneapolis Quarterly Review*, no. 5, 1–17.

6. Beyond the Current Crisis: How Should Europe Deal with Government Deficits and Public Debt in Future?

Fabian Zuleeg and Hans Martens

1. INTRODUCTION

The current financial crisis, triggered originally by the sub-prime crisis in the US, has necessitated many governments around the world taking over banks' assets and liabilities and guaranteeing debts. Governments have responded to the 'credit crunch' by injecting capital into the financial sector to combat the lack of lending. By the end of 2008, the financial crisis had clearly spilled over into the real economy, with most economies being hit by lower growth. Europe and the US have moved into recession, accompanied by a marked deterioration in labour markets. In response to the deteriorating economic environment, many governments have put together fiscal stimulus programmes, in essence cutting taxes and/or increasing government spending.

These government responses to the financial sector crisis have required large injections of capital and governments taking over bank liabilities. At the same time, the fiscal stimulus, in combination with the deteriorating real economy, has led to a deterioration of public finances. This has largely been financed by increases in government debt with the deficit and debt situation likely to deteriorate further in the coming months.

Instead of focusing on the current crisis,[1] this chapter examines the long term implications of the crisis for European fiscal policy. In particular, it argues that the long-term focus of the EU should be on reinforcing the need for more 'prudent' public finances once the current crisis has passed.

1.1 The Impact of the Crisis on Public Deficits and National Debt

Current debt and deficit forecasts vary significantly and it is difficult to obtain reliable economic data. But what is clear is that current levels of deficits and government debts in the EU and the US will be revised upwards rapidly in the coming months as governments start to spend more and tax less to deal with the economic downturn. In addition, significant doubts remain over the longer-term impact of governments taking over bank liabilities and guaranteeing saving deposits or inter-bank loans. This might add a significant amount of debt if governments are forced to prop up the financial sector even further.

It is already clear that the deficit and debt levels which will be reached, especially in the US and the EU, are very significant. For example, recent estimates in Germany speculate that the current stimulus programmes could increase debt by €200bn over the next four years, not even taking into account the additional measures being discussed in January 2009 (*Der Spiegel* 2008). In January 2009, a German fiscal stimulus package of €50bn was announced, as well as a €100bn loan guarantee scheme for businesses (BBC Online 2009b). Similarly, in the UK, as far back as in October, there was speculation that the budget deficit might be as high as £ 64 billion next year (McNeill, 2008). Public borrowing is set to increase dramatically from £ 37bn in 2007–2008, to £ 78bn in 2008–2009 and £ 118bn in 2009–2010, equivalent to 8 per cent of Gross Domestic Product (GDP) in 2009–2010. Net debt will rise from 36 per cent of GDP in 2008–09 to 57 per cent in 2012–2013 (*The Economist* 2008). The US situation is even more dramatic – the projected deficit is $1.2 trillion in 2009, more than 8 per cent of GDP. The fiscal stimulus programme proposed by Barack Obama will add further to this, going well beyond a deficit of 10 per cent of GDP (Guha, Luce and Ward 2009).

It is important to emphasise that this chapter, like others in the volume, does not argue against using fiscal policy proactively in the current crisis. The current crisis is not a 'normal' cyclical downturn and government responses have to be adapted accordingly. The action of governments to prop up the financial sector was necessary to prevent the drying up of flows of capital and loans, which are the lifeblood of modern economies. Equally, there is a requirement to use fiscal policy proactively to mitigate some of the impact of the current crisis. A detailed examination of the EU fiscal stimulus programmes is beyond the scope of this chapter (although the authors believe that such a coordinated EU response is desirable, see Zuleeg and Martens 2008). Chapter 5 in this volume provides a detailed examination of the impact of the crisis on EU fiscal policy and the compatibility of the fiscal stimulus programmes with the Lisbon Agenda.

The focus in our chapter is on the longer term – what principles should underpin long-term fiscal policy in the EU?

1.2 Focus of the Chapter

Even though there are justifiable pressures for a more expansive fiscal policy as a part of combating the effect of the economic crises, in the long term such an approach is not sustainable. The US approach, discussed later in this chapter, should serve as an example not to be followed. While in the short term, additional debt to finance tax cuts and higher public spending might be necessary, in the medium to long-term countries should return to more prudent fiscal policies, not least to reduce the debt which is being accumulated now. This chapter focuses on the political economy of discretionary fiscal policies, examining its interaction with fiscal consolidation and long term sustainability of public finances. There is a particular focus on the management of fiscal balances and national debt within the euro-area context.

The chapter examines the question of how to best design economic governance mechanisms in the EU to ensure such a return to more prudent policies. Currently, within the EU governance structure, these issues are almost exclusively managed at member state level but in light of the increasing interdependence of European economies, especially in the euro-area, a new approach is necessary. One country's fiscal policy decision will now have a direct impact on other countries through the common interest rate and through spill-over effects, for example trade flows, competition and even business and consumer confidence, raising the question of fiscal policy coordination within the euro-area to potentially overcome economic governance issues.

This chapter does not attempt an econometric examination of the relationship between the different factors, driven by a conviction that there is only limited continuity in the macroeconomic framework, for example with the creation of the EMU (Economic and Monetary Union) and the current financial crisis. Rather this chapter focuses on the political economy questions, investigating political incentives and mechanisms which drive decisions in the EU and using empirical data to illustrate the arguments.[2] The chapter also explicitly attempts to come up with policy recommendations to improve the long-term governance of fiscal policy in the EU.

2. GLOBAL AND EU POLICY CONTEXT

To examine the EU's current and future fiscal policy position, it is useful to contrast the EU position with the US. The US has come out of a recent period of deficit-financed expansion, which has led to a significant deterioration of its debt situation even before the current crisis hit.

2.1 The US Experience: From Bad to Worse

This economic and financial crisis was triggered by a crisis in the sub-prime mortgage market in the US, where personal debt was available to people even on low incomes, based on a rising property market. Much of the recent growth in the US was consumption-led, often financed by debt and securitised on speculative assets. But it was not just households that indulged in debt-financed expansion: businesses also financed expansion through loan-financing. The fiscal policy pursued by the Bush administrations did little to counterbalance the developments in the private sector with government running an unprecedented deficit. The additional goods and services consumed in the US were produced abroad and as a result the balance of trade deficit for the US also increased to unprecedented levels. This resulted in a triple deficit in the US economy: the current account deficit, the government deficit and the household deficit.

Although there have been periods of slight improvement, the Bush administration has overseen a US government deficit equivalent to a permanent 'fiscal stimulus package'. The economic stimulus arising from a large government deficit has contributed to the jobs and growth performance in recent years, but it has also meant an accumulation of public debt, which makes it more difficult to face the challenges of the current financial and economic crisis. Fiscal policies have led to the US deficit outpacing the EU's annual deficit in recent years:

This has also resulted in the overall level of US public debt now being higher (as a percentage of GDP) than that in the EU.

The American experience illustrates that the real economy can be boosted by debt-financed spending for a period of time, but at the cost of fiscal stability. It also illustrates the resulting danger of not being able to react adequately to a downturn without further jeopardising public finances. The US deficit will reach above 10 per cent of GDP during 2009 because of the costs of the various financial and economic rescue packages in combination with a pre-existing imbalance between spending and revenue. This creates a position for the US, which makes recovery difficult with repayment of debt needing to start as soon as the economy picks up again. It could also put a strain on monetary policy if higher interest rates are needed to raise the necessary debt.

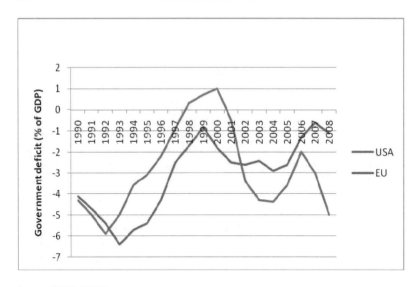

Source: OECD (2008).

Figure 6.1 US and EU Government Deficit

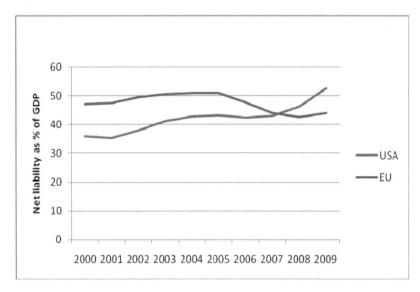

Source: OECD (2008).

Figure 6.2 Central Government Net Liability

There are clear political economy explanations for these past policies. Firstly, there can be no doubt that stimulating growth and jobs through consumption has been politically popular in the US – at least until the crisis began. Secondly, there was additional pressure on public finances through steep increases in public expenses arising from new public policy priorities: to finance the war against terror, including military and rebuilding operations in Afghanistan and Iraq. Thirdly, there appears to be a bias against tax increases in the US political system. In fact, in the recent past, populist tax cuts have been more common. Often, these cuts went alongside a belief that they would sufficiently stimulate the economy to be revenue-neutral. However, it is clear that this has not been the case. The result of this overall bias towards deficit-financed spending has resulted in the record deficits that are now recorded.

Given the strong aversion to tax increases in the US population, it will be difficult to re-balance the budget by tax increases in the future. This reduces the ability to focus efforts on proactive fiscal policies as fiscal consolidation will have to rely on cutting expenditure, which can be difficult to achieve within the context of a relatively small state (in relation to GDP).

But in the medium term, once the current crisis has passed, the US will have to address these serious fiscal imbalances. To do this will require political leadership as well as setting the right strategic direction now: 'higher spending and tax cuts will only make a big budget deficit even bigger. This danger does not justify penny-pinching now: that could merely prompt a bigger collapse in economic activity and even larger deficits. But Mr Obama should do what Mr Bush never did and link the upcoming splurge to long term fiscal reform' (*The Economist* 2009).

2.2 The European Experience: From Bad to Slightly Better

Many European countries face similar issues. Europe has had its share of unsustainable fiscal policies, resulting in very high levels of public debt relative to GDP in countries like Italy, Greece and Belgium. But it is noticeable that recent fiscal policies in Europe have been significantly different from the US. Table 6.1 shows that public debt as a percentage of GDP has gone down significantly.

The table clearly shows that, with the exception of the new member states which generally started at a lower level of debt, most member states have reduced debt over the last decade. The exceptions are France, Germany and Portugal, as well as Greece where the ratio has remained at about the same level. Very significant reductions have taken place in Denmark and Belgium (almost 35 percentage points), Ireland, Sweden and Spain (almost 30 percentage points) and the Netherlands (20 percentage

Liberalism in Crisis?

points). It also shows that some countries are still above 60 per cent: of the old member states, Italy, Greece and Belgium are significantly above 60 per cent, with Portugal, France and Germany just above this level.

Table 6.1 Nominal Government Debt (per cent of GDP)

	1998	1999	2000	2001	2002	2003	2004	2005	2006	2007
EU27	66.4	65.8	61.9	61.0	60.3	61.8	62.2	62.7	61.3	58.7
Belgium	117.1	113.6	107.8	106.5	103.5	98.7	94.3	92.1	87.8	83.9
Bulgaria	79.6	79.3	74.3	67.3	53.6	45.9	37.9	29.2	22.7	18.2
Czech Rep.	15.0	16.4	18.5	25.1	28.5	30.1	30.4	29.8	29.6	28.9
Denmark	60.8	57.4	51.5	48.7	48.3	45.8	43.8	36.4	30.5	26.2
Germany	60.3	60.9	59.7	58.8	60.3	63.8	65.6	67.8	67.6	65.1
Estonia	5.5	6.0	5.2	4.8	5.7	5.6	5.0	4.5	4.3	3.5
Ireland	53.6	48.5	37.8	35.5	32.2	31.1	29.4	27.3	24.7	24.8
Greece	94.5	94.0	103.4	103.7	101.5	97.8	98.6	98.8	95.9	94.8
Spain	64.1	62.3	59.3	55.5	25.5	48.7	46.2	43.0	39.6	36.2
France	59.4	58.8	57.3	56.9	58.8	62.9	64.9	66.4	63.6	63.9
Italy	114.9	113.7	109.2	108.8	105.7	104.4	103.8	105.9	106.9	104.1
Cyprus	58.6	58.9	58.8	60.7	64.6	68.9	70.2	69.1	64.6	59.5
Latvia	9.6	12.5	12.3	14.0	13.5	14.6	14.9	12.4	10.7	9.5
Lithuania	16.6	22.8	23.7	23.1	22.3	21.1	19.4	18.4	18.0	17.0
Luxembourg	7.1	6.4	6.2	6.3	6.3	6.1	6.3	6.1	6.6	7.0
Hungary	62.0	61.1	54.2	52.1	55.8	58.1	59.4	61.7	65.6	65.8
Malta	53.4	57.1	55.9	62.1	60.1	69.3	72.1	69.9	63.8	62.2
Netherlands	65.7	61.1	53.8	50.7	50.5	52.0	52.4	51.8	47.4	45.7
Austria	64.8	67.2	66.5	67.1	66.5	65.5	64.8	63.7	62.0	59.5
Poland	38.9	39.6	36.8	37.6	42.2	47.1	45.7	47.1	47.7	44.9
Portugal	52.1	51.4	50.5	52.9	55.6	56.9	58.3	63.6	64.7	63.6
Romania	16.6	21.9	22.6	26.0	25.0	21.5	18.8	15.8	12.4	12.9
Slovenia	n/a	n/a	n/a	26.8	28.0	27.5	27.2	27.0	26.7	23.4
Slovakia	34.5	47.8	50.3	48.9	43.4	42.4	41.4	34.2	30.4	29.4
Finland	48.2	45.5	43.8	42.3	41.3	44.3	44.1	41.3	39.2	35.1
Sweden	69.1	64.8	53.6	54.4	52.6	52.3	51.2	50.9	45.9	40.4
UK	46.7	43.7	41.0	37.7	37.5	38.7	40.6	42.3	43.4	44.2

Source: Eurostat (2008a).

There are a number of reasons for these trends. It is clear that in some countries the positive development can be clearly attributed to a booming economy. For example, Ireland experienced a period of high sustained growth in recent years and had consequently reduced the debt to GDP ratio significantly. Countries which had slower economic growth, such as Germany and France, have had the opposite experience. Other countries have put strong domestic political emphasis on reducing debt, for example Belgium. Scandinavian countries have also been successful in reducing debt for different reasons. Outside the EU, Norway has been very successful in running surpluses, driven by oil and gas revenues. For the other Scandinavian countries the sound position of public finances as a public policy priority has emerged through a combination of the success of labour market policies (such as the Danish Flexicurity model) which have reduced unemployment, and a political decision of governments to not reduce taxation (despite reasonably good economic circumstances) at least until national debt will have been substantially reduced.

Clearly, one of the driving forces behind more 'prudent' public finances has been Economic and Monetary Union. The Maastricht Treaty, signed in 1992, set the course for the introduction of the euro in 1999. By early 2009, the majority of EU countries had joined the euro,[3] being governed by a common monetary policy administered by the European Central Bank.

To join the euro-area, countries have to fulfil the so-called Maastricht criteria, which contain explicit rules about debt: a country should have a debt-to-GDP ratio of less than 60 per cent (or if the country has higher debt due to special circumstances, the ratio should show a significant trend in the right direction) and an annual deficit not exceeding 3 per cent (with possible temporary exceptions in case of special circumstances).

These rules are enshrined at European level in the Stability and Growth Pact (SGP). The SGP was signed in 1997 at the insistence of the German Government to underpin the euro with an economic framework designed to ensure the strength of the new currency. However, the Framework proved to be too strict for most European countries. France and Germany struggled with the 3 per cent limit repeatedly, particularly from 2003 onwards. As a result there was a revision of the SGP in 2005. The result was more flexibility and a more long-term focus but also a distinctive role for the Commission in monitoring member states' public finances and in making policy recommendations to address imbalances.

The SGP sets out how the Excessive Deficit Procedure (EDP) is applied to member states when they have a deficit in excess of 3 per cent of GDP. If a decision is taken that the deficit is excessive, 'the Council issues recommendations to the member states concerned to correct the excessive deficit and gives a time frame for doing so. Non compliance with the recommendations triggers further steps in the procedures, including for euro-area member states the possibility of sanctions' (European Commission, Stability and Growth Pact 2008).

Up until the economic and financial crisis, the Maastricht Criteria and the SGP seem to have encouraged countries to move in the right direction. While certain countries have struggled, the average EU annual deficit has been kept close to or within the bounds of the SGP:

Liberalism in Crisis?

Table 6.2 Net Lending (+) and Net Borrowing (−) (per cent of GDP)

	1998	1999	2000	2001	2002	2003	2004	2005	2006	2007
EU27	−1.9	−1.0	0.2	−1.4	−2.5	−3.1	−2.9	−2.5	−1.4	−0.9
Belgium	−0.9	−0.6	0.0	0.4	−0.1	−0.1	−0.3	−2.7	0.3	−0.3
Bulgaria	1.7	0.4	−0.5	0.2	−0.8	−0.3	1.6	1.9	3.0	0.1
Czech Republic	−5.0	−3.7	−3.7	−5.7	−6.8	−6.6	−2.9	−3.6	−2.7	−1.0
Denmark	0.0	1.4	2.3	1.2	0.2	−0.1	1.9	5.0	5.0	4.4
Germany	−2.2	−1.5	1.3	−2.8	−3.7	−4.0	−3.8	−3.3	−1.5	−0.2
Estonia	−0.7	−3.5	−0.2	−0.1	0.3	1.7	1.7	1.5	2.9	2.7
Ireland	2.3	2.6	4.7	1.0	−0.3	0.5	1.4	1.7	3.0	0.2
Greece	−3.8	−3.1	−3.7	−4.4	−4.8	−5.7	−7.4	−5.2	−3.1	−3.8
Spain	−3.2	−1.4	−1.0	0.7	−0.5	−0.2	−0.4	1.0	2.0	2.2
France	−2.6	−1.8	−1.5	−1.6	−3.2	−4.1	−3.6	−3.0	−2.4	−2.7
Italy	−3.1	−1.8	−0.9	−3.1	−3.0	−3.5	−3.6	−4.4	−3.4	−1.5
Cyprus	−4.1	−4.3	−2.3	−2.2	−4.4	−6.5	−4.1	−2.4	−1.2	3.5
Latvia	0.0	−3.9	−2.8	−2.1	−2.3	−1.6	−1.0	−0.4	−0.2	0.1
Lithuania	−3.1	−2.8	−3.2	−3.6	−1.9	−1.3	−1.5	−0.5	−0.4	−1.2
Luxembourg	3.4	3.4	6.0	6.1	2.1	0.5	−1.2	−0.1	1.3	3.2
Hungary	−8.2	−5.5	−2.9	−4.1	−9.0	−7.2	−6.4	−7.8	−9.3	−4.9
Malta	−9.9	−7.7	−6.2	−6.4	−5.5	−9.8	−4.7	−2.8	−2.3	−1.8
Netherlands	−0.9	0.4	2.0	−0.3	−2.1	−3.2	−1.8	−0.3	0.6	0.3
Austria	−2.5	−2.4	−1.9	−0.2	−0.9	−1.6	−4.5	−1.6	−1.7	−0.5
Poland	−4.3	−2.3	−3.0	−5.1	−5.0	−6.3	−5.7	−4.3	−3.8	−2.0
Portugal	−3.4	−2.8	−3.0	−4.3	−2.9	−3.0	−3.4	−6.1	−3.9	−2.7
Romania	−3.2	−4.5	−4.4	−3.5	−2.0	−1.5	−1.2	−1.2	−2.2	−2.6
Slovenia	−2.4	−3.1	−3.7	−4.0	−2.5	−2.7	−2.2	−1.4	−1.2	0.5
Slovakia	−5.3	−7.4	−12.3	−6.5	−8.2	−2.7	−2.3	−2.8	−3.5	−1.9
Finland	1.7	1.6	6.9	5.0	4.1	2.4	2.2	2.7	4.0	5.3
Sweden	1.2	1.2	3.7	1.7	−1.4	−1.2	0.6	2.1	2.2	3.5
UK	−0.1	0.9	1.4	0.6	−1.9	3.3	−3.4	3.3	−2.6	−2.7

Source: Eurostat (2008a).

But this masks a wide divergence in approaches. Focusing on the old member states, there are a number of countries which have run a deficit persistently over the last decade: Germany (with the exception of 2000 but above the 3 per cent from 2002 to 2005), Greece (which has been persistently above the 3 per cent), France (above 3 per cent from 2002 to 2005), Italy (3 per cent or above for the majority of the period), Austria (above 3 per cent in 2004) and Portugal (3 per cent or above for the majority of the period). A few countries have run surpluses for most of the period: Denmark, Ireland, Luxembourg, Finland and Sweden.

Overall, the data seems consistent with the 3 per cent limit helping to control deficits but domestic policy issues still play a significant role in the fiscal policy field: 'Domestic economic and political conditions are crucial determinants of fiscal policy and fiscal adjustment strategies despite the strict provisions of the Stability Pact' (Mulas-Granados 2006).

It is also noticeable that there seems little direct link between the business cycle and fiscal consolidation in most countries. Rather, certain countries seem to have long periods of imbalance while others seem to have made a political decision to consolidate public finances over the period. Only the Nordic countries and Ireland seemed to be committed consistently to fiscal consolidation in the last decade while the large continental economies and the Mediterranean economies – with the exception of Spain – have struggled.

But overall, progress has been made in the EU. This progress reflects, in part, the political commitment made under the SGP but domestic policy priorities also clearly played a part. In the UK, the Labour Government which came to power in 1997 pledged to keep 'prudent' public finances and introduced the so-called Golden Rule which states that over the economic cycle, any borrowing will only be used to invest and not to fund current spending. The German Grand Coalition which came to power in 2005 included plans to cut spending and increase VAT (Value Added Tax) to bring the deficit under the Maastricht limit and subsequently committed to achieving a balanced budget. Consequently, the German budget deficit reduced significantly in 2006 and 2007.

However, not all administrations have been as supportive of the objectives of the SGP. The 2008 French budget, proposed in September 2007, still contained a deficit of 2.3 per cent of GDP despite being based on a positive growth forecast of 2–2.5 per cent for 2008 – and this growth rate was over-optimistic even then (*The Economist* 2008). President Sarkozy argued in the middle of 2007 that the French Government could not achieve a balanced budget by 2010 and that the rules should be relaxed for France (BBC Online 2007).

This, in part, reflects the difference in economic situation which still persists across Europe. Economically, the last decade has been a difficult period for the big euro-area economies – France, Germany and Italy. Not only were these countries affected by cyclical downturns but they have also suffered from significant structural problems. For example, all these countries have persistently high levels of unemployment, which also affects public finances negatively.

But even when member states have argued for a relaxation of the SGP, it shows the step change which had been achieved before the current crisis hit. The mere fact that member state deficits are discussed and that individual governments have to justify their approach at the EU level is a significant departure from the past. With the SGP, fiscal consolidation had become a more generally accepted part of economic policy in Europe and better public finances have also enabled EU economies to respond to the crisis with greater freedom of movement.

While many EU countries had made significant progress in addressing their fiscal imbalances in recent years, the economic and financial crisis has the potential to undo much of what has been achieved. The current debate on the SGP is illustrative in this context. The Commission has already noted that the provisions will be applied flexibly in line with the 'special circumstance' clause which is already included. But some countries have argued strongly that the long-term goals of the SGP need to be set aside in the current crisis: 'the Growth and Stability Pact should be implemented flexibly. This would not demand any lengthy discussion since the Pact provides room for manoeuvre in the short term which must be used. The time for developing a genuine budget recovery plan will come later' (Merkel and Sarkozy 2008). Presumably this is to give themselves more freedom of movement without boundaries being imposed at EU level.

There has also been an argument that fiscal consolidation is not possible in the current climate. This might well be true in the short term but in the medium to long term, the current spending spree will have to be paid for. Recent European experience demonstrates that fiscal consolidation is possible even in difficult economic times if there is political will. The experience of a number of EU countries, especially in Scandinavia, shows that neither the overall size of public spending nor the decision to invest heavily in public services necessarily goes hand-in-hand with higher deficits.

The current crisis should thus not be taken as a signal that fiscal consolidation and sound public policies are no longer required. Rather, it emphasises that it is necessary to take a fresh look at fiscal policy and, in particular, to examine what principles should underpin fiscal policy once the current crisis has passed.

3. FISCAL POLICY LIMITATIONS

After the current crisis has passed, there will be a political and economic debate in Europe on how to deal with the accumulated debt and whether fiscal policy should be more countercyclical on a permanent basis. There are already voices which see the current crisis as permanently reintroducing Keynesian demand management to European economic policy.

There are serious limitations to this approach, not least because of the debt which will be accumulated in the coming months. The EU should also not just focus on the short term but should start preparing for the long-term future challenges such as demographic change and its implications for health and pension provision, as well as challenges of adapting to climate change and moving towards a low carbon economy.

The key questions examined in this section are:

- How effective is countercyclical fiscal policy likely to be in Europe once the current crisis has passed?
- Are current debt and deficit levels (pre- and post-crisis) consistent with Europe's economic structure and long-term trends?
- Can European governments accumulate assets to deal with future challenges and to deliver the high levels of public services citizens want?

In examining these questions, the chapter will look into the changing nature of the political economy of EU fiscal policy, as well as attempting to identify salient features which will play a prominent role in future. In doing this, it is important to acknowledge that current data and policy only provides us with limited information about the future, given the changing nature of the economic and political environment.

3.1 Traditional Counter-cyclical Policy

The current crisis has triggered a revival of more traditional fiscal policy approaches, marking to some extent the return of countercyclical fiscal policy, often labelled Keynesian demand management, as a proactive tool to manage the economy: 'after more than three decades in the wilderness, Keynesian-style fiscal policy seems to be making a come-back' (*The Economist* 2008d). Countercyclical policies explicitly aim to stabilise economic cycles by providing a boost to demand in the economy in economic downturns, balancing the books through higher revenue in the upturn. Higher spending and lower taxes provide a boost in times of an economic downturn, bringing under-utilised resources into economic activity. In the boom, higher taxes and lower spending can reduce inflationary pressure, as well as reducing speculative bubbles. The current crisis has also highlighted the potential role of fiscal policy in immediate crisis management, in particular by providing liquidity to financial markets.

Traditionally, the way this is financed is by debt-financing the higher spending/lower taxes in a downturn, helped by the lower financing costs arising from loose monetary policy with lower interest rates. Public finances are then rebalanced when times are good. Countercyclical fiscal policy thus has a direct impact on the net fiscal balance – there should be a net surplus and a reduction in the debt-to-GDP ratio in a boom, and a deficit and an increase in debt in a downturn. The debt-financing cost required to finance the stock of debt will lower the amount of money government can use for higher spending or lower taxation. However, the reduction in debt is accelerated in a boom as economic growth reduces the debt-to-GDP ratio.

To some extent, countercyclical spending and taxation happens automatically. In addition to governments' discretionary policy decisions to change expenditure and taxes, there are also a number of automatic stabilisers, that is, expenditure increasing in a downturn with tax revenues decreasing and vice versa in the upturn. The key automatic stabilisers are social security spending and tax revenues. Social security spending (for example unemployment benefits) will increase as the economy slows, through for example increased unemployment requiring support to a greater number of people. Most tax revenues are also dependent on the overall level of economic activity – either directly as in the case of corporate taxes and VAT or through the labour market as in the case of income taxes and social security contributions.

If countercyclical policy is balanced out over the business cycle, it can bring the best of both worlds – a smoother business cycle with sound public finances. In certain circumstances it can even be self-financing – if tax cuts or active labour market policies increase overall economic activity or help more people stay in work, the overall effect on the fiscal balance might be positive.

3.2 The Political Economy of Discretionary Fiscal Policy

The renewed emphasis on discretionary fiscal policy represents a shift away from the focus on monetary policy in the latter part of the twentieth century, which led to the creation of independent central banks with a remit for price stability across most developed economies. Monetary policy pursued by an independent central bank was often seen as being better able to deal with cyclical variations with the automatic stabilisers being sufficient fiscal policy levers. At the EU level, fiscal policy stability was seen as one of the key cornerstones for the EMU, being enshrined in the Treaty in the form of the Maastricht Criteria and in the Stability and Growth Pact (see Chapter 5 in this volume for further details and an examination of the impact of the economic crisis on EU fiscal policy).

Lately, the focus in Europe has been on structural policies, aimed at increasing long-term productivity, competitiveness and efficiency and effectiveness of public services as embodied in the Lisbon Agenda. Excessive and persistent deficits, and more generally an imbalance between spending and revenue and the accumulation of national debt, were seen as one of the structural issues which needed to be addressed in a number of countries, to ensure sound public finances and minimise the burden of debt repayments.

The return of discretionary countercyclical fiscal policy to the forefront of economic policymaking has reawakened the debate around economic governance of fiscal policy. One of the reasons why discretionary fiscal policy had fallen out of favour is that it is directly controlled by politicians – unlike monetary policy, which is mostly under the control of independent central banks. As a result, one of the key issues in countercyclical policies is how far decisions are driven by electoral cycles rather than economic rationale. This also raises a time inconsistency problem: spending in a crisis is easier than committing to future repayments.

This time inconsistency can be aggravated over the long-term if there is a requirement to address long term challenges such as climate change (see Chapter 7) and demographic change. This can lead to a lack of sustainability in the long term, negatively affecting inter-generational equity by compromising future generations' ability to meet their own needs through the accumulation of national debt. In the long-term, this can impact on the delivery of public services and the sustainability of European economic and social models.

Even if politicians are genuinely aiming to use a balanced countercyclical policy, taking into account long-term sustainability issues, there are information failures which make it difficult to meet these objectives. The macroeconomic environment is characterised by significant uncertainty and time lags. In addition, the impact of policy is often uncertain and might alter the underlying trend development. This has led to some commentators arguing that, at best, countercyclical policy is ineffective; at worst it can be counterproductive.

The use of a more proactive fiscal policy also raises the broader question of the role of the state in economic policy and the impact of the size of government spending. There is no consensus among economists what this impact might be with some pointing out crowding-out effects while others maintain that the correction of market failures, for example under-supply of public services, can increase economic efficiency. Most economists do, however, agree that the size of the public sector is, at the margin, not as important as the quality of public spending, in particular what the money is spent on.

3.3 Limitations of Counter-cyclical Fiscal Policy

Countercyclical fiscal policy, which pays due respect to long-term sustainability issues and 'prudent' management of public finances, aims to achieve multiple objectives in an environment of significant uncertainty and with a significant political economy influence. But these political economy issues make it difficult for fiscal policy to be both debt-neutral over the economic cycle and to be effectively countercyclical.

Government decisions can suffer from a range of difficulties. It is hard to know where exactly the economy is at any given point in time and there are time lags between spending and taxation decisions until they start affecting the economy. It is also difficult to assess exactly what impact these decisions have on the economy and on the overall deficit. This is aggravated by the interaction of fiscal policy with monetary policy – if a fiscal stimulus creates inflationary pressure, this is likely to be met by central banks raising interest rates. In addition, fiscal policy decisions will be affected by political considerations, for example the electoral cycle and a 'ratchet' effect, which makes it more difficult to reduce spending than to increase it as citizens come to expect the additional services or public servants expect to maintain their wage levels.

Past responses to economic crises have also highlighted that it is not sufficient to simply finance any activity. Money which is not spent productively – for example boosting public sector wages without increasing the quality and/or quantity of public service provision – has at best a temporary effect. Individual consumers and businesses also assess any spending or taxation programmes to determine whether the changes will lead to a temporary impact on their revenues or income and, if not, may not increase investment or consumption in response.

What the funding is spent on also has significant impact. Productive investments which increase the capacity of the economy in the long run will have greater effect but have the disadvantage of taking time to start and to manage effectively. The overall economic state of the economy will also potentially negate any spending programmes – for example the large-scale investment in infrastructure as happened in Japan was not sufficient to kick-start the economy as domestic demand for goods and services remained low and businesses remained reluctant to invest despite record low interest rates. As Hamish McRae notes 'cutting interest rates and boosting public spending will not of themselves solve the problem. Japan did both, with near zero interest rates for 20 years and the huge public borrowing noted above. The government spent on supposed 'pump-priming' schemes, building new bridges, roads and rail links, but while this pumped things up for a bit, it failed to establish sustained growth' (McRae 2008).

3.4 A Changing Economic Policy Environment

In addition to the traditional criticisms of countercyclical spending, it should also be recognised that the way we look at economic policy has been changing. Traditional countercyclical fiscal policy considers fiscal policy purely as a lever which can be increased and decreased as macro-economic conditions change.

This treatment of fiscal policy as 'public finance accounting' at a macroeconomics level has its limitations. It does not recognise that how this money is spent matters and that more and more emphasis is on the delivery of public services, such as education, health or local government services. For example at the EU level, in 2006 18.7 per cent of GDP was spent on social protection but expenditure on health services was at 6.4 per cent, education at 5.2 per cent and general public services stood at 6.5 per cent (Table 4.14, Eurostat 2008b).

For significant parts of public spending, longer-term commitments exist which need to be honoured which implies that the bulk of public spending cannot be reduced, limiting changes to the margin. It is also generally difficult to make significant reductions without cutting back on the services provided. Spending more money tends to be relatively easy but it can be difficult to spend the money quickly and productively. This limits the usefulness of spending and taxation on public services as a countercyclical instrument.

3.5 Structural Policies

Recent years have also put a much higher emphasis on structural reform in the policy mix. Structural policies aim to move the economy as a whole to a higher potential growth path and to eliminate inefficiencies. Carrying out reforms entails making difficult choices even in bad times, for example ensuring that there are clear incentives for labour market participation. This can be politically difficult and it can also undermine countercyclical spending as reform might entail cutting spending to increase efficiency, regardless of the current state of the economy.

Improving the quality of public finances is an essential part of addressing Europe's long-term challenges. This can be either 'directly, through fiscal consolidation, pension and expenditure reforms or indirectly by creating conditions in support of long-term growth as expenditure and revenue systems become more efficient and less distortionary' (Barrios and Schaechter 2008).

As noted above, higher spending on public spending might just increase the take-home pay of public workers rather than increasing productivity. This runs counter to the structural reform agenda as it not only means that the spending does not add to GDP but it also creates a ratchet effect – it will be hard to bring down numbers or wage levels of public sector workers at a later stage. Mostly this can only be done gradually through, for example, inflation erosion or through retirement schemes but strong public sector unions are likely to prevent this to some extent.

In many countries, systems have had to be redesigned to create strong labour market incentives. Individual payments for being out of work have been 'minimised' as much as possible to ensure that people have clear financial incentives to be in work, taking low-paying jobs which are available rather than ending up economically inactive and, for example, relying on social security or public pensions in early retirement. Similarly, there are benefits for those at the lower end of the income scale (for example tax credits in UK) to make sure that there are increasing benefits from work. In many countries there have recently been attempts to close the gap between different groups receiving transfers – for example to reduce the difference between those receiving unemployment benefit and those receiving social security payments – to ensure people do not get removed too far from the labour market.

Countries are unlikely to change the nature of such systems according to the economic cycle. While the numbers in the different groups might change, there is little scope to increase individual benefit levels without distorting incentives to work and there is also a more gradual impact on spending as a larger group of people receive support on a differential scale (for example moving from receiving tax credits to unemployment benefit rather than in the past on/off benefits, that is unemployed or not).

3.6 The Difficulty of Assessing when Times are Good

The identification of what constitutes 'good' or 'bad' times has become increasingly difficult. The traditional view of the business cycle is a number of periods of healthy growth, followed by a relatively short period of recession, with similar patterns over time. Looking at recent European growth experience shows very different patterns in many countries for example with irregular business cycles and long periods of low growth, as demonstrated in the Table 6.3.

The table suggests that since an upturn at the start of the millennium, there has been a period of relatively low growth in most European countries. The situation in 2006 and 2007 improved somewhat but the forecasts for 2008–2010 show a marked deterioration. Overall growth performance in Europe has not been high in recent years, with only a few exceptions. Even when taking out the forecast data for 2008–2010, average growth has been below 2.5 per cent in the EU-27, with Germany and Italy at around 1.5 per cent. With this forecast data included, average growth is clearly below 2 per cent, with Germany and Italy barely above 1 per cent. This is particularly worrying, given that some of these forecasts are starting to be revised downward already. This raises the question of whether growth in good times is sufficient to outweigh the debt increases in bad times. Some countries have seemingly entered a period of prolonged low growth, which raises questions about whether the trend growth line around which the business cycle is moving has moved permanently downwards.

Table 6.3 Real Growth Rates in the EU-15, 1999–2010

	1999	2000	2001	2002	2003	2004	2005	2006	2007	2008	2009
EU (27)	3	3.9	2	1.2	1.3	2.5	2	3.1	2.9	0.2(f)	1.1(f)
Belgium	3.4	3.7	0.8	1.5	1	3	1.8	3	2.8	0.1(f)	0.9(f)
Denmark	2.6	3.5	0.7	0.5	0.4	2.3	2.4	3.3	1.6	0.1(f)	0.9(f)
Germany	2	3.2	1.2	0	-0.2	1.2	0.8	3	2.5	−0.0(f)	1.0(f)
Ireland	10.7	9.2	5.8	6.4	4.5	4.7	6.4	5.7	6	−0.9(f)	2.4(f)
Greece	3.4	4.5	4.2	3.4	5.6	4.9	2.9	4.5	4	2.5(f)	2.6(f)
Spain	4.7	5	3.6	2.7	3.1	3.3	3.6	3.9	3.7	−0.2(f)	0.5(f)
France	3.3	3.9	1.9	1	1.1	2.5	1.9	2.2	2.2	−0.0(f)	0.8(f)
Italy	1.5	3.7	1.8	0.5	0	1.5	0.6	1.8	1.5	−0.0(f)	0.6(f)
Luxembourg	8.4	8.4	2.5	4.1	1.5	4.5	5.2	6.4	5.2	1.2(f)	2.3(f)
Netherlands	4.7	3.9	1.9	0.1	0.3	2.2	2	3.4	3.5	0.4(f)	0.9(f)
Austria	3.3	3.7	0.5	1.6	0.8	2.5	2.9	3.4	3.1	0.6(f)	1.3(f)
Portugal	6.8	3.9	2	0.8	-0.8	1.5	0.9	1.4	1.9	0.1(f)	0.7(f)
Finland	3.9	5	2.6	1.6	1.8	3.7	2.8	4.9	4.5	1.3(f)	2.0(f)
Sweden	4.6	4.4	1.1	2.4	1.9	4.1	3.3	4.2	2.5	−0.2(f)	1.6(f)
UK	3.5	3.9	2.5	2.1	2.8	2.8	2.1	2.8	3	−1.0(f)	0.4(f)

Source: Eurostat (2008d).

Determining what constitutes 'good' times is thus fraught with difficulties. This is aggravated by the relationship between growth and labour market performance. Just having positive growth is not sufficient to impact positively on labour market performance – a more significant positive growth rate is needed.

The German example is illustrative in this context. Figure 6.3 shows that the unemployment rate tends to increase when German growth dips below 1 per cent and vice versa:

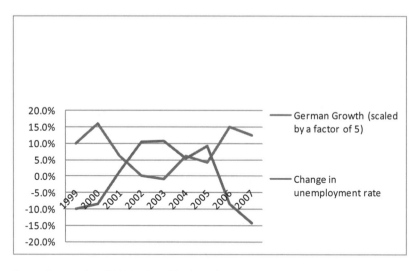

Source: Eurostat data (2008c), adapted by the authors.

Figure 6.3 Relationship between German Growth and Changes in the Unemployment Rate

This suggests that for Germany even a growth rate of around 1 per cent is not sufficient to improve labour market performance. A counter-cyclical policy would thus have to intervene in the whole period 2001–2005, raising fiscal sustainability issues. This also raises the question of whether governments have the necessary information to get it right over the cycle – they need to know when times are good and when times are bad to make the right discretionary choices but with irregular patterns this is difficult to identify.

3.7 A Potential Weakening of Automatic Stabilisers

Automatic stabilisers might also not be as effective as they were previously. The above-mentioned ratchet effect also affects social security: it is easy to increase funding per person in boom (for example one-off payment for pensioners) but hard to take away again at a later stage. Consequently, rather than varying in both directions, the only possible changes are upwards. A similar issue can arise with people exiting the labour market in the downturn, if they drop out entirely for example through early retirement schemes. It is very difficult to move these groups back into the labour market in the upturn, potentially creating labour shortages and constraining growth.

More generally, there is a shift in the numbers from those affected by cyclical movements (for example unemployed who are relatively close to the labour market) to those permanently receiving support (pensioners and to some extent the economically inactive, for example those on permanent sickness or disability benefits). In many large European economies, there is also a stock of unemployed now which does not vary significantly in a boom. This creates a requirement of large upfront social security transfers, regardless of the stage in the economic cycle.

Arguably, the recent focus of public spending on providing public services such as health and education might also weaken the counter-cyclical nature of spending. However, a study of data for the OECD (Organisation for Economic Co-operation and Development) from 1980 to 2001 suggests that 'age- and health-related social expenditure as well as incapacity benefits all react to the cycle in a stabilising manner' (Darby and Melitz 2008), suggesting that automatic stabilisers are also at work within these public services.

Arguably, in future, tax revenues might weaken as an automatic stabiliser if there is a shift away from sources which are highly cyclical (for example VAT, income tax) to those which are not necessarily as closely tied to the cycle (for example green taxes or taxes on properties). However, this shift is slow to happen and a significant countercyclicality will still be apparent. It is more likely that the cyclical or countercyclical nature of taxes is affected by political consideration as described earlier in relation to US policy.

3.8 Changing Expectations

Expectations of the population on what fiscal policy should deliver might also be changing. Not only might there be preferences for more stability in certain countries, there can even be expectations for more public spending (or tax cuts or both) in a boom. Again, the ratchet effect might limit the amount by which public sector wages or transfer payments such as pensions can be reduced and only gradual erosion through inflation might be possible. But there might also be higher inflation in the upturn which could lead to higher expectations to compensate those on fixed incomes.

Europeans also inherently perceive 'fairness' as an important consideration. As in many European countries, public sector wages and transfer payments are under pressure in the downturn as overall budget constraints are reached, the expectation can be that these groups in society will receive higher payments in the upturn when this becomes more affordable. Equally, there is pressure that those who have had to pay additionally in the downturn (for example through increased social security contributions) will now be able to pay less.

There is also now political pressure to spend additional tax receipts when they become available as policy priorities get postponed rather than cancelled in the downturn due to overall budget constraints. Rather than a balanced budget, this could result in a deficit being accumulated over time and a weakening of the countercyclical nature of fiscal policy.

In certain countries, there is also a limitation arising from the legacy of past policies. A number of countries still pay for significant debt accumulated in the past, which limits their freedom of movement in a downturn and imposes a significant burden in terms of interest payments. For example, Belgium pays almost 4 per cent of GDP on annual interest payments, Italy 5 per cent and Greece 4.4 per cent, pre-committing around 10 per cent of government revenue to interest payments (Eurostat 2008a). Having large levels of debt might also reduce the ability to act countercyclical: 'As the dynamics of debt accumulation become, or come to be perceived as, unsustainable, fiscal consolidation may become necessary, regardless of the economy's position in the business cycle' (OECD 2003).

3.9 Fiscal Policies to Address Long-term Challenges

Public services need to focus more on investing in long-term structural change, that is, investing in the future. This type of investment should not vary too much with the economic cycle. For example, lifelong learning should take place at all times and health should be promoted regardless of economic cycles. Even in policy areas such as infrastructure development, contracts are long term and often difficult to alter.

Investment of this nature should be part of a long-term strategy, rather than being subject to cyclical variations. While some of this investment will react in a countercyclical manner (for example money for training those who become jobless) this is a relatively small part of overall expenditure on education in most countries. Similarly, some health problems will increase in worse economic times (for example mental health or some poverty-related illnesses) but the big trends persist regardless of the stage of the economic cycle (for example cancer or heart disease).

Public services are also not easily scalable and 'increasable'. It needs time to build up provision – for example, medical staff have to be trained over a number of years. Increasing services too quickly can also lead to skills mismatch if in a downturn such as people getting locked into a career in public services (education, health) or activities funded by public money (for example construction of public infrastructure). In better times, it will be difficult to entice these workers into other sectors.

Many public services are also no longer universal or supplemented by private funding, for example in health, education and also certain social insurances. Driven by levels of disposable income, many people will contribute additionally in the upturn but have no incentive to do so in a downturn or lack the necessary funds. A shortfall in private investment in, for example, education or health might require additional spending by governments in a downturn.

In addition, governments need to take account of long-term societal and economic change. The current crisis has shown that in a globally interdependent economy, contingencies have to be created to cope with rapidly spreading shocks affecting global markets. Climate change will also require expenditure in future to adapt to increases in extreme weather events and to deal with the health impact, as well as ensuring that Europe can fulfil its responsibilities globally (see Chapter 7 on fighting climate change).

The impact on public spending of demographic change is also underestimated. It will result over time in a deterioration of receipts and additional spending pressures in areas such as healthcare and pensions. A European study projects an increase of public spending due to ageing of 4 percentage points of GDP in the EU-15 over the period 2004–2050 and 'most of the projected increase in public spending will be on pensions, health care and long-term care' (Economic Policy Committee 2006). In the long term, in terms of intergenerational equity, the current generation should be saving to finance future pensions and healthcare.

This implies that rather than aiming for an overall balanced budget in the near future, there might be a need to aim for a budget surplus to be invested. It might also be necessary to introduce new methods and measurements of debt which include long term liabilities to make visible long term deficits in pensions and healthcare. Current social security contributions could be seen as a form of borrowing in return for future provision of public services, creating liabilities for governments, not dissimilar to government bonds, rather than public sector income. Government policy can change the value of the outstanding liabilities (by, for example, changing pension ages). This would make some of the trade-offs between current and future social spending more visible.

The above discussion suggests that traditional tools for dealing with different stage in the economic cycle might be inappropriate in dealing with the multi-faceted nature of the problems facing many economies today. If we are serious about achieving fiscal consolidation and countercyclical spending objectives at the same time, it is necessary to rethink fiscal policy approaches and the governance of fiscal policy.

4. FUTURE POLICY APPROACHES

The discussion of the changing environment in which fiscal policy finds itself raises serious doubt about the ability of national governments to reach goals of effective countercyclical spending and fiscal prudence over the economic cycle. Germany's Finance Minister, Steinbruck, made the following comment about the UK's rescue programme: 'All this will do is raise Britain's debt to a level that will take a whole generation to work off' (BBC Online 2008). The Czech Finance Minister Kalousek warned that 'there is a risk that if discipline is not adhered to, we'll have real problems' (BBC Online 2009a).

But the debt being accumulated now is a reality and even Germany is now starting to spend more freely. For better or for worse, the world economies have chosen to attempt to kick-start their economies through fiscal stimulus programmes. National agendas need to shift now to a discussion of how fiscal policy will be handled in future and whether it is possible for Europeans to benefit from countercyclical fiscal policy and sound public finances simultaneously.

4.1 Common Action or Country-by-country?

The key governance questions are how much of fiscal policy will be dealt with at the European level and what governance mechanisms can be put in place to support objectives of fiscal policy. Many governments will undoubtedly argue that spending and taxation is at the heart of the member states and that further 'encroachment' of Europe in this field is not welcome. But subsidiarity should cut both ways: if there are good arguments for why an EU level response represents the best options to address some of the policy questions, then more competence should move to the European level.

There are a number of good reasons why joined-up European action might be desirable within this field:

- A growing interdependence of EU economies, especially in the euro-area which implies that fiscal policy in one country has significant knock-on effects in others;
- Businesses, including financial institutions, operating across borders;
- The benefit of scale and focus in dealing with financial and economic crisis: being able to draw on significant pooled resources is likely to be more effective than a country-by-country approach and resources can be focused on where they are needed most;

- The ability to quell panic and to affect confidence in all member states simultaneously, preventing a contagion effect; and
- A range of common challenges, including demographic change and climate change which require a European response.

4.2 The Political Economy of Fiscal Policy at EU Level

The EU level can, to a certain extent, also overcome some of the political economy issues discussed earlier in this chapter. EU institutions, and peer review by other member states, can potentially be more objective and independent, as they are not driven by the same political economy issues as member states. There are parallels here to the inflation debate. The creation of independent central banks was to a large extent driven by the perceived need to have monetary policy focusing only on price stability, without the temptation for politicians to boost the economy with unsustainably low interest rates and paying for it in the long run with permanently higher inflation. Similarly, it can be argued that governments can find debt-financed expansionary policies too alluring, resulting in long-term fiscal imbalances without the benefit of higher growth. These unsustainable fiscal policies then reduce the ability of governments to react in a downturn, potentially making policy procyclical as governments meet the downturn already in deficit, with a large stock of debt.

This can be aggravated by a tendency to overestimate future growth in certain countries and circumstances. In countries with low growth performance, there is the tendency to hope for imminent brightening of prospects. For countries with a sustained period of healthy growth, the temptation is for politicians to believe that 'bad days will never come', believing that their economy is no longer subject to a business cycle. In addition, many of the policies which are required to maintain fiscal discipline are not necessarily popular in the short term and some countries have developed a strong bias against running surpluses in good economic times, instead handing out any additional revenue in tax cuts or additional spending. This can be aggravated if perception of longer-term growth is higher than the actual trend, as this will create an expectation that current cutbacks will be rewarded in future, rather than recognising that these cutbacks are necessary in any case.

This implies that it is necessary to create governance systems at the EU level which can ensure that EU countries are 'prudent' in their fiscal policy, as well as ensuring that countercyclical spending and taxation is effective without jeopardising long-term public finances. Such governance mechanisms would enable EU member states to continue with countercyclical taxation and spending policies, helping to smooth out the business cycle and support macroeconomic management of the euro-area.

It would also necessitate taking into account the need to have a sound fiscal balances to manage future risks, be it an economic and financial crisis such as the current one or the risk that the future growth performance is lower than what is expected or hoped for. Finally, European governments need to prepare for common future challenges such as demographic change and climate change by minimising liabilities (and the unproductive interest payments associated with national debt) and starting to invest in and accumulate assets for the future.

There are political choices here – not all governments might agree with these policy priorities, highlighting, for example, the need to maintain and expand current levels of public services. There is also a question of how future risk is assessed and the overall confidence in the national economy's ability to produce high growth rates in future. It also has to be acknowledged that for some countries such a policy approach might be more painful than for others: those countries already having high public debt, slowing economic growth and a significant challenge from an ageing population, such as Italy, will have to adjust their spending and taxation patterns more radically. They have to bring public finances under control as a priority. There might even be a risk of defaulting on debt payments (although the current situation in Italy is not quite this critical – see for example *The Economist* 2008a). Other countries have done better in recent years, putting their fiscal policy on a much more sound footing, but there is no room for complacency.

The reality is that all EU countries will be required to follow a more prudent course in future. Not making the difficult choices which are required now simply postpones the inevitable adjustments, and aggravates them in the process. Current practice also puts a significant burden on future generations and will jeopardise the ability of European governments to finance Europe's social provision, which is valued highly by its citizens.

It is, however, difficult to see how we can have a common regime which imposes strict boundaries on member states at the European level in the near future. Any move towards a pan-European fiscal policy is not likely to be acceptable to member states. In political accountability terms, it is also important to recognise that governments have to remain responsible in accounting for their spending-taxation decisions to the national electorates.

But there are ways in which governments can coordinate their action more effectively at the EU level. Having this higher level can also be a tool which governments can use to commit themselves credibly within a European framework, being assessed objectively and publicly against their commitments. This will need leadership to make sure that politicians not only commit their economies to future actions but that concrete and difficult policies are detailed in any such commitment and that they are carried out by current administrations.

4.3 Concrete Policy Recommendations

What does this mean in practice? There is a need to rethink the SGP to ensure that it takes into account the political economy issues and the changes in the nature of spending and taxation discussed above. The mechanism should not only focus on excessive debt but should assess whether any level of deficit and indeed surplus is in line with the long-term trends and the current state in the economic cycle. Here, caution is needed to ensure that economic prospects are assessed realistically and cautiously, preferably by an independent expert body.

On the basis of that assessment, a fiscal sustainability programme should be drawn up which sets out how sound public finances will be achieved, with governments being required to commit to such a programme. Such a programme would vary according to country and situation, aiming to ensure that hard choices are made in those countries where policies have been on an unsustainable trajectory. Governments ought to create new 'automatic stabilisers', for example earmarking additional tax revenues above a certain level for debt repayment.

The SGP should focus on longer-term sustainability, discouraging governments from attempting to 'fine-tune' the economy with fiscal policy in the short term. There needs to be a re-evaluation of the desirable level of debt being accumulated over the business cycle. Given the need to address already existing stocks of debt (which will further increase due to the current crisis), coupled with future challenges such as population ageing and climate change and the need to set aside contingencies to deal with future crisis, a balanced budget over the economic cycle is no longer sufficient.

European governments also need to renew their efforts to enhance competitiveness and drive forward structural reform. The follow-up to the Lisbon Agenda post-2010 should contain a strong emphasis on fiscal sustainability, including monitoring the long-term liabilities associated with health and pension systems, as well as debt. This is necessary to drive up Europe's growth and jobs performance but sound public finances should also be recognised at the EU level as being a critical part of future competitiveness. With public finances being tighter in future in many cases there will no longer be the same freedom of deciding how much to spend. Instead, the focus will need to shift on how the funding can be spent more effectively. Spending and taxation needs to be focused on increasing public sector productivity to ensure that public services remain sustainable. Spending and taxation also need to be recognised as playing an important role in setting microeconomic incentives for households and businesses which will reduce their use as macroeconomic levers.

European governments also need to consider ways and means by which they can invest in future economic growth and to accumulate assets to deal with future challenges. This could be spearheaded by the establishment of a European public pension fund, similar to the establishment of the Oil Fund in Norway. Having such a fund at the European level would remove the temptation for governments to use funds for short-term priorities and it would make the accumulation of assets visible. Countries would commit a certain percentage of GDP (or tax revenues) on an annual basis, owning the long-term rights to the returns in proportion to pay-ins. Such a fund could be administered by the EIB (European Investment Bank), according to cautious investment rules. The Funds should be voluntary at the outset, only including those countries which are wiling to take part.

It is in the nature of such a chapter that we can sketch out only some of the policy implications at this stage, without being able to present a 'masterplan' for the future economic governance of fiscal policy at the EU level. However, it is argued that a fresh look at fiscal policy is required and that there is a need for an enhanced role for the European level. The current crisis makes it difficult to plan too far ahead but this chapter argues that the sound management of fiscal policy should be on the European agenda as soon as the immediate crisis has passed.

5. SUMMARY AND CONCLUSIONS

In the short term, fiscal stimulus programmes will continue and it is likely that many countries will expand them in the near future. For most countries, this will have to be financed through increased debt. While there is little which can be done to limit the accumulation of debt, governments should try to ensure that this money is not simply used to try to increase consumption but also to increase future productivity.

Even in the short term, a degree of fiscal discipline is necessary: as Trichet warns, 'Fiscal indiscipline could threaten already fragile economic confidence and increase the nervousness of capital markets about governments' funding needs' (Atkins and Barber 2008). In the medium to long term, once the current crisis has passed, there will need to be a return to more sustainable fiscal policies. It will also be important to ensure that there is a political constituency for fiscal consolidation.

This chapter has demonstrated that countercyclical spending to smooth out business cycles is in principle a good idea but difficult to implement in current and future economic circumstances. In particular, the political economy issues and the potential changes in the nature of expenditure and taxation, as well as future challenges, imply that countercyclical spending policies might end up undermining fiscal sustainability.

The policy implications for national governments are politically difficult to implement: in 'normal' times, governments should stop running deficits and should generally aim to run a surplus over the whole cycle apart from periods of recession. Surpluses can be used to eliminate debt and to start saving and investing to meet future liabilities, as well as serving as a contingency to deal with future crisis. The current German proposal to limit German deficits to 0.5 per cent of GDP in normal economic times (*Der Spiegel* 2009) is a step in the right direction.

Economic governance at EU level needs to be strengthened to help drive governments in the right direction. In particular, there are three concrete policy suggestions:

- To revise the Stability and Growth Pact to take into account the limitations of countercyclical spending and to explicitly build in mechanisms to drive forward fiscal consolidation;
- To ensure that fiscal policies are taken into account as one of the key components of structural reform; and
- To establish a European Futures Fund to start accumulating assets to deal with future challenges.

Given the political economy issues underpinning the sound management of fiscal policy, only a European governance mechanism can successfully ensure that fiscal consolidation and countercyclical policies are compatible. The authors acknowledge that progress will be difficult, not least because of the pressures arising from the current economic crisis. But in the medium to long term, European fiscal policies have to be put on a more sustainable level. Otherwise our future ability to deal with crises and to supply the public services and social protection Europeans desire will be jeopardised.

NOTES

1. Please see Altomonte, Passarelli and Secchi in Chapter 5 of this volume for an examination of the current crisis and its immediate effect on EU fiscal policy.
2. In Chapter 5 of this volume the authors discuss the changes brought about by the economic crisis to the EU fiscal and monetary policy stance.
3. By the end of 2008, Austria, Belgium, Cyprus, Finland, France, Germany, Greece, Ireland, Italy, Luxembourg, Malta, Netherlands, Portugal, Slovenia and Spain were part of the euro-area, with Slovakia about to join.

BIBLIOGRAPHY

Atkins, Ralph and Lionel Barber (2008), 'Trichet warns of fiscal discipline', *Financial Times*, 14 December.

Barrios, Salvador and Andrea Schaechter (2008), *The Quality of Public Finances and Economic Growth*, European Commission, Economic Papers no. 337, September.

BBC Online (2007), 'Sarkozy pleads for deficit room', 9 July, http://news.bbc.co.uk/2/hi/business/6283702.stm.

BBC Online (2008), 'Germany questions UK rescue plan', 11 December, http://news.bbc.co.uk/2/hi/business/7776718.stm.

BBC Online (2009a), 'Czechs warn on EU fiscal plans', 8 January, http://news.bbc.co.uk/2/hi/business/7818474.stm.

BBC Online (2009b) 'Germany agrees 50bn euro stimulus', 13 January, http://news.bbc.co.uk/2/hi/business/7825513.stm.

Darby, Julia and Jacques Melitz (2008), *Social Spending and Automatic Stabilisers in the OECD*, Discussion Paper no. 18, Centre for Public Policy for Regions (CPPR), May.

Der Spiegel (2008), 'Konjunkturhilfen könnten Bund 200 Milliarden Euro kosten', 17 December, http://www.spiegel.de/wirtschaft/0,1518,597001,00.html.

Der Spiegel (2009), 'Koalition beschließt drastische Begrenzung der Nettokreditaufnahme', 13 January, http://www.spiegel.de/politik/deutschland/0,1518,600956,00.html.

Economic Policy Committee (2006), 'Impact of ageing populations on public spending on pensions, health and long-term care, education and unemployment benefits for the elderly', ECFIN/EPC(2006)REP/238 final.

The Economist (2009), 'After the recession, the deluge', 8 January.

The Economist (2008a), 'The ogre in the attic', 13 December,

The Economist (2008b), 'Coming soon to a screen near you', 29 November.

The Economist (2008c), 'Unausterity programme', 29 September.

The Economist (2008d), 'A stimulating notion', 16 February.

European Commission, Stability and Growth Pact (2008), December, http://ec.europa.eu/economy_finance/sg_pact_fiscal_policy/index_en.htm?cs_mid=570.

Eurostat (2008a), *Annual Summary Government Finance Statistics*, December.

Eurostat (2008b), *European Economic Statistics*, Glasgow University Library.

Eurostat (2008c), 'German Unemployment Rate', December

Eurostat (2008d), Real Growth Rates, December.

Federal Trust (2006), *The Governance of the Eurozone*, October, http://www.fedtrust.co.uk/admin/uploads/FedT_Eurozone.pdf.

Guha, Krishna, Edward Luce and Andrew Ward (2009), 'Budget deficit set to make US postwar record', *Financial Times*, 8 January.

McNeill, Sabine (2008), 'Gordon Brown defends level of national debt', *Guardian*, 20 October, http://www.guardian.co.uk/politics/2008/oct/20/gordonbrown-economy.

McRae, Hamish (2008),'Can we avoid the years of stagnation suffered by Japan?', *The Independent*, 29 October, http://www.independent.co.uk/opinion/commentators/

hamish-mcrae/hamish-mcrae-can-we-avoid-the-years-of-stagnation-suffered-by-japan-976792.html.

Merkel Angela and Nicolas Sarkozy (2008), 'International financial crisis joint article', *Le Figaro* and *Frankfurter Allgemeine Zeitung*, 26 November, http://www.ambafrance-se.org/spip.php?article2021.

Mulas-Granados, Carlos (2006), *The Political Economy of Fiscal Consolidations in Europe*, Palgrave MacMillan.

Organization for Economic Co-operation and Development (OECD) (2003), *Economic Outlook 74*, http://www.oecd.org/dataoecd/58/19/23466327.pdf.

Organization for Economic Co-operation and Development (OECD) (2008), *Economic Outlook 84*, November, http://www.oecd.org/dataoecd/41/33/3575 5962.pdf.

Zuleeg, Fabian and Hans Martens (2008) 'The stimulus package: how much is enough – and what for?', *Commentary EPC*, 27 November.

7. Feeling the Heat: Towards a Revised Governance of Climate Change

Antonio Villafranca

1. INTRODUCTION

The search for a new economic governance, not reflecting the post-war order but rather the new balance of power which is emerging in the era of globalization, lies at the core of the current international debate. The economic crisis has made this search more urgent. The world economy needs a revised and better-shared governance which also allows the qualified participation of big emerging countries. This seems to be a prerequisite for solid and sustainable recovery leading to a new era of economic cooperation. But the recovery of industrialized countries and the return of emerging countries to a path marked by impressive growth rates raise doubts on their future sustainability in global warming terms. As a consequence, the anomalous and striking rise in world temperatures has included the climate change issue in the seeking of a new world governance. It is now quite clear that climate change is at least partially a human-induced phenomenon, and as such it requires human intervention which cannot be limited to 'business as usual'. In other words, the debate over the new world economic order needs to be coherent with a more intense and shared fight against climate change.

The high costs borne to exit today's crisis must not hamper individuation of new, stronger tools with which to face this challenge. Indeed, the intensive use of renewable resources and the development of new 'green technologies' represent a unique economic opportunity, especially in view of the inevitable depletion of fossil fuels and increase in their world demand (and price) over the coming decades.

But unfortunately one of the most disappointing features of fighting climate change is its capacity to produce positive effects that can be felt only decades ahead (according to the most optimistic scenario), whilst the costs start to be borne today. The required long-run vision can clash with firms' and politicians' attitudes of looking to the short–medium run, especially in the context of a severe economic crisis with potentially enormous social consequences.

Nonetheless, growing consciousness of the urgency of the phenomenon and the need for an effective fight against climate change have already contributed to the creation of a 'semi-spontaneous' multilevel governance. The United Nations Framework Convention on Climate Change (UNFCCC), the Kyoto Protocol and actions taken at any level (global, regional, state and sub-state) all over the world may be considered examples of such governance. In addition, the significant initiatives promoted by the European Union and the positive signals sent by the Obama administration and many emerging countries are raising hopes for the future, especially in the wake of the definition of the post-Kyoto targets (from 2013 onwards). In this regard, this chapter will devote specific attention to the European Union, which has already set its own post-Kyoto targets and intends to play a leading role in fighting climate change and developing 'green technologies'. It can be seen as a best practice to be duplicated, 'mutatis mutandis', in other regions.

But today's 'spontaneous' model of multilevel governance exhibits many drawbacks, as it appears unfit to manage effectively the complex – and in many respects new – phenomenon of climate change.

This chapter intends to define a revised multilevel governance, which on the one hand is coherent with a better-shared economic governance and on the other is compatible with a significant reduction of greenhouse gases. In particular, section 2 will provide an overview of the main features which make climate change a particularly complex phenomenon, including in terms of individuation of the most appropriate governance for it. Section 3 will place emphasis on the current 'spontaneous' governance, by analyzing all levels of intervention (global, regional, state and sub-state) with the aim of highlighting inconsistencies at any level. Building on this analysis, section 4 will suggest changes in the current multilevel governance of climate change, by seeking solutions which are viable and effective, rather than revolutionary intervention.

2. A TRULY GLOBAL CHALLENGE

The first noticeable effects of climate change (melting ice, growing number and intensity of hurricanes, droughts, desertification etc.) and, above all, its staggering and potentially catastrophic consequences are changing priorities in political agendas all over the world. The vast majority of scientists agree that climate change is a global phenomenon, and as such requires an equally global human intervention. But it is difficult to identify weapons to be used in fighting climate change since its peculiar features render it a unique, unprecedented challenge. In this respect, its most important feature is obviously the urgency and extreme significance of the phenomenon. Over the last 30 years, average world temperatures have grown by 0.6°C, thus probably reaching the highest levels since the last ice age (Hansel et al. 2006). Besides, greenhouse gases could double from 2030 to 2060 (compared to pre-industrial levels) and may cause a 2–5°C increase in average world temperatures (however some scientists provide worse scenarios).

The Intergovernmental Panel on Climate Change (IPCC) has repeatedly maintained that most of this warming can be attributed to human activity.[1] As shown in Figure 7.1, 'radiative forcing' (the warming effect defined in terms of the equivalent concentration of carbon dioxide) is rising constantly for all six Kyoto greenhouse gases.[2]

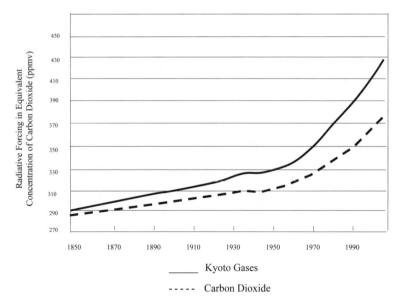

Source: Laila K. Gohar and Keith P. Shine, Dept of Meteorology, University of Reading.

Figure 7.1 Rising Levels of Greenhouse Gases

In particular, over the past 20 years the concentration of carbon dioxide in the atmosphere has increased from 280 to 368 parts per million and by

2100 this concentration may be in the range of 540 and 970 parts per million, thus committing the world to 3–10° warming (see IPCC Report 2001). This may imply a significant rise in temperatures and unknown effects on human beings, animals and plants.

According to Stern,[3] 1 per cent of global GDP (Gross Domestic Product) is required in order to stabilise emissions (at 550 parts per million of CO_2 equivalent) in the next 20 years and reduce them 1–3 per cent afterwards. But this calculation has been criticized by others who are less or more optimistic. In particular, some authors stress that Stern's estimates assume unrealistically efficient government spending and technological developments which cannot be taken for granted today, whilst others have criticized the Stern Review for spreading unbalanced alarmism. Either way, it is broadly acknowledged that climate change is a major challenge and that fighting it requires many financial, human and natural resources.

Although this phenomenon is directly linked to worldwide emitted greenhouse gases, it is noteworthy that its effects can differ in every region. In this regard, great attention should be afforded to the growing intensity of the water cycle. Some regions, such as the Mediterranean, will probably experience a dramatic reduction in rainfall which may in turn lead to draught and desertification. On the other hand, other regions (for example the US and the Caribbean) could be hit by more catastrophic hurricanes and typhoons, partly owing to warmer air and oceans.

Adaptation policies therefore require different tools and actions, which also imply different costs. The economic literature on adaptation costs is still limited and chiefly focused on sea-level rise (for example Fankhauser 1995; Nicholls and Tol 2006) and agriculture (for example Adams et al. 2003; Reilly et al. 2003). In particular, the Stern Review puts the overall cost (the additional investment and financial flows needed in 2030) at 'tens of billions of dollars per year', while the UNFCCC increases this cost to 'several tens of billion United States dollars' (UNFCCC 2007).

To make things worse, many other 'side-effects' are directly or indirectly linked to global warming: nutrition and food-water safety, environmental refugees (mass migrations caused by climate change), infectious diseases etc.

In a nutshell, a very complex and dangerous situation involving the entire world is emerging and it is difficult to quantify the costs of the required policies (both in terms of adaptation and mitigation) in advance.

2.1 Room for Free Riding

Another feature characterizing the fight against climate change is the purely global dimension of its causes and effects (in relation to mitigation at least). The rise in temperatures is (at least partially) caused by overall human-produced pollution. It is therefore crystal clear that only a global effort can fight this phenomenon.

In addition, whoever bears the cost of this fight, its effects will be enjoyed by all others, and consequently some will be tempted to maintain a low profile and wait for others to take action (and bear costs).

In other words, there is a real risk of free-riding behaviour, making the definition of a transparent model of governance in which everyone will be asked to make a sacrifice proportional to their produced pollution and relative wealth even more necessary.

Climate change, in particular, may be considered a human-induced phenomenon, and those who cause it impose a cost on others who are not fully responsible for it. This issue can therefore be included in studies on 'public goods' (climate) and negative externalities (climate change), for which much literature is available.[4] Like any other negative externality, climate change cannot be corrected by market forces alone and consequently requires policy intervention. Nonetheless, this phenomenon shows peculiar features requiring analysis that differs, at least partially, from that traditionally provided by the economic literature (see Stern Review Parts I and IV).

As mentioned above, climate change is characterized by being 'global' both in its causes and consequences. Greenhouse gases are diffused in the atmosphere no matter where they are emitted (in Europe, Australia or China). The marginal local damage of greenhouse gases is potentially the same all over the world, since local climate changes depend strictly on the global climate system.

Another feature of climate change is its persistency over time. Once diffused in the atmosphere, gases may remain there for hundreds of years. In economic terms this implies that the cost of today's emissions can only be estimated precisely (and their consequences felt fully) in the future, and perhaps the long-term future. So it is quite difficult to consider the number of tools (and their cost) we can use today to face challenges whose effects will be estimated fully only in future decades or even centuries. This means that there are lags in the environmental and economic-social responses to climate change. Therefore, uncertainty about the potential size, type and timing of its impacts (and again the related costs) makes the situation worse.

Such peculiarities require intervention which can be only partially based on traditional measures used to solve market failures. Indeed, as will be shown below, these measures are necessary and can contribute to the fight, but they alone are not sufficient to secure a full victory over climate change. On the one hand, the above-mentioned features require a sufficiently flexible response to adapt today's expectations to tomorrow's reality. On the other, the required intervention is so wide-ranging that the consequent rethinking of world governance cannot be limited to the strict economic and environmental field but must also encompass redefinition of international equilibria. In other words, it is an unprecedented challenge not only in economic terms but also in political terms.

2.2 A Political Conundrum

The largest problem related to global warming is not simply its effects in climate change terms, but above all the speed of this phenomenon. If spread over several centuries, it would be easier to manage as there would be time to make the necessary political changes. But since significant effects may occur in just one century, we run the risk that adequate political responses will not be provided in time.

Indeed, it is not the first time in human history that climate has profoundly influenced events; 'Muslim expansion into the Mediterranean and Southern Europe in the eighth century was to some extent driven by persistent drought in the Middle East ... and a changing climate may have been responsible for the collapse of China's Tang dynasty and the disappearance of the Mayan world in Central America a thousand years ago' (Dupont 2008). Therefore, the relationship between climate and historical-political events is anything but new. Nonetheless, some current features (its urgency, purely global dimension and the fact that it is, at least partially, a human-induced phenomenon) are making today's global warming an unparalleled event. As a consequence, the potential effects in terms of political and social changes might be extremely significant.

In brief, the urgency of this global phenomenon and its high speed (as opposed to the traditional slowness of political change) require a revised global governance, which political scientists have been discussing in recent years.

Although international security and the global economy are traditionally the two main issues addressed by International Relations (as a discipline), some scholars underline the emergence of the environment and climate change as a third major issue (Porter and Brown 1996).

To put it simply, the specific International Relations debate on climate change is between two extreme groups of scholars: modernists and ecoradicals (Jackson and Sorensen 2007). Modernists believe that the continuous development of science and technology will inevitably lead to an improved ability to solve environmental problems. For instance, today's industrial production requires fewer CO_2 emissions per unit than in the past, and a growing number of agricultural products are cultivated using new sustainable methods.

On the other hand, ecoradicals warn that the increase in world population has already gone well beyond world limits and that its environmental impact will be anything but negligible. As a consequence, demographic control and a new world governance will be required in the near future. The current international system and the 'old-style' balance of power are unable to face these challenges, and a new and even revolutionary world order will emerge.

Either way, these two approaches seem too 'out of line', therefore it would be wise to seek a mid-way solution. In this regard, the more traditional debate between realism and liberalism can encompass the issue. For realists (Morgenthau 1948; Waltz 1979; Gilpin 1987; Grieco 1993) the environment, pollution and global warming can be simply considered as other problems to be added to the long list of potential conflicts between states. Crudely speaking, the emergence of a superpower would be a 'first best' solution for fighting climate change. Since that is not easy to achieve, the seeking of a 'balance of power' between the major countries in the international system is the main tool that may be used to reduce inevitable international conflicts, including climate change. Besides, states are the main actors in the international system and are mainly interested in 'relative gains' for each option at the international level. In other words, they compare their pay-offs with those of other states and will be reluctant to cooperate even in the presence of positive, but disproportionate, pay-offs. As a consequence, formal or informal international cooperation – including in the field of climate change – is very difficult to achieve. Even if institutions are set up to deal with this problem, they cannot be very influential as only states have the powers (and responsibility) to tackle climate change and other international challenges.

In our view, it is key to attach great importance to the implications of climate change in terms of international conflict and the impact on the distribution of power, but realism fails to grasp the complexity of the problem, considering the number of actors (institutional and non-institutional) involved in fighting global warming at any level (global, regional, state and sub-state).

Conversely, the liberal tradition and more particularly the regime theory approach (Keohane and Nye 1977; Krasner 1983) point out that international institutions can lower international conflicts even in a realistic anarchical world, and allow cooperation by putting emphasis on absolute rather than relative gains. Indeed, cooperation on climate and the environment at the international level is already taking place today, as the UNFCCC demonstrates. With this approach, international cooperation should be enhanced and reinforced in order to fight climate change better.

The regime theory can be considered a good starting point for the theoretical analysis of climate change because it helps explain the recent efforts made internationally in this field. However, it needs to be enlarged to consider the above-mentioned complexity of the phenomenon and to provide better understanding of its consequences.

Other approaches go beyond the international regime theory and provide new insights. Even if they may be considered too extreme in many respects, the neo-Gramscian approach and the governmentality perspective allow other relevant elements, such as non-state actors, to be included in the scheme of analysis. They may be considered the outcome of a 'self-limiting state' and a more or less explicit agreement between the leading elites of a state and the rest of its society in the neo-Gramscian approach (Gramsci 1971, Cox 1983). They can even be considered new 'technologies of government' (that is, new, open and shared processes of government) in the governmentality approach (Foucault 1978). To put it simply, in this case the emphasis is placed on the processes with which governance is accomplished, rather than on the actions and institutions that undertake it (Okereke and Bulkeley 2007). Both approaches leave room for a form of power which goes beyond the zero-sum concept, moving us towards a plural and multiple conception which is one of the constituents of modern social relations. In other words, the intervention of these actors does not imply a decrease in state power but rather the sharing of new objectives (including the environment) for which joint action can be more successful.

In order to take the complexity of the phenomenon into account, it would therefore be wise to follow a multilevel governance approach which, on the one hand, does not yield to pointless alarmism (as the ecoradicals seem to), and on the other does not underestimate problems by hoping that technology or state intervention (with or without strong international institutions) will solve them.

Evidently, the solution of this political conundrum is not easy. The best way to address this issue is to put it in very concrete terms. Climate change will undoubtedly give rise to new tensions between states, which still remain the most important actors at the international level (realism). But at the same time international institutions (regime theory) and other not necessarily institutional actors (neo-Gramscian approach and governmentality perspective) will be required to make their contribution. What we basically need is not a political revolution but a revised world governance, which already exists today to some extent. In this respect, the definition of governance which probably fits best with the complex measures to be undertaken in fighting climate change is that of the Commission on Global Governance (*Our Global Neighborhood* 1995), where governance is defined as 'the sum of the many ways individuals and institutions, public and private, manage their common affairs. It is a continuing process through which conflicting or diverse interests may be accommodated and cooperative action may be taken. It includes formal institutions and regimes empowered to enforce compliance, as well as informal arrangements that people and institutions either have agreed to or perceive to be in their interest'.

In the context of this definition, this chapter suggests a revised multi-level model (global, regional, state and sub-state) in which all the relevant actors (institutional and non-institutional) can make their contribution by jointly defining the objectives, scope of intervention and measures to be undertaken at any level. The role of individuals (which clearly emerges from the above-mentioned definition of governance) will not be developed specifically. This is partly due to the possibility to link the action of individuals to two groups – Non-Governmental Organizations (NGOs) and the international business community – whose role will be included in the suggested multi-level governance of climate change.

3. GOVERNING CLIMATE CHANGE

Global warming and climate change are becoming top priorities for political leaders around the world. All large emerging and industrialized countries have at least tried to tackle these issues, even though their responses (if any) may vary in size or commitment terms.

Moreover, the first noticeable effects of climate change and the personal commitment of illustrious personalities (including Mr Al Gore) have contributed to spreading awareness of these issues. For example, what emerges from a recent Eurobarometer survey requested by the European Commission and the European Parliament is striking. It was found that the majority of Europeans are highly concerned about climate change and aware that they need to change their behaviour. According to 62 per cent of respondents, climate change scores number 2 – after poverty, lack of food and drinking water – in the list of the most serious world problems.[5] This is certainly an astonishing result, partly as these concerns have emerged clearly only in recent years.

Such specific development of the debate on climate change (from scientific to mass media focus) has inevitably influenced its governance. In the early stages (around 20 years ago), the science of climate change was the dominant topic and consequently discussion was driven mainly by climate and meteorological specialists. In Canada, for example, the group negotiating the UNFCCC was initially the Atmospheric Environmental Services, which is responsible for weather forecasts and atmospheric sciences. The same holds true for many other countries, with the exception of the United States where the State Department was involved immediately as it leads all US international negotiations, including those on climate change.

In this context it comes as no surprise that the Intergovernmental Panel on Climate Change – the first significant international initiative on climate dating back to 1988 – was founded by the World Meteorological Organization (WMO) and the United Nations Environment Programme (UNEP). But the IPCC's mandate was not limited to assessing scientific and technical information relevant to the understanding of human-induced climate change, it also included provision of socio-economic information and evaluation of potential impacts and options for mitigation and adaptation. Clearly, economic and political competencies are necessary to accomplish these tasks (allocated to Working Group III) but the initial composition of the IPCC did not match these needs.

Later on, the IPCC staff was reinforced with economists and political scientists who gave considerable added value to the IPCC Reports. The significance of the data provided by the IPCC was essential for the United Nations Conference on Environment and Development (UNCED) held in Rio de Janeiro in 1992. The UNFCCC – the current most important tool in fighting climate change – was created on that occasion.

The current governance of climate change is presented schematically in Figure 7.2. The UNFCCC is the central actor of the first level of intervention in this scheme. Various international organizations – from the World Bank (WB), the International Monetary Fund (IMF), G8 to OECD (Organisation for Economic Co-operation and Development) and UN programmes/agencies interact with it (albeit not exclusively), making their contribution to the following four aspects:

- definition of objectives on a global scale;
- coherence with other global objectives (including the growth of international trade);
- fundraising of necessary financial resources;
- implementation of concrete measures.

The second level of intervention is via Multilateral Environmental Agreements (MEAs) and various regional actors (including the European Union in particular), that can either stimulate – or in the European case compel – provision of an adequate state/sub-state answer which is hopefully, but not always, in line with the global objectives.

At the next level are the states, which are the key actors for implementation of policies with which to fight climate change concretely.

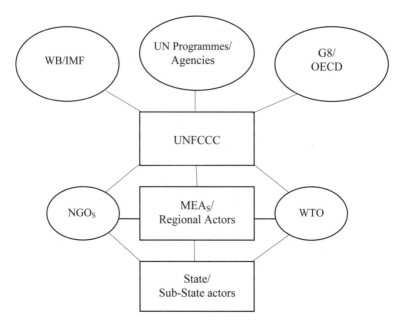

Figure 7.2 Current Multi-level Governance of Climate Change

In this regard, it is noteworthy that the levels described in the figure are not intended to be strictly hierarchical. States represent a good example as on the one hand they are the obvious 'makers' of environmental policies, but on the other they play a leading role in defining global objectives and actions to be taken at regional, state and sub-state levels.

Growing attention has been devoted to sub-state actors recently. They can promote initiatives with a strong territorial impact, but they run two risks when doing so; firstly the interventions may be disconnected from higher levels and secondly the size of their initiatives may be too low if they are not included in a horizontal cooperation framework with other sub-state actors or in vertical cooperation with state/regional/international actors.

As shown below, the WTO (World Trade Organization) and NGOs play a very specific role as their action can impact on the three levels and four aspects mentioned above.

In summary, Figure 7.2 shows a multilevel governance model which presumably represents the best answer in governance terms to the complex issue of climate change. Unfortunately this model is not the outcome of conscious 'a priori' construction, but rather the 'spontaneous' effect of a series of competencies and initiatives which have piled up in recent decades. As a consequence, there is much confusion over the four aspects mentioned, which makes the current model of governance quite ineffective and inefficient.

In the subsections below we shall analyse the three levels of intervention in order to emphasize the inconsistencies and overlaps at any level which hamper more conscious and mature multilevel governance.

3.1 The International–Global Level: Searching for Coordination

The cornerstone of current international governance is the UNFCCC, which came into force in 1994 and aims to 'achieve stabilization of greenhouse gas concentrations in the atmosphere at a low enough level to prevent dangerous anthropogenic interference with the climate system' (Art. 2 of the UNFCCC).

To date, the Kyoto Protocol – ratified by 182 countries – is the UNFCCC's biggest accomplishment. In accordance with the 'common but differentiated responsibilities' principle, industrialized countries (the so-called 'Annex I countries') are requested to lower, on average, their emissions by at least 5.2 per cent from 2008 to 2012 (compared to 1990), while developing countries (including large emerging countries such as China and India) have no binding targets. The Bush Administration decided not to ratify the Protocol, so the US economy is not required to contribute to its objectives. Annex I countries can also pursue their targets by using the global carbon market created by the Kyoto Protocol. This market includes the following: Assigned Amount Units (AAUs) that a country has not used for its own target and can therefore sell to another country which has not met its target; Emission Reduction Units (ERUs) that a country can earn for emission-reduction projects in developing countries under the Clean Development Mechanism (CDM); Certified Emission Reduction for projects in other industrialized countries under Joint Implementation (JI); Removal Unit (RU) on the basis of land use, land-use change and forestry (LULUCF) activities, such as reforestation.

The global carbon markets have increased their importance and in 2007 they reached 40 billion euros, up by 80 per cent from 2006.[6]

Countries are the most important actors in the UNFCCC and they lead it through the Conference of the Parties (COP) which meets annually and defines the main objectives of the Convention. But the UNFCCC exchanges inputs–outputs (information, guidelines, objectives, initiatives etc.) with many other actors which are schematically presented in Figure 7.2. The first group of actors is obviously UN agencies and programmes (also as the UNFCCC itself is part of the UN constellation).

A number of measures in many sectors (science, energy, agriculture and fisheries, trade, education, health etc.) is required to mitigate and adapt to climate change. It is therefore inevitable that many UN agencies and programmes try to make their part. But the growing number of these actors is creating a problem in efficiency terms. As a consequence, duplications, overlappings and conflicting actions may emerge. Bearing this in mind, in November 2007 the General Assembly asked the Secretary-General to prepare a report providing an overview of the activities of the UN system in relation to climate change.

The report underlines the lack of coherence of the actions (often with relatively small size) taken by the UN.[7] For example, 15 actors are involved in dealing with water scarcity.[8] What is more, the type of non-hierarchical relationship which exists between them is anything but clear. Notwithstanding the intention of the General Assembly to 'deliver as one' in relation to global warming, the current UN framework is quite confusing.

As mentioned above, this is due to the process that has led the fight against climate change so far. The current governance, even at the UN level, emerged as a simple sum of the existing actors and competencies and not as an *ex novo* search for the most efficient institutional framework. The United Nations System Chief Executives Board for Coordination is currently making an attempt at higher integration and coherence at the UN level, but this may be considered merely a first step. There is a need to initiate reorganization of the entire UN system, to lead to different attribution of competencies and simplification of the framework (by reducing the number of the actors). In particular, for each specific intervention it would be wise to identify a UN programme-agency to take the lead and have responsibility for coordinating the actions undertaken by all the other actors. Therefore, in view of the further efforts needed in the post-Kyoto period, it is necessary to reorganize the complex UN system to deliver better in response to climate change.

Furthermore, successful delivery depends on the financial resources raised for such a challenge. In this respect, 'global investments in the magnitude of from 15 trillion to 20 trillion United States dollars may be required over the next 20–25 years to place the world on a markedly different and sustainable energy trajectory'.[9] Clearly, the bulk of these investments will be provided by states and private sectors, nonetheless international and regional actors will be required to make their own contribution.

The Global Environment Facility (GEF) serves as the financial mechanism of the UNFCCC, providing financial assistance to developing countries and economies in transition. From 1992 to 2007, the GEF allocated $6.2 billion for more than 1,800 projects in 155 countries. It also leveraged co-financing of more than triple that amount. The GEF has three implementing agencies: the United Nations Development Programme

(UNDP), UNEP and the World Bank (WB).[10] The WB, which has already developed the Clean Energy Investment Framework (CEIF) in 2005–2007,[11] may play a particularly important role. While poverty is still the WB's main target, it is attaching growing importance to climate change (including a robust carbon finance business). Indeed, new funds (Climate Investment Funds) have been created recently to scale up energy efficiency, low carbon technologies and the use of renewables in national energy mixes,[12] but the WB should be requested to make new efforts, especially in view of the post-Kyoto regime.

Conversely, another relevant important institution – the International Monetary Fund – is not expected to take a lead in the work on climate change. But, given its specific mission, it can contribute to the objectives of the leading institutions, for instance by providing its member countries with advice and instruments for dealing with economic and financial problems related to climate change. Concretely, these problems may require fiscal measures (that is, emission taxes, cap-and-trade schemes, public spending etc.) and may impact on financial markets (that is, design of innovative instruments, such as catastrophe bonds and weather derivatives to manage climate-related risks).[13]

Trade is another field in which climate change has a significant impact. In this regard, it is noteworthy that climate change 'per se' is not an issue for the World Trade Organization and consequently no specific rule has been created in the latest rounds of trade negotiations.

But WTO rules do intersect with climate change measures and policies in different ways. The WTO can improve the efficiency of the international distribution of resources (including natural resources), lower barriers for environmentally-friendly goods, services and technologies, and contribute to raising living standards around the world (thus increasing demand for a cleaner environment). These effects help both mitigation and adaptation policies.

However, freer trade can also increase global industrial output (the so-called 'scale effect') and transportation services (but the International Maritime Organization noted that around 90 per cent of global merchandise traded by volume is transported by sea, whereas CO_2 emissions are mainly generated by road transport). In brief, it is very difficult to determine the positive or negative effect of trade liberalization on climate change in advance.

At the same time, the impact on international trade of measures and projects undertaken at any level to mitigate and adapt to climate change should be considered. These can alter trade conditions (that is, carbon leakage, environmental dumping etc.) and give rise to unfair competition. This represents one of the biggest challenges of the WTO and requires the creation of new norms and rules.

As shown in Figure 7.2, the WTO is an important actor at the international level but it may also work in cooperation with macro-regions and countries which can call for the respect of its rules.

The role of the WTO is essential especially in view of the (hopefully) more stringent constraints in the post-Kyoto period. Consequently, higher emphasis should be placed on the role it can play in a revised multilevel governance of climate change.

Eventually, the role of the leading world countries on the delicate and wide-ranging issue of climate change needs to be explored. They share a considerable power in the current international institutions and are consequently responsible for the reorganization and redefinition of targets in line with the fight against climate change (not to mention their availability of adequate financial resources).

Indeed, the issue of climate is present in the rhetoric of the G8 meetings, but no concrete result has been achieved so far. In particular, on the occasion of the Tokyo summit in July 2008, the G8 members declared 'we seek to share with all Parties to the UNFCCC the vision, and together with them to consider and adopt in the UNFCCC negotiations, the goal of achieving at least 50 per cent reduction of global emissions by 2050, recognizing … differentiated responsibilities and respective capabilities'. Besides, this Declaration maintains that 'all major economies will need to commit to meaningful mitigation actions to be bound in the international agreement to be negotiated by the end of 2009'. The intention to include all the major world economies (including emerging countries) is crystal clear. This is important not only because joint actions are requested to achieve considerable results but also to prevent free-riding behaviours.

To conclude, the analysis of the international level provides new elements for the definition of a revised, more effective multilevel governance of climate change: reduction of actors and overlappings in the UN system; higher (financial) responsibility for the most powerful and richest countries; involvement of developing and, above all, emerging countries (in the context of new international aids); scaling-up of trade-related issues on climate change in the future WTO negotiations.

3.2 The Regional Level: Searching for Coherence

There are many forms of international cooperation among states, ranging from simple informal agreements to international treaties, institutions and organizations. The European Union represents an unprecedented example of cooperation because such deep-level integration (including competencies and powers entirely handed over by states) has never been experienced in the course of human history.

EU integration has led to the creation of a macro-region which acts as a single, powerful player in some fields (for example trade).

Following this example, other macro-regions with limited scope and depth of integration (compared to the EU) have been created all over the world in recent decades (that is, NAFTA, MERCOSUR, ASEAN, etc.).

These actors can play a relevant role in the field of climate change as well. They are the ideal intermediaries between the global and national levels and can consequently contribute to a better understanding of internationally defined objectives, making them more coherent with the peculiarities of state and sub-state actors.

In addition, they can provide tools (that is, emission trading schemes) to lower the costs of state interventions, and which may result in these costs being more equally distributed among member states (for example according to GDP levels).

Over recent decades, states have also signed many MEAs. They do not imply the same level of coordination of macro-regions as they usually take the form of simple international agreements-treaties, with or without binding targets. Negotiation, development and implementation of MEAs are not necessarily included in the UNFCCC framework, thus creating a problem of coherence.

Nonetheless, MEAs and (even more) macro-regions can play an important role in defining a revised multilevel governance of climate change.

In this section, great attention will be attached to the European Union as it can provide best practices to be shared with other less developed international organizations and/or states.

Many reasons help explain the recent actions taken by the EU in fighting climate change. Firstly, the EU depends heavily on foreign imports of fossil fuels. It will import 94 per cent of oil and 84 per cent of gas from abroad in 2030.[14] In particular, gas demand will face the biggest growth (if compared to other energy sources) in the next decades. About 60 per cent of gas imports will come from Russia, whilst the remaining 40 per cent will come from Norway and Algeria.[15] This emphasizes another crucial point: the limited number of extra-European suppliers (with whom relationships are often anything but simple). In principle, the more a country is able to diversify its energy sources the more it will improve its security of supply. In this regard, the Shannon-Weiner (SW) Index is a diversity index which can allow for the quantification of the security of supply. This index can be adjusted to take into consideration also the political risk of the exporting country.[16] This index increases as the number of exporting countries increases. It assumes values in the range 0 (no diversification) and 2 (full diversification). Table 7.1 shows the SW index for some European countries, the US and Japan in 1996, 2000 and 2005.[17] Data show that

Liberalism in Crisis?

European countries have tried to diversify their growing imports over the last decade but have not succeeded (as the value of the index is still quite low).

Table 7.1 Adjusted Shannon–Weiner Index

Country	SW Index 1996	SW Index 2000	SW Index 2006
France	0.61	0.88	0.78
Germany	0.63	0.60	0.66
Italy	0.19	0.26	0.80
Poland	0	0.13	0.25
United Kingdom	0	0	0.52
Czech Republic	N	0.34	0.35
Spain	0.16	0.52	0.73
Japan	N	1.12	1.21
United States	0	0.02	0.05

Note: Calculations by the author.

The situation is even worse for Eastern European countries (such as Poland and the Czech Republic) whose dependence on Russian gas is heavier for obvious historical reasons. Beyond the European borders, the US and Japan represent two extreme cases. The low SW Index for the US does not necessarily imply a bad situation in terms of security of supply. It can be explained not only by high levels of national production (the ratio between national production and consumption is 0.84) but also by a privileged relationship (85 per cent of the US gas imports) with Canada (a country with a high political stability).

On the opposite, Japan's high SW Index is the outcome of a highly diversified gas import (from nine different countries). Therefore, interruptions of gas supply from a single country cannot seriously hamper Japan's security as its biggest supplier (Indonesia) originated only 24 per cent of its gas imports in 2005.

These data help explain the European Union's decision to take a decisive step towards a 'greener' Europe, but there are other reasons behind this decision.

Together with the extreme urgency of the phenomenon, the internationally set-up schedule plays a crucial role in defining the European position. At the conference held in Bali in December 2007, it was agreed to pave the way to a post-Kyoto agreement (from 2013 onwards) to be reached at the 2009 UNFCCC conference in Copenhagen (with the 2008 Poznan conference as an intermediate step). The EU needs a strong, clear position if it is to play a leading role at this conference. From this particular point of view, the EU can rely on a favourable international situation. On the one hand, the US is lagging behind the EU (partly as it does not face the same security of supply problem), and on the other the large, emerging countries are more focused on supporting their high growth rates than on tackling environmental issues seriously. Therefore, there is room for a leading European role at the international level, including in the context of the current international crisis. This role would also lead to development of new green technologies and know-how to be sold to extra-EU countries. In the medium term, this would help turn European standards into world standards (as is already happening with trade standards under the Single Market). New opportunities for competitiveness and growth in Europe would ultimately arise. Unilateral European action is therefore necessary if the EU is to be in the forefront in fighting climate change and leading the pending multilateral negotiations on the post-Kyoto agreements.

These are the reasons for Europe's strong position on renewables and climate change. With a view to analysing the mechanism initiated by the EU to tackle these issues, the starting point is the European Emission Trading Scheme (EU ETS) which was approved in 2003.

Each member state must contribute to these targets through a National Plan, identifying the burden in energy and industrial sectors for fulfilment of state commitments. The ETS has already experienced a warm-up phase in 2005–2007 and has started a second phase (for 2008–2012 – the real commitment period of the Kyoto Protocol). It is based on a 'cap-and-trade' mechanism[18] which already covers 40 per cent of the total CO_2 emitted by European firms.[19] So far, over 90 per cent of the European Union Allowances (EUAs) – given to firms for their emissions under the ETS – have been allocated for free.

The EUAs covered more than 62 per cent of the worldwide negotiated allowances in 2007. In financial terms their value represents 70 per cent of the world allowances (the prices of the EUAs are generally higher), thus creating the most important carbon market in the world. About 70 per cent of the EUAs (equivalent to 1Gt of CO_2) has been negotiated in over-the-counter markets, while the remaining 30 per cent has been traded in stock exchanges. Among these, the European Climate Exchange (based in London) is definitely the most important market (in 2007 it traded 87 per cent of EUAs and grew 11 per cent).[20]

In December 2008, the EU approved an Environmental Package[21] for the post-Kyoto period. This Package is two-fold: it increases the number of firms included in the ETS (thus covering 50 per cent of CO_2 emissions) and suggests auctioning up to two thirds of the EUAs. But this will happen gradually over the entire 2013–2020 period.[22]

However, the decision to opt for auctions has laid itself open to criticism, especially as other possible options have been excluded. For instance, free allocation of allowances could be provided by an administrative procedure gradually reducing the allowances up to a fixed target, or pollution could be reduced through a European tax.

But auctions do have undisputed positive aspects. Firstly, they allocate EUAs efficiently because allowances are purchased by those who value them most. Secondly, they can show in advance the future abatement costs of the firms involved in the ETS (neither an administrative procedure nor a tax on pollution could achieve the same results). In real terms, firms will be required to evaluate their future ability to curb CO_2 emissions in order to make adequate bids. They will not be willing to enter auctions until the price of the auctioned allowances exceeds their marginal abatement cost. Moreover, this early information will be very valuable both for decision-makers and managers. In particular, firms will be increasingly asked to move from the current 'compliance thinking' to a full 'emissions strategy' which takes all available options into consideration (investments to reduce abatement costs, purchase of auctioned allowances, purchase in secondary markets).

Conversely, an administrative procedure would not provide essential information in terms of abatement costs and could allocate allowances efficiently only with liquid, mature secondary markets (which is not the case today). Moreover, member states could re-invest auction revenues into their economies, thus reducing their national burden. In any case it is noteworthy that auctions cannot be designed taking national revenues as a main target, since they must deliver chiefly in terms of the acquisition of price signals and the efficient allocation of allowances, as described above.

Furthermore, the Package is not limited to those sectors involved in the ETS but also encompasses other sectors whose emissions are considerable (household heating, transport, agriculture). In this regard, each member state has a national target, set taking its own per capita GDP into account (countries with a per capita GDP below the European average will have lower reduction targets). In particular, by 2020 Italy will have to cut its emissions by 13 per cent (versus 2005). Other large countries have similar targets (Germany and France –14 per cent, Great Britain –16 per cent, Poland +14 per cent). Specific national targets are also set for renewables. Their share of total energy consumption is expected to be 17 per cent in Italy, 23 per cent in France, 18 per cent in Germany and 15 per cent in Poland. These targets include both a flat-rate increase in each country and a GDP-weighted rate increase modulated to consider the national starting point and the efforts already made.[23]

In addition, Guarantees of Origin (GO) can be issued in order to guarantee renewable sources in electricity generation. These guarantees can be negotiated among member states and contribute to their targets in terms of renewables.

Eventually the Package – as envisaged by the Kyoto Protocol – will allow member states to partially meet their national targets through the Clean Development Mechanism and Joint Implementation (JI). As explained in section 3, these two initiatives allow European firms to earn tradable credits by putting in place projects aimed at reducing CO_2 emissions in emerging and developed countries respectively. The trading of these credits creates new secondary markets with relatively low prices, as compared with the EUAs. As a consequence, these mechanisms are potentially very attractive for firms and, if fully exploited, can contribute to cutting the total cost of the environmental Package. We can calculate this cost by using the Total Compliance Cost (TCC), which is defined as the additional direct and indirect energy-related cost compared to business as usual. In other words, the TCC is the additional effort needed in order to meet the 2020 environmental targets. However it is necessary to bear in mind that various scenarios (and costs) could be taken into consideration, depending on the measures to be undertaken to meet the targets.

For instance, the cost-efficiency scenario could be a viable alternative to the mechanism envisaged in the Package. In this case, goals would be pursued taking into account the overall EU-27 contribution (and not the contribution of each member state). Initiatives would be promoted in the EU territory wherever they are more convenient in terms of CO_2 reduction or renewables production, and no national target would be defined 'a priori' for each member state. This scenario would ensure the lowest TCC (about 0.58 per cent of European GDP by 2020). Conversely, this cost rises to 0.71 per cent in the scenario foreseen by the Commission (even allowing for GOs, CDM credits and recycling auction revenues into the European economic system).

However there is a major problem with the cost-efficiency scenario: the unfair distribution of costs among member states damages low GDP countries and favours rich ones. It is therefore clearly unacceptable, as it would mainly hit the new EU countries and go against the solidarity principle which the EU has repeatedly reaffirmed in fighting climate change.

In conclusion, the Package offers the fairest option in terms of cost-sharing, and is therefore the preferred option. Comparing the national costs of the largest EU countries in this scenario, it emerges that Germany should pay 0.56 per cent of GDP, France 0.47 per cent, Great Britain 0.42 per cent, Italy at least 0.66 per cent and Poland 0.06 per cent (which would rocket to 1.24 per cent in the cost-efficiency scenario).[24] According to data provided by the European Environment Agency[25] Italy, Denmark and Spain are the only European countries which have not met their Kyoto targets so far (-6.5 per cent, –21 per cent, +15 per cent respectively versus 1990) and which will probably be unable to do so by 2012.

In brief, the analysis of the European intervention shows that the regional level may be considered as an important transmission belt of objectives set at the global level. In concrete terms, it makes these objectives more coherent with the actions to be taken at the state and sub-state level. Besides, macro-regions show other undisputed advantages as they can lower the cost of fighting climate change (if compared to single country measures) and can allow for solidarity (if requested) inside the region. Still, other problems may arise both for macro-regions and MEAs: the compatibility of their rules with those envisaged by other agreements and international institutions (for example the WTO).

3.3 The State–Sub-state Level: Searching for Effectiveness

Whatever the theoretical approach to International Relations, it is hard to deny that states are the most important actors in the current international system. They define the limits of their cooperation at the international level jointly and choose whether or not to reach regional agreements. In addition, they are responsible for the implementation in their territory of decisions taken at the regional or international level.

Indeed, many initiatives have been started by states in recent years. Most have usually taken the MEA form but some are genuine state projects which have already been started or should be introduced in the near future (for example Australian Carbon Trading Scheme, Canadian Climate Change Accountability Act, United Kingdom Climate Change Programme etc.).

But often the scope and dimension of these initiatives are not adequate even because of free-riding problems which are mainly felt at this level. Moreover, these interventions are often linked to wider national targets (for example the reduction of various pollutants) and greenhouse gases are just a part of them. Consequently, objectives may not be coherent with those defined at higher levels in terms of dimension, scope, timing and involved actors.

More broadly, there is a problem of effectiveness of national interventions in relation to global objectives (that is, fight against climate change). The same holds true when moving from the state to the sub-state level, where emphasis is mainly put on the various sources of local pollution and not simply to greenhouse gases. In this regard, the following issue should be addressed: why should citizens and local politicians strive for climate change initiatives whose costs will be borne locally but whose benefits will be shared with the entire world? To put it simply, free-riding could emerge as the typical response to climate change (as shown in section 3.1), not only at the national level but also at the local level (and perhaps even more so there).

Surprisingly enough, in the United States of the Bush Administration, the majority of states and hundreds of cities have adopted local climate change initiatives and regional collaboration between states and/or cities is taking place throughout the entire USA.[26] Various forms of horizontal and vertical collaboration have been initiated all over the world and especially by cities (for example the Swedish 'Klimatkommunerna', the C40 Cities including the world's largest cities, the US Mayors' Climate Protection Agreement, etc.). The number of these initiatives is growing, even though climate change policy is predominantly a voluntary task in most countries.

Cities are also developing new forms of urban governance to adopt their own targets to climate change. These modes range from soft forms of governing to traditional forms of intervention (Bulkeley and Kern 2006). In particular, Gotelind Alber and Kristine Kern (2008) consider four forms of urban governance: 'self-governing' (implying very soft intervention for example energy efficiency improvements in municipality-owned buildings); 'governing through enabling' (coordinating and facilitating partnerships with private actors); 'governing by provision' (creating infrastructures that generate less greenhouse gas emission, especially when municipalities own or hold stakes in local utility companies for energy, transport, water and waste services); 'governing by authority' (using traditional forms of authority, such as regulation and sanctions) (Alber and Kern 2008).

Each city will choose one of these forms of governance, depending on its institutional competencies/powers and the amount of state activity in fighting climate change.

Clearly there are reasons for this seemingly irrational behaviour of citizens and local authorities. Engel and Orbach (2008) try to solve this puzzling issue by considering the supply and demand sides of local climate change initiatives. Citizens' demand for these initiatives depends on various factors: the importance usually attached to symbolic statements (not necessarily involving binding targets) and the prestige given by environmental policies; the role of 'strategic voting' (trying to achieve the primacy of climate change initiatives and hoping that other jurisdictions will make the same choice); asymmetric presentation of information to the public (the emphasis usually being put on the reduction of CO_2 emissions rather than on the real impact on the global concentration of greenhouse gases); the underestimation of unknown costs and growing pressure on local suppliers of energy for efficient products and services. On the supply side, one obvious explanation of the willingness of many local politicians to consider this kind of initiative depends simply on the existence of demand for such actions in their constituency. Other reasons are administrative and political entrepreneurship (civil servants or politicians may gain good media coverage and awards for their efforts in this field) and by piggybacking on the popularity of climate change actions (for example promoting policies such as new transportation plans, whose primary objective is not the reduction of greenhouse gases).

Following the definition of multilevel governance given in section 2.2, we can elaborate on these reasons further by introducing the notion of a state which does not consider itself a single, united actor but rather the sum of the many internal forces and processes expressed by its own citizens and the complex net of cultural, economic and political relationships they put in place both within national borders and externally.

In this context, NGOs are playing a crucial role in spreading awareness of the risks related to global warming and are undoubtedly influencing these forces and networks.

Besides (as shown in Figure 7.2), their role cannot be limited to the state and sub-state level, because many NGOs take transnational civil society (as a whole) as their main target and try to make their contribution to defining global and regional objectives. For instance, a growing number of NGOs are asking the UNFCCC to be admitted to the Convention bodies. Over time, more than 600 NGOs have been admitted to the various bodies (the Conference of the Parties is in charge of admittance of new applicant organizations, see Art. 7, UNFCCC). Under the UNFCCC framework, NGOs sharing the same interests usually work together through so-called 'constituencies' in order to increase the effectiveness of their participation in the Convention. Initially there were two constituencies, the Business and Industry Non-Governmental Organizations (BINGO) and the Environmental Non-Governmental Organizations (ENGO), but three other constituencies have since been created and admitted.[27] They obviously facilitate the relationship between the complex network of NGOs and the Secretariat of the Convention.

Clearly, the official contribution that NGOs can make to defining global objectives and actions is limited, as they are admitted to the UNFCCC only as observers. Nonetheless, their role is becoming increasingly important due to their continual influence on national and transnational civil societies. Their role may be particularly important in those countries that did not agree to binding national targets. In these cases, NGOs may influence citizens and local authorities to take their own action to fight climate change, notwithstanding state inactivity or unwillingness.

To conclude, NGOs and local authorities must be considered essential players in the revised multilevel governance of climate change, not only because they can amplify the actions taken by states and international institutions, but also because they can work together with sub-state actors to adopt local climate change policies when state intervention is absent or negligible.

4. TOWARDS A REVISED MULTI-LEVEL GOVERNANCE

With a view to assessing the distribution of powers and competencies in a multilevel governance model, Bruni (2008) builds on the previous literature (Hooghe and Marks 2001) and suggests two types of governance. In the first, multilevel governance emerges as the outcome of the continuous handing over of state powers to the sub-state and international levels. The issue can therefore be tackled in terms of federalism, including for its implications on international relations. The problem of coordination through the levels is usually solved by hierarchy (with the state government playing the leading role). Conversely, the second type of multilevel governance requires a wide distribution of powers in a net of structured, overlapped levels with different sizes and targets. In this less precise but more flexible model, the levels of governance are not connected through hierarchy, thus raising the problem of how to coordinate them efficiently. One possible solution is the individuation of either an 'arbiter' or a specific level of coordination. Bruni suggests that the first model – based simply on the state (that is, its government) and a clear and rigid relationship with local authorities and supranational entities – is not fit to manage a very complex sector. In particular, Bruni takes international financial regulation into consideration and opts for a second type of multilevel governance. The same might also hold true in relation to climate change, whose complexity stems mainly from the unprecedented global challenge, the growing number of actors (not only institutional), and the various tools to be used and targets to be pursued.

So far, we have focused our attention on the multilevel governance which has emerged spontaneously in the last two decades, with a view to identifying its features and weaknesses.

The previous critical analysis of these elements can now help us identify the main features of a revised multilevel governance which does not necessarily imply a complete redesign of the model but rather its improvement and the scaling-up of targets. In particular, we should define new elements of a revised governance that allow for more coherent functioning of the international/global level, better coordinated action within macro-regions and a more effective role for state–sub-state actors.

This will be achieved in accordance with a 'second-type' model of multilevel governance. The coordination problem will be solved by taking the UNFCCC as the 'arbiter'. As a consequence, any intervention at any level should be coherent with UNFCCC targets and any relevant dispute should be solved in the framework of the Convention itself. The flexibility of this type of governance will allow the Convention to have direct links with lower levels (that is, the sub-state level) and non-institutional actors (NGOs), not necessarily involving intermediate levels (macro-regions and states). These guidelines are clearly in line with the more general principles expressed in section 2.2.

Bearing all this in mind, we can start analysing those changes which are presumably needed at the international-global level. As mentioned in section 3.1, the entire UN system should be revised in order to increase its efficiency and improve its ability to deliver in the field of climate change. As a first step, the number of UN programmes and agencies dealing with global warming should be reduced, and a UN programme/agency should take the lead and be considered as the focal point of the actions taken by all actors at any level for each specific intervention (for example biodiversity, water and food scarcity, etc.).

But the main purpose of a revised post-Kyoto multilevel regime is to increase the number of states adopting binding targets (starting from those with the highest emissions). In this regard, Mr Obama's willingness to consider security of supply and environmental issues as priorities for his administration raises hopes for full US commitment in the coming years. Hence, the biggest challenge is now to include emerging countries in the post-Kyoto regime. As shown in Figure 7.3, non-OECD countries will be responsible for the highest rise in CO_2 emissions over the coming decades. This implies that no post-Kyoto regime will be successful unless non-OECD countries are fully involved, starting from emerging countries which are still heavily reliant on coal (that is, China). Besides, Figure 7.4 shows that per-capita and per-US$ emissions will remain much higher in OECD countries (which are also responsible for the bulk of the current stock of CO_2 in the atmosphere). Since these are also the world's richest and most powerful countries, they should attract emerging countries by providing an 'all-inclusive package' in which binding emission reduction targets are jointly negotiated with financial support, power-sharing in international institutions and more favourable trade agreements.

Under new guidelines provided by the UNFCCC for the post-Kyoto period, the GEF (Global Environment Facility), the WB and other international institutions (including regional development banks) should jointly provide aid and assistance for the full engagement of non-OECD countries. Some could be offered the possibility to join the WTO in exchange for environmental commitments. The same might hold true in relation to the G8. The debate on its enlargement should consider the willingness of would-be members to adopt binding targets on climate change. In a nutshell, the sharing of the global burden should be considered a condition for joining such a club.

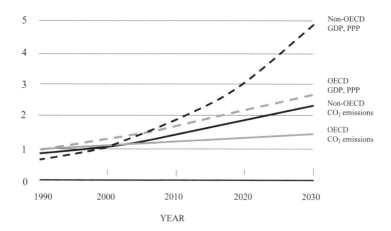

Figure 7.3 Projected Growth of GDP and CO₂ Emissions Relative to 1990 (OECD=1)

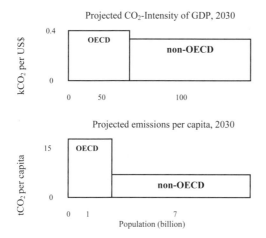

Source: Energy Information Administration, US Department of Energy (2007).

Figure 7.4 Projected CO₂-Intensity of GDP and Projected Emissions Per Capita, 2030

The world 'carbon market' – initiated by the Kyoto Protocol – should be further extended and the enormous cost-effective opportunities offered by many developing countries should be fully exploited. In this regard, the CDM has to be reinforced by reducing its high transaction costs (complexities, delays and uncertainties) which, by and large, have been its biggest constraint to date.

Moreover, the WTO and UNCTAD (United Nations Conference on Trade and Development) should make their contribution to the post-Kyoto regime by making technology transfer from developed to developing countries easier (know-how, skills, methods of manufacturing, manufacturing and facilities from industries, universities, governments and other institutions), and by lowering constraints and barriers to freer trade of environmentally-friendly products and services. This would represent a win–win situation; on the one hand, technology transfer would help emerging and developing countries to fulfil their environmental commitments and avoid 'technology lock-in' in a period in which they are investing heavily in new infrastructures to accommodate rapid economic growth. On the other, OECD countries would benefit from fewer barriers to their environmentally-friendly products and services (that is, water heaters, hydropower turbines, tanks for biogas production, etc.). A World Bank study shows that complete removal of both tariff and non-tariff barriers would result in a 14 per cent increase in trade. Moreover, the consequent reduction in the price of these products and services would also make them more accessible to developing countries.

But these actions raise many problems in terms of trade policies. The Convention addresses its relations with the trade regime underlining that 'measures taken to combat climate change, including unilateral ones, should not constitute a means of arbitrary or unjustifiable discrimination or a disguised restriction on international trade'.[28] Nonetheless, these measures will affect production costs and consequently have an impact on international competitiveness. As shown by the long discussion in the EU, those countries that may be affected by cheaper imports could call for offsetting measures (that is, tariffs), thus creating a WTO rule coordination problem.

Similarly, discrimination between products because of the manner in which they are produced may arise. Moving to the regional level, preferential agreements between some countries (that is, MEAs) may raise other concerns in relation to WTO rules (see Sampson 2008b). Many countries have signed up to the rules of both the WTO and the largest MEAs, thus creating legal uncertainties which constrain the optimal global governance of both trade and environment targets. The clash between the WTO and MEAs will probably be fiercer in the post-Kyoto regime, hopefully implying more stringent economic obligations to combat global warming.

Negotiations at the WTO level should give priority to climate-friendly goods and services, possibly identified in cooperation with UNFCCC and IPCC, and to MEA–WTO relations. But the 'single undertaking' procedure – implying commitments by all members on all items under negotiation – could make negotiations on these products and services hostage to other more controversial issues (see Palmer and Tarasofsky 2007). A possible solution could be to include these issues in the UNFCCC framework (for example the Copenhagen COP may address them). But this would require a much stricter dialogue between the UNFCCC and the WTO, whereas at the moment each takes part in some of the other institution's bodies mainly as an observer.

To conclude with the regional level, the European Union (as indicated in section 3.2) can be taken as an example for other macro-regions that intend to take further steps towards environmental policies in the UNFCCC framework. The 'cap-and-trade' mechanism and the auction of allowances can be regarded as the most effective way to achieve concrete results, but the EU model can be changed (allowances could be distributed through an administrative procedure) and adapted to the other macro-regions depending on their priorities (that is, efficient versus fair distribution of the burden of the intervention).

As far as the state and sub-state levels are concerned, cooperation between them should be strengthened in order to increase the size of their intervention and coherence with the regional (if applicable) and international targets. If a state adopts binding targets under an international agreement, the national government and the local authorities may set up an 'ex ante' dialogue aimed at distributing the burden of these targets across all the actors. Following the example of the 'internal pacts' signed by European governments with their local authorities to respect the European Stability and Growth Pact, a similar internal pact specifying objectives for each actor and sanctions for non-compliance could be signed in the climate change field. But if no binding target has been adopted by a national government, the UNFCCC bodies could negotiate ad hoc targets with local authorities, including large cities (which often produce a country's highest emissions). NGOs can play a significant role in making sub-state levels (including individuals, groups, associations etc.) more sensitive to these targets.

In conclusion, no revolutionary approaches are probably required in order to address the issue of climate change governance effectively. However, in view of the hopefully more ambitious and comprehensive post-Kyoto period targets, the spontaneous model of multilevel governance which has emerged so far should be revised to make it more flexible (according to a 'second-type' model) and able to involve new actors at any level.

Owing to the future depletion of fossil energy resources, the fight against climate change and the related development of renewable energies and green technologies are more than a moral imperative for everybody. They are also a way to escape from a world in which growing tensions and fearful conflicts may explode, more as the consequence of a 'clash on resources' than a consequence of Huntington's 'clash of civilization'.

NOTES

1. See the Fourth Assessment Report *Climate Change 2007: Impacts, Adaptation and Vulnerability*. The same conclusions have been drawn by the Joint Statement of Science Academies in 2005 and in a Report from the US Climate Change Science Program (2006).
2. Carbon dioxide, methane, nitrous oxide, sulphur hexafluoride, hydrofluorocarbons, perfluorocarbons.
3. The *Stern Review on the Economics of Climate Change* is a highly comprehensive report (over 700 pages) issued on 30 October 2006 by the economist Lord Stern of Brentford for the British government. It is mainly focused on the effect of climate change and global warming on the world economy. Although it is not the first report on this issue, over the last two years it has by and large become the most known, discussed and criticised report of its kind.
4. Samuelson, *The Pure Theory of Public Expenditure* (1954); Cornes and Sandler, *The Theory of Externalities, Public Goods and Club Goods*, 2nd edn (1996); Olson, *The Logic of Collective Action: Public Goods and the Theory of Groups* (1965); Stigler, *Free Riders and Collective Action: An Appendix to Theories of Economic Regulation* (1974).
5. See 'Europeans' attitude towards climate change', *Special Eurobarometer 300*, September 2008.
6. 'Carbon 2008', *Point Carbon*, March 2008.
7. See Annex II, Paragraph III D 'Overview of United Nations activities in relation to climate change', A/62/644, January 2008
8. UN-Water, UNEP, UNDP, UNESCO, WMO, Department of Economic and Social Affairs of the United Nations Secretariat, Office for the Coordination of Humanitarian Affairs of the United Nations Secretariat, FAO, World Bank Group, IFAD, UNIDO, United Nations Human Settlements Programme (UN-Habitat), UNICEF, IAEA, Convention on Biological Diversity.
9. See 'Overview of United Nations activities in relation to climate change', op. cit.
10. See www.theGEF.org.
11. It currently aims to increase access to electricity in Sub-Saharan Africa from 25 per cent to 35 per cent by 2015 (47 per cent by 2030). It is also considering interventions for mitigation measures in India, Mexico, Brazil, South Africa and Indonesia.
12. See the report *Development and Climate Change: a Strategic Framework for the World Bank Group* for the Development Committee (the Joint Ministerial Committee of the Boards of Governors of the Bank and the Fund on the Transfer of Real Resources to Developing Countries), September 2008.
13. See www.imf.org/external/np/exr/facts/enviro.htm.
14. *Green Paper*, COM 2006 105 final, SEC (2006) 317/2, Brussels 2006.
15. Ibid.

16. In ecology, the diversity index is intended to measure the biodiversity of an ecosystem. More generally, diversity indices can be used to assess the diversity of any population in which each member belongs to a unique species. In particular, we will use the following index:

$$SW = - \left(\sum_i x_i \ \ln \ x_i \ b_i \right) (1 + g_j)$$

where x_i is the market share of the supply country i in country j (for which we want to calculate the security of supply), $\ln x_i$ is the natural logarithm of x_i, b_i is the index of political stability of exporting country i, gj is the share of national gas production of country j.

17. For further details about the European security of gas supply and the Shannon-Weiner Index see Villafranca (2007).

18. The central authority sets a limit (*cap*) on the amount of the pollutant that can be emitted. Allowances are given to firms with a *grandfathering provision* (rights are issued in proportion to historical emissions). Firms that need to increase their emission allowances must buy credits (*trade*) from those who pollute less.

19. The EU ETS includes some 12,000 installations covering energy activities (combustion installations with a rated thermal input exceeding 20 MW, mineral oil refineries, coke ovens), production and processing of ferrous metals, mineral industry (cement clinker, glass and ceramic bricks) and pulp and board activities.

20. Other important markets are the Nord Pool, based in Oslo (6.3 per cent), and the French Powernext (5.5 per cent). Data *Point Carbon* included in the Report published on the occasion of 'Point Carbon's 5th Annual Conference', March 2008.

21. Directive amending Directive 2003/87/EC so as to improve and extend the EU greenhouse gas emission allowance trading system; Directive on the promotion of use of renewable energy sources; Decision on the effort of member states to reduce their greenhouse gas emissions to meet the EU commitments up to 2020.

22. In the warm-up phase only three countries (Ireland, Hungary, Lithuania) chose auctions, but the situation will be different in the second phase. Many countries have already expressed their interest in auctioning their allowances (partly as Directive 2003/87/EC allows them to auction up to 10 per cent of allowances in the second phase).

23. See European Commission, *Impact Assessment of the Package of Implementation Measures for the EU's Objectives on Climate Change and Renewable Energy for 2020*, January 2008.

24. Calculations provided by the Report of the European Commission, *Model-based analysis of the 2008 EU Policy Package on Climate Change and Renewables*, June 2008.

25. See 'Gas Emission Trends and Projections in Europe 2008', *EEA Report*, The Regional Greenhouse Gas Initiative (RGGI), no. 5, 2008.

26. For instance which includes North-Eastern and Mid-Atlantic states; the Western Climate Initiative (WCI) which was set up in 2007 and involves not only US states but also the Canadian Provinces of British Columbia and Manitoba.

27. The Local Government and Municipal Authorities (LGMA), the Indigenous Peoples' Organizations (IPO) and the Research and Independent Non-Governmental Organizations (RINGO).

28. See Art. 3.5 of the Convention.

BIBLIOGRAPHY

Adams, Richard M., Bruce A. McCarl and Linda O. Mearns (2003), *The Effects of Spatial Scale of Climate Scenarios on Economic Assessments: an Example from U.S. Agriculture*, Kluwer Academic Publishers.

Alber, Gotelind and Kristine Kern (2008),'Governing climate change in cities: modes of urban climate governance in multi-level systems', Organisation for Economic Co-operation and Development (OECD), www.oecd.org/dataoecd/22/7/41449602. pdf.

Alexander, Douglas (2008), 'Climate change and global social justice', Foreign Policy Centre, Annual Lecture, 6 February.

Balkeley, Harriet and Kristine Kern (2006), 'Local government and the governing of climate change in Germany and the UK', *Urban Studies*, **43** (12), 2237–2259.

Beckerhoff, Constanze (2008), *EU Emission Trading Scheme: Use Permit Revenues to Fund Climate Change Protection, says Environment Committee*, European Parliament Press Release, 7 October, http://www.europarl.europa.eu/sides/getDoc.do?pubRef=//EP//TEXTIMPRESS+20081006IPR38798+0+DOC+XML+V0//EN&language=EN.

Capros, Pantelis et al. (2008), *Report of the DG ENV: Model-based Analysis of the 2008 EU Policy Package on Climate Change and Renewables*, European Commission, June.

Carbajosa, Ana et al. (2008), 'Europa asume el coste de ser verde', *El Pais*, 24 January.

Caretto, Ennio (2008), "USA e Europa, via all'accordo. 'Una serie di vertici anti-crisi'", *Corriere della Sera*, 20 October.

Carter, Robert M. et al. (2006), 'The Stern Review: a dual critique', *World Economics Journal*, **7** (4), October–December.

Chatham House (2007), *Changing Climates: Interdependencies on Energy and Climate Security for China and Europe*, London: the Royal Institute of International Affairs.

Council of the European Union (2008), 'Contribution to the European Council, 2911th Economic and Financial Affairs', Brussels, 9 December.

Council of the European Union (2008), '17215/08, Presidency Conclusions', Brussels, 12 December.

Cosbey, Aaron and Richard Tarasofsky (2007), *Climate Change, Competitiveness and Trade*, Chatham House Report, London: The Royal Institute of International Affairs.

Cox, Robert W. (1983), 'Gramsci, hegemony, and international relations: an essay in method', *Millennium: Journal of International Studies*, **12**(2).

Dijkstra, Bouwe R. and Marco Haan (2001), 'Sellers' hedging incentives at EPA's emission trading auction', *Journal of Environmental Economics and Management*, Academic Press.

Drexhage John (2008), *Climate Change and Global Governance. Which Way Ahead?*, Global Environmental Governance (GEG) Briefing Paper.

Dupont, Alan (2008), 'The strategic implications of climate change', *Survival*, **50** (3), June–July.

Engel, Kristen H. and Barak Y. Orbach (2008), 'Micro-motives for state and local climate change initiatives' Arizona Legal Studies Discussion Paper no. 07–19, *Harvard Law & Policy Review*, vol. 2, 119–137.

Fankhauser, Samuel (1995), *Valuing Climate Change: the Economics of the Greenhouse*, London: Earthscan.

Gilpin, Robert (1987), *The Political Economy of International Relations*, Princeton N.J.: Princeton University Press.

Gramsci, Antonio (1971), *Selections from the Prison Notebooks*, International Publishers.

Grieco, Joseph (1993), *Anarchy and the Limits of Cooperation: a Realist Critique of the Newest Liberal Institutionalism*, in D.A. Baldwin (ed.), *Neorealism and Neoliberalism: the Contemporary Debate*, New York: Columbia University Press, 116–140.

Hansel, James et al. (2006), 'Global temperature change', *PNAS*, **103** (39).

Hedegaard, Connie (2008), 'Negotiating a new international response to climate change: the prospects for COP-15 in Copenhagen 2009', speech delivered at London School of Economics, 1 October.

Hooghe, Liesbet and Gary Marks (2001), *Multi-level Governance and European Integration*, Rowman & Littlefield.

IPCC (2001), *Climate Change: Synthesis Report*, Contribution of Working Groups I, II, and III to the Third Assessment Report of the Intergovernmental Panel on Climate Change.

IPCC (2007), *Climate Change 2007. Working Group II Report: Impacts, Adaptation and Vulnerability*, IV Assessment Report.

Jackson, Robert and George Sorensen (2007), *Introduction to International Relations*, Oxford: Oxford University Press.

Kawaguchi, Yoriko (2008), *Japan as a Leader in Tackling Climate Change*, AJISS Commentary, July.

Keohane, Robert and Joseph Nye (1977), *Power and Interdependence: World Politics in Transition.* Boston: Little, Brown.

Kempf, Hervé (2008), 'La crise s'invite aux négociations sur le climat', *Le Monde*, 1 December.

Krasner, Stephen D. (1983), 'Structural Causes and Regime Consequences: Regimes as Intervening Variables', Ithaca, NY: Cornell University Press.

Marta, Lucia, 'Il nuovo orizzonte strategico dell'Unione Europea', *Affari internazionali*, 18 November, http://www.affarinternazionali.it/articolo. asp?ID=995.

Maung, Zara (ed.) (2008), *Special Report: the Real Cost of Climate Change*, Climate Change Corp, 9 April http://www.climatechangecorp.com/content.asp? ContentID=5253.

McCreery, Stuart (2007), *Possible Design for a Greenhouse Gas Emissions Trading System*, Evans & Peck.

Mendelsohn, Robert O. (2006), *A Critique of the Stern Report*, SSRN Regulation, **29** (4).

Morgenthau, Hans J. (1948), *Politics Among Nations*, New York: Alfred Knopf.

Nicholls, Robert J. and Richard Tol (2006), *Impacts and Responses to Sea-level Rise: a Global Analysis of the SRES Scenarios over the Twenty-first Century*, Philosophical Transactions of the Royal Society, **364** (1841).

Organization for Economic Co-operation and Development (OECD) (2009), *Climate Change Mitigation. What Do We Do?*.

Offeddu, Luigi (2008), 'Clima via al piano UE. Lite sulle industrie con licenza d'inquinare', *Corriere della Sera*, 24 January.

Okereke, Chukwumerije and Harriet Bulkeley (2007), *Conceptualizing Climate Change Governance Beyond the International Regime*, Tyndall Centre, Working Paper no. 112, Durham University, October.

Palmer, Alice and Richard Tarasofsky (2007), *The Doha Round and Beyond: Towards a Lasting Relationship Between the WTO and the International Environmental Regime*, London: the Royal Institute of International Affairs.

Porter, Gareth and Janet Welsh Brown (1996), *Global Environmental Politics*, Westview: Boulder.

Reilly, John et al. (2003), U.S. agriculture and climate change: new results, *Climatic Change*, **57**, 43–69.

Røine, Kjetil et al. (eds) (2008), 'Carbon 2008 – Post-2012 is now', *Point Carbon*.

Sampson, Gary P. (2008a), *Developing Countries and the WTO: Policy Approaches*, United Nations University Press.

Sampson, Gary P. (2008b), *The WTO and Global Governance: Future Directions*, Brookings Institution Press.

Stern, Nicholas (2006), *The Stern Review on the Economics of Climate Change*, HM Treasury.

United Nations Development Programme (UNDP) (2001), *Sustainable Development, Energy and the Environment: UNDP's Climate change initiatives*, UNDP.

United Nations Framework Convention on Climate Change (UNFCCC) (2004), *The First Ten Years*, UNFCCC.

United Nations Framework Convention on Climate Change (UNFCCC) (2007), *Investment and Financial Flows to Address Climate Change*, UNFCCC.

US Climate Change Science Program for the U.S. Department of Agriculture (2008), *The Effects of Climate Change on Agriculture, Land Resources, Water Resources, and Biodiversity*.

Villafranca, Antonio (ed.), (2008), *Le Sfide della Governance Economica Europea*, Bologna: il Mulino.

Waltz, Kenneth N. (1979), *Theory of International Politics*, Cambridge: Cambridge University Press.

Index